D0076866

Life Beyond the Line

A Front-of-the-House
Companion for Culinarians

Noel C. Cullen, Ed.D., CMC, AAC
Boston University

Prentice
Hall

Upper Saddle River, New Jersey 07458

Library of Congress Cataloging-in-Publication Data

Cullen, Noel C.
    Life beyond the line : a front-of-the-house companion for culinarians / by Noel C. Cullen
        p.   cm.
    Includes index.
    ISBN 0–13–907585–2
    1. Hospitality industry—Management.   2. Cooks.   I. Title

TX911.3.M27 C8497 2001
647.95′068′—dc21

00–057101

Publisher: Dava Garza
Acquisitions Editor: Vern Anthony
Associate Editor: Marion Gottlieb
Production Editor: Bruce Hobart, Pine Tree Composition
Production Liaison: Barbara Marttine Cappuccio
Director of Manufacturing and Production: Bruce Johnson
Managing Editor: Mary Carnis
Manufacturing Manager: Ed O'Dougherty
Art Director: Marianne Frasco
Cover Design Coordinator: Miguel Ortiz
Marketing Manager: Ryan DeGrote
Editorial Assistant: Susan Kegler
Cover Design: Joe Sengotta
Cover Art: Dick Patrick/Workbook Co/Op Stock
Interior Design: Pine Tree Composition
Printing and Binding: R. R. Donnelley & Sons

Prentice-Hall International (UK) Limited, *London*
Prentice-Hall of Australia Pty. Limited, *Sydney*
Prentice-Hall Canada Inc., *Toronto*
Prentice-Hall Hispanoamericana, S.A., *Mexico*
Prentice-Hall of India Private Limited, *New Delhi*
Prentice-Hall of Japan, Inc., *Tokyo*
Prentice-Hall Singapore Pte. Ltd.

10 9 8 7 6 5 4 3 2 1
ISBN 0-13-907585-2

Dedication

For Linda

Contents

Foreword

To meet current and future challenges in the culinary profession, chefs will need the knowledge and comprehensive understanding of all facets of the hospitality industry. Whether in hotel, restaurant, or distinguished dining, a chef will require a well-rounded education in all aspects of management to have a successful career.

From the age of thirteen onward, I was fortunate to have a broad spectrum of experience. Beginning my career in the industry as dishwasher, then to busboy, bartender, executive chef, maitre d', accountant, general manager, and finally the fulfillment of ownership gave me the confidence and encouragement to succeed in business and enjoy the successful ownership of many restaurants over the past thirty years. However, for you, this invaluable information is here in this text.

By reading, learning, and using this text as a reference you will find that Noel Cullen has created an excellent manual for the hospitality industry. The text is in easily understandable terminology. If you are to succeed as a chef or in management in this great hospitality industry in the future, the contents of this text and the knowledge you gain will be your guiding light to a most successful and gratifying career. Education, education, and more education will be with you as long as you remain active in a professional career or as an entrepreneur.

Finally, I can repeat that Dr. Cullen has achieved the preamble for anyone to reach their goals in this book. I wish this wonderfully written comprehensive text had been available when many of us began our careers. In the past the hospitality industry was not as bright as it is today. How wonderfully brilliant it can be for you in the future. You will benefit greatly by gaining the years of knowledge encompassed in *Life Beyond the Line*. It will help you develop an attitude of success and gain the prestige deserved by today's chef in the culinary profession.

Bert P. Cutino, CEC, AAC
Chairman, American Academy of Chefs
Co-owner, Sardine Factory Restaurant, Monterey, California

Noel Cullen has done an exemplary job with this text. He has taken the mystique out of how to be a successful restaurant operator, whether that person be an owner, manager, wait person, chef, or any other of the myriad individuals who contribute to the success of a restaurant operation.

Any person, whether in the front or back of the house, who takes time to read this book, will be surprised at how comprehensive it is; it is practical, as well as technical, and has been presented in a logical and easy-to-understand format.

Noel has put together one of the first reference books that focuses on the importance of educating and training chefs in front of the house service and management in order to bring an understanding of the complete dining experience to the guest.

Benjamin Franklin once said, "The taste of the roast depends on the handshake of the host." This book is a practical guide to achieving this goal, and should be recommended reading for all those who aspire to enter the food service and hospitality profession.

Ted Balestreri, FMP
Co-owner, Sardine Factory Restaurant, Monterey, California
Past President, National Restaurant Association

Preface

The foodservice industry in the United States continues to grow and change, rapidly offering significant employment opportunities for culinarians. According to 1998 figures, the industry employs 9 million people, and according to the National Restaurant Association, this figure will grow to 13 million by the year 2005.

The culinary profession is a large segment of this number which is projected to reach over 1.9 million participants during the year 2000. It is expected that against this background of explosive growth a significant shortfall of culinarians will exist.

Therefore, the foodservice industry in the future will present ever challenging, rewarding, and demanding efforts for culinarians. Just consider the size and scope of the foodservice industry in the United States: in 1998 the food service industry reached sales of over $300 billion, and there are over 720,000 locations that might qualify as foodservice establishments.

With regard to the foodservice market—that is, all the people that visit or are expected to visit a foodservice outlet—whether it be table service or fast food, two important statistics are worth mentioning:

1. Consumers will spend almost 45 percent of every dollar they have available for food on meals and other food *away from home.*

2. Almost 50 percent of all adults in the United States will visit a foodservice establishment on any typical day. (National Restaurant Association data)

So what will all this mean for the chef in this new millennium?

According to U.S. Bureau of Labor Statistics data, over one million additional trained chefs will be required to meet planned restaurant expansions. Added to this is the changing role and new demands being placed on culinarians. Foodservice industry leaders have pointed out that a chef's culinary talent will not be sufficient for the new millennium. Today the major portion of a culinarian's skills are defined in mostly technical terms. Conceptual, creative, leadership, team building, managerial skills, and a front of the house focus are just a few examples of the required skills.

Studies in the United States have shown culinarians not only will have significant responsibility for planning, organizing, directing, and controlling foodservice operations, but also will play critical roles in assuring a "total" customer-satisfaction, quality-dining experience.

Chefs not only have discovered that they are expected to be outstanding culinarians, but they also need to share in the leadership of the entire guest dining experience. The old foodservice management notion of managing kitchen operations from the back door to the front door has been replaced by management from the "front door to the back door" with the main emphasis on customer satisfaction and retention.

As foodservice operators seek competitive advantage in a very crowded market, many operators have embraced quality-management strategies. It has been said that quality management is at the business base of the twenty-first century; it will give foodservice operators a competitive edge.

It is therefore reasonable to assume that chefs of the future will become customer-driven—not only skilled in all aspects of high-quality food production but also in the essential elements of what is generally known as "front of the house" skills. The principal driving force behind the modern chef is satisfying guests and retaining them as customers.

As the foodservice industry continues to grow, Mike Hurst, former president of the National Restaurant Association and owner of the highly successful 15 Street Fisheries in Fort Lauderdale, believes that:

> The foodservice sector of the hospitality industry now at 9 million employees, and growing very fast, clearly there will be a greater need for culinarians with people developmental skills along with great culinary talent *and* a guest focus. These elements together will produce a formidable combination in any future chef.

Life Beyond the Line presents practical and technical aspects of "front of the house" duties which traditionally were only marginally treated as part of a culinarian's training. It is therefore intended that this text not only serve as an informational resource companion for culinarians but also as the basis of a curriculum in front of the house skills to augment culinary skills.

Additionally this text offers practical guidelines in the areas of dining room service, wine and bar service, elements of guest interactions, and an overview of the legal environment in which service is provided. It also examines the issues of team building, the dynamics of leadership, respect and diversity, and the origins of quality management. A positive team environment—so necessary for today's integrated approach success—is discussed in detail.

Life Beyond the Line is different than most texts in the area of education and training for chefs in that it concentrates on noncooking elements. Culinary students are offered a practical framework so as to understand the relevant issues and modern approaches to the complete dining experience for the guest—not just as a view from the cooking line. As students progress through *Life Beyond the Line,* they will find the text "user friendly" in that it uses a rich depth of treatment to the essential and desirable elements of guest relations, dining room service, wines and their service, along with background information on liqueurs, beers, mixology, and training intervention procedures for servers. This text is appropriate for students pursuing an associate-level degree in culinary arts and for practicing culinarians at all levels.

In today's foodservice arena, those culinarians with a broad knowledge of the aspects of quality, teamwork, leadership, and a guest focus, along with the technical skills in service of wine, alcoholic beverages, and guest relations will be highly sought by foodservice operators.

ACKNOWLEDGMENTS

I wish to thank the following friends and colleagues for their encouragement and practical assistance with ideas, suggestions, and technical help. My special thanks to Jim Needell, Dennis Ellis, Klaus Friedenreich, Frederick Dame, Gerard Murphy, Edward Kelly, and Linda Hebach, and my extra special thanks to Dellie Rex for her guidance and superior technical advice with the wine section.

Noel C. Cullen
Boston University

Objectives

GENERAL

After reading this text, you will be able to:

1. Understand the concept of hospitality and guest relations, know and understand the impact of quality management on the foodservice and hospitality industry.
2. Identify the various elements of team building, quality service, and empowerment.
3. Describe the essentials of professionalism in the field of guest relations, mixology, and the service of food, wines, beers, spirits, and liqueurs.
4. Exercise the social skills to meet and exceed guest expectations and satisfaction.
5. Know, understand, and apply the skills required to present oneself professionally.
6. Know and understand the expectations of guests and be able to interact with them in a polite, courteous, and caring manner.
7. Understand the importance of personal grooming, safety, and sanitation.
8. Know the safety procedures in the event of emergencies and be able to recognize and take appropriate actions.
9. Know the laws in relation to a server's responsibility in regard to serving alcoholic beverages; be aware of alcohol and drug abuse. Understand TIPS—the training intervention procedures for servers.

10. Know and understand the basics of wine making, wine apprecia-
    tion, and aspects of tasting and evaluating wine; know the major
    grape varietals and the service of wine.

11. Know and understand the effects of alcohol on the body and aspects
    of bar fraud, theft, and the special problems associated with liquor
    shortages.

12. Know and understand the potential of fraud and civil lawsuits rela-
    tive to guest service.

SPECIFICS

Know and understand:

1. The significance of the modern foodservice industry in the United
   States and the changing roles for culinarians.

2. The various departments within the hospitality and foodservice industry, and how they interact with each other.

3. Individual attitudes and their effects on guest relations.

4. Effective communication with other team members and guests.

5. Meeting, greeting, and seating guests in an efficient, effective, courteous, and respectful manner.

6. How to deal with awkward guests and handle complaints.

7. How to serve disabled persons.

8. Safety procedures in the event of fires or other emergencies.

9. Sanitation, grooming, and personal hygiene.

10. Identification of service equipment.

11. Wines, their origins, opening and service of wine—handling and
    pouring skills.

12. The methods of Russian, French, American, and English service.

13. Technology and computer systems used in dining rooms and bars.

14. Practical aspects of safety; dealing with accidents, spillage, and
    breakages during service.

15. The marriage of wine and food.

16. Dining room staffing—the various positions and the duties associ-
    ated with each.

17. Use of equipment associated with the service of wines.

18. Steps in bar service.

19. Duties of the sommelier.

20. Merchandising and salesmanship.

21. Using the telephone to take guest reservations.

22. Tableside preparations.

23. Spirits, liqueurs, beers, cocktails—their quality points, pouring and serving.

24. Buffet service.

Lessons in Life

Take time to work,

It is the price of success.

Take time to think,

It is the source of power.

Take time to play,

It is the secret of perpetual youth.

Take time to read,

Is is the foundation of wisdom.

Take time to be friendly,

It is the road to happiness.

Take time to share

Life is too short to be selfish.

Take time to laugh,

For laughter is the food of the soul.

—Anon.

People Are the Hospitality Product!

Front-of-the House

Comprises all the areas guests will have contact with

Hospitality

The cordial and generous reception of guests

Empowerment

People

Team Members

Quality Service

Back-of-the House

Areas and individuals who are part of the support team behind the scenes

Teamwork

About the Author

Noel C. Cullen, Ed.D., CMC, AAC, developed his culinary skills to become one of 54 Certified Master Chefs in the United States. Noel Cullen has over thirty years' experience in the foodservice/hospitality/education and culinary arts field as a culinarian, chef patron, executive chef, manager, and professor of hospitality administration. He holds unique combinations of food service and education degrees, including the Licentiate of the City and Guilds of London Institute, a Master of Science degree in Managerial Technology, and a Doctor of Education degree from Boston University.

Named the 1995 "National Educator of the Year," Noel is also the recipient of three "Distinguished Visiting Chef Chairs" from Johnson & Wales University. CHRIE awarded him the "Chef Herman Breihaupt Award" for excellence in hospitality education in 1997. In addition, he has accumulated more than forty-five major international awards for his culinary art, including seven Olympic gold medals.

Dr. Cullen is an associate professor in the School of Hospitality Administration at Boston University, teaching culinary arts, food & beverage, and human resources management. He holds the unique combination of an earned Doctoral Degree and Certified Master Chef status.

Part One

The Imperative
of Customer Service

An Overview of:

Culinarians and Their Roles in Quality Service

The New Challenges for Chefs

The Significance and Legacy of "Service"

Methods of Table Service

Tableside Service and Buffets

Guest Relations and "People" Skills

Suggestive Selling and Merchandising

Legal Issues and Dining Room Service

1

Chefs and the Future

Outline

Life Beyond the Line has been written to provide culinarians with an overview of front of the house functions which contribute to the total dining experience of a guest.

In today's customer-driven, high-quality foodservice industry, culinarians must come to terms with the notion that good service and ambience has often rescued mediocre culinary creations. Guests are becoming increasingly discriminating in their choice of dining establishments. Most guests don't care how famous you are or about organizational charts or how many units or other restaurants you have. In simple terms they want the person standing in front of them to be able to solve their problems.

Each member of the foodservice establishment must understand what brings value to guests and provide this value better than their competition. Guest satisfaction is the result of this transaction. Culinarians have a most important part in this team effort.

CULINARIANS AND QUALITY SERVICE

The vast majority of practicing culinarians are committed professionals who view culinary success from the standpoint of satisfied guests, rather than simply the satisfactory completion of complex menu items during a busy service period. These culinarians derive their "Oscars" from the empty plates and dishes returning from the dining room and are happy in the knowledge that those serving their food are also interested in the diners' gastronomic satisfaction and enjoyment. They understand the philosophy and concept of a professional and total dining experience.

Excellent food poorly served can result in the failure of a restaurant, whereas average food served in an outstanding manner often results in success. Professional hospitality is a complete experience, from the moment guests enter the establishment to the time they leave, and every employee interaction is part of the dining experience.

It is vital in this environment that culinarians not only view quality and guest service in terms of the quality of prepared menu items, but also the integration of all the elements that contribute toward guest satisfaction.

Guest service and guest retention not only is the function of the dining room staff but also the chefs. Culinarians who focus on end-user satisfaction are acutely aware of data that show that for every guest who bothers to complain, there are twenty-six others who remain silent. The average displeased guest will tell eight to sixteen people, and 91 percent of unhappy guests will never come to your restaurant again. It costs about five times as much to get a new guest as to keep a current one.

MOMENTS OF TRUTH

Jan Carlzon, group president of Scandinavian Air System, accomplished a remarkable turnaround for his airline in the recessionary 1980s. His innovative idea was that he saw the business as "moments of truth." Carlzon pointed out, "SAS has ten million passengers a year. The average passenger comes in contact with five SAS employees. Therefore, SAS is the product of ten million times five. SAS is fifty million "moments of truth" per year. Fifty million, unique, never to be repeated opportunities to distinguish ourselves in a memorable fashion, with every one of our customers."

Foodservice fits perfectly into the Carlzon's rationale of "moments of truth." Rarely do guests separate food preparation from service; they react holistically. If the ambience of the restaurant is great and the food perfectly cooked and presented, but service is slow and sloppy and performed with indifference to guest enjoyment, a negative dining experience results.

It has been determined that one of the major reasons why guests stop patronizing a restaurant is employee indifference to guest service. Research has also shown the reasons why guests stop coming to our establishments: 1 percent die, 3 percent move away, 5 percent form other friendships, 9 percent have reasons for patronizing competitors, 14 percent cite product dissatisfaction, and 68 percent quit because of the attitude of indifference toward guests by some employees.

Competition in the foodservice industry has increased enormously, and foodservice organizations are pursuing more discerning and diverse guests who have an acute awareness of good service, good food, and value for money.

It is, therefore, impossible to effect quality service without first understanding the elements that contribute to the *complete* dining experience.

Guest service (the meeting, greeting, seating of guests; attention to their needs to meet or exceed their expectations of the dining experience) is a major part of the chef's job. The old belief that service is only the responsibility of the wait staff, the maitre d', or the manager is a fallacy. This attitude has no place in the modern, competitive, market-driven team approach to satisfying restaurant guests.

In a quality foodservice environment, the service staff are the chef's internal customers. These are the people who play a vital role in supporting the chef's efforts—*they are not the enemies*. Traditional training for culinarians did not include elements of guest relations, social skills, or the techniques of dining room service. This, however, has all changed. In the quality management arena, these areas of training are not an option anymore—they are a must for culinarians.

It has been said chefs were conditioned to thinking of food quality from the "back of the house," that is, the receiving and processing of food product through its various stages. Now the focus is on the "front door." This "front door" philosophy requires the chef to think in terms of getting guests into the restaurant and compelling them to return.

NEW CHALLENGES

Chefs have always been able to attract guests with their culinary creations; now they not only must meet and exceed the guests' gastronomic expectations but also they have a new role in striving to retain them as customers. Modern diners are forcing culinarians to look at them in a new light. Today for foodservice establishments to be successful, culinarians must become customer driven.

To meet this new industry challenge, many culinary schools and colleges have recognized the additional requirements of the elements of quality service in their culinary core curricula. Many of these curricula now include guest relations, dining room service, wine service, and knowledge of bar service, along with an understanding of quality management as part of a culinarian's training.

This resource text is designed to reinforce and enhance training efforts in this area, and to demonstrate that there is truly a *Life Beyond the Line* to which culinarians not only should be aware, but be skilled in its principles and processes. This text has been designed for chef students so they may know and understand how to interact with guests in a real and meaningful way.

TEAMWORK

Throughout this text, all employees and others who work in the hospitality industry are referred to as "team members" or the "team," irrespective of whether they are chefs, waiters, or other employees. Apart from the modern management philosophies of total quality, the restaurant, foodservice, and hotel industry cannot function without the total involvement of all parties through teamwork. Servers, chefs, and others make up the total guest dining experience; therefore a holistic team approach to guest satisfaction is necessary.

A team focus facilitates the modern approach to quality and begins to ensure that there are no negative guest interactions for chefs. Successful quality guest service includes building a strong rapport with the dining room team members and visiting the dining room regularly especially by speaking with guests, introducing yourself to guests, and having guests evaluate new dishes. It's amazing what chefs can learn from these interactions and regular visits to the dining room.

Effective teamwork has no level. It is just as important among top executives as it is among the kitchen and dining room employees. If high value is not placed on teamwork, it does not occur. Teamwork takes conscious efforts to develop and continuous efforts to maintain.

Some of these conscious efforts include the following:

1. Kitchen staff and other team members commit to support each other to make the team successful.
2. Team members understand priorities and support one another when difficulties arise.
3. Communication is open; the expression of new ideas, improved work methods, and articulation of problems and concerns are encouraged.
4. Problem solving is more effective because the collective expertise of the team is available.
5. Performance feedback is more meaningful because team members understand what is expected and can monitor their performance against expectations.
6. The team is recognized for outstanding results—as are individual team members.
7. Learning to work as a team in one department is good preparation for interacting as a team with other foodservice departments.
8. Collective wisdom is virtually always superior to individual wisdom.

A foodservice organization can serve its customers only as well as it serves its own employees. The organization must be committed to developing and supporting a highly motivated team.

UNDERSTANDING WINE AND WINE SERVICE

Wine sets the tone for dinner and enhances the flavor of food. It improves the entire dining experience for the guest and increases revenue for the restaurant. Wine can draw more guests, particularly that desirable upscale segment who look for that special dining experience. Wine contributes to that expectation.

The production of "fine" distinctive wine results from integrity and dedication, much as the chef devotes to a fine culinary achievement. Frequently the chef student will miss its essence because that student may lack the "fundamental" understanding of what's important in wines. The guidelines contained in this text assist in the development of a personal perspective on the appreciation of wine.

Among the many reasons why chefs need to become knowledgeable about wines is the wisdom of being well informed about an integral part of the professional hospitality experience. Besides personal and professional satisfaction, knowledge of wine also enables chef students to distinguish wine varieties and to determine which foods they complement. Additionally wine sales are important to the foodservice establishment itself because they increase the profit margin.

The best way to learn about wine is simply by looking at it, smelling it, and tasting it. Knowing how to read a wine label, how to talk about wine, and how to evaluate it enables an appreciation of the quality points of wine. Also this text helps chef students to gain an understanding of liqueurs, beers, and other spirits, including important information about their composition and history. This information serves the chef student as a basis for studying flavor compatibility in food recipes.

FOOD AND BEVERAGE SERVICE

Within this text the student also discovers the essential techniques and qualities of service currently in use in the United States. There are traditional protocols, unique to each style of service. The text outlines and discusses the qualities and elements relative to each service method, and how to serve guests food, wine, and other beverages.

It has been said that sometimes servers can become so wrapped up in the technical aspects of service that they can fail to see the guest as a person. The text not only outlines for each student an understanding of the expectations of the service techniques but also, most importantly, the attitudes, knowledge, and skills necessary to meet and exceed guest expectations every time.

These elements include:

1. Being attentive and anticipating guests' needs.
2. Displaying excellent communication skills with guests and fellow team members.
3. Promoting teamwork.
4. Being detail oriented.
5. Having confidence, a positive attitude, and an outgoing personality.
6. Having an appropriate knowledge of the food and beverage products, as well as their description, prices, and methods of service.
7. Having a complete knowledge of the elements of service.
8. Being technically competent.

The opinions or attitudes that guests develop toward the foodservice establishment may be determined for a long period of time by the actions of the service providers. It is sometimes easy to take a guest for granted, but when we do, we not only run the risk of losing that guest, but also their associates—their friends, family, and other prospective guests.

Remember guests are not always right, but they are always guests.

ISSUES SURROUNDING THE SERVICE OF ALCOHOL

In today's hospitality and foodservice industry, the bartender and server are legally responsible for serving either a minor (even with "proper" identification) or an intoxicated patron; therefore, they need to understand the legal requirements placed on them. Because of today's legal environment, servers and bartenders need to take their responsibilities even more seriously and always make the decision whether to serve alcoholic beverages on the side of caution.

Overconsumption of alcohol should never be encouraged or tolerated. Servers and bartenders need to be constantly aware of what and how much alcohol is served to each guest. Strict and sensible policies promote and encourage responsible drinking, and every reasonable effort should be taken to prevent visibly intoxicated guests from driving.

Visibly intoxicated guests should not be allowed to enter the restaurant or bar. A certain amount of tact and professionalism and a knowledge of intervention strategies must be used when it becomes necessary to end the service of alcohol to guests. TIPS (Training Intervention Procedures for Servers) outlines steps and practices to be adopted. This training includes handling guests in a diplomatic manner, explaining why guests are being denied further service, and that legally, morally, and for their personal safety, as well as the safety of others, you cannot, in good conscience, serve them any more.

Chapter 18 treats this subject area in detail, as well as outlines the various warning signs of intoxication and provides procedures and strategies to be adopted in this serious and important area.

Against this background new strategies of working together in the foodservice establishment must be put in place. A greater awareness of respect, diversity, leadership, and team building are necessary to accommodate the new dimensions of the modern culinarian. This modern culinarian not only is a first-rate cook but also one who can recognize all the elements that must come together to have an understanding of the guest, contributing to a complete dining experience and making a successful restaurant.

REVIEW QUESTIONS

1. Explain the changed role of the chef relative to quality and service.
2. List the challenges that face chefs in the new millennium.
3. Describe why chefs require a knowledge and understanding of the service of wines and other beverages in the new paradigm.
4. Outline the important issues surrounding the service of alcohol.
5. Indicate why Carlzon's "moments of truth" are relevant to the foodservice industry.

2

The Legacy of Service

Outline

HISTORICAL NOTES ON RESTAURANT SERVICE

The moment our ancient ancestors gathered around cook fires, from then on gatherings at a table became possible, and the era of dining and banquets began. The Renaissance period saw a rise in elegant dining. Contrary to popular thought, elegant dining truly began in Italy. However, its move to France took it to its highest level thanks mainly to Catherine de Medici and her marriage to Henry II of France. When Catherine arrived in France, she brought with her the master "Medici" cooks. Foods never before seen in France were soon being served. She introduced the French to eating with knives, forks, and spoons instead of using their fingers or daggers. She had brought these utensils with her from Florence and introduced them to the nobility. Soon it became a custom for guests to carry their own eating utensils when they went to dine outside their homes.

In the Middle Ages, the traveling public ate at inns and taverns. When people of wealth or high rank traveled and stayed in these inns, they often had their servants prepare the food. Religious orders continued to care for travelers, but places for common people to go and dine did not exist. People ate largely in private homes.

At first only taverns were allowed to serve drinks. Later they were allowed to serve such foods as appetizers (which they in turn had bought from Charcuterie); eventually they were allowed to serve full meals.

During the sixteenth century, coffee and tea were imported into Europe, and over the next hundred years, coffeehouses sprang up all over Europe. These coffeehouses became the social and literary centers of the day, and were the forerunners of the modern cafés and coffee shops.

Tour d'Argent Restaurant opened in Paris in the mid-sixteenth century, and for over four hundred years, it has remained unique, and is the oldest restaurant in the world. Inns served meals, but were not primarily eating places as was the Tour d'Argent. However, during the sixteenth century, only the *traiteurs* (caterers) were allowed by law to sell cooked meats to the public.

In 1760, during the reign of France's King Louis XV, a man named Boulanger decided to sell soups and a special dish made from sheep's feet or trotters in a white sauce. The advertisement for his dishes read: *"Walk up everybody who has a weak stomach. I'll restore you."* The French word for restore is *restaurer*. These nourishing dishes gradually became associated with the word *restorante*, meaning restorative foods, which is what Boulanger called his enterprise. The *traiteurs* sued Boulanger, and the case went to the French Parliament. Boulanger won. We have to thank Boulanger for the beginning of what we now know as the restaurant and foodservice industry.

One of the dishes Boulanger prepared was a dish of sliced potatoes baked in stock in his bread bakers' oven. Boulanger allowed the people from his town to use the heat of his oven to cook their potatoes after the bread was done, and so began one of the classic potato dishes. Boulanger potatoes are still included on many menus today.

In 1782 The Grande Tavern de Londres, a true restaurant, opened in Paris; it was followed three years later by Aux Trois Freres Provencaux, and by the time of the French revolution, there were 500 restaurants in France.

With the demise of the French aristrocacy following the French revolution, the servants who had worked for the nobility were out of work. These dispossessed chefs and servants scattered, eventually forming the basis of what became the modern French restaurant and foodservice industry.

CHANGES IN SERVICE STYLES

French service was a most elegant form of service which originated in the courts and palaces of the nobles. Originally this type of service consisted of three courses:

- The first course consisted of soups, *relevé* (a large roast of meat), the *entrée*, (several types of dishes), and various hors d'oeuvres.
- The second course included roasted chicken or fowl and entremets. (Initially, there were two types of entremets—light vegetable or garnishes and sweets.) Entremets are now generally considered side dishes and more appropriately desserts.
- The third and last course included various kinds of desserts and fruit. For each course the dishes were not served individually; instead they were placed on the table all at one time.

With French service, very often the abundance and beauty of the dishes became more important than the taste.

BRINGING ETIQUETTE AND STYLE TO THE TABLE

In medieval times knives had always been a part of a man's everyday wear. They were used mainly for hunting but also for personal protection. The inns and taverns of the times did not supply any eating utensils when they served their dishes. When dining, men placed their knives at the right hand while they ate, so in case of an attack the knife was in a perfect position to be grabbed for protection.

(In ancient times when the monarch sat at the head of the table no other person could sit within a six-foot radius—the reason was that the average length of a sword was three feet and the length of a man's arm was three feet. Therefore if an excited diner decided to take swipe at the monarch, there was a good chance they would miss him.)

Later on knives became a standard feature at most taverns and inns. History has it that Cardinal Richelieu of France observed an individual using his pointed knife to pick his teeth in a public restaurant. Shortly after he issued an edict that all knives in restaurants henceforth be rounded off at the tip instead of being pointed.

The early type of forks consisted of two prongs. Although history suggests it was originally introduced to Venice in the eleventh century, there is no doubt that Catherine di Medici brought it with her to France. The fork replaced the practice of eating food with the fingers and daggers. At first it was treated with great amusement. Later forks were to become very ornate and elaborate, and when people were invited to dinner, they brought their own forks with them in specially designed carrying cases.

The spoon is the oldest of all the eating utensils. The earliest spoons were made from wood. Ancient examples of spoons include those that were elaborately decorated in precious metals and intricately carved in ivory. The spoon was a mark of rank in society. Wealthy parents had special spoons commissioned for their children at birth, which is where the expression to be "born with a silver spoon in your mouth" comes from.

In medieval times it was the custom for diners at royal courts to keep long-haired dogs at their feet while they were dining. The dogs' role was twofold: to eat the scraps and, more importantly, to act as a "towel" or napkin for the diner to wipe and dry his hands. The use of napkins began when wealthy individuals began to cover their dining table with expensive linen or silk drapes.

At that time dining room tables were long and narrow, and the cloths were laid across the table diagonally; therefore, a corner piece would hang over for each guest. Because of the manner in which a piece of the cloth hung over the table, it became common practice for guests to "tuck" the corner of the tablecloth under their chins to prevent food from falling into their laps and to use to wipe their hands and faces at the end of the meal. It was a very simple step from there to presenting square pieces of accompanying linen on the table. Later the manipulation of these "napkins" became an art form for dining room table decorations. (See Appendix 3 for examples of napkin folds.)

THE ORIGINS OF MODERN TABLE SERVICE

In the early 1800s, Kourakine, the Russian ambassador to France, noticed faults with the French service and decided to introduce his particular brand of service. He believed that guests would better appreciate the taste of their dishes if each dish was served individually—hot dishes served hot and cold dishes served cold as was the practice in Russia.

This style of service took over fifty years to be fully embraced by the French. Urbain Dubois, the famous chef and author, worked for a Russian duke. In his book titled *La Cuisine classique* (1856), he extolled the benefits of Russian service. Dubois outlined his belief that Russian service was a much better form and style of service than that of the traditional French. According to Dubois, its main virtue was that food served from a platter was at its best. With this serving method, guests could have as much food as they desired and in pristine condition. Throughout the nineteenth century, Russian service was introduced into an increasing number of restaurants, and it grew tremendously in popularity.

THE DAWNING OF ELEGANT SERVICE AND THE LEGACY OF CESAR RITZ

Cesar Ritz began his hotel career in the hospitality industry at the age of fifteen as an "Apprenticed Hotelkeeper." By the age of nineteen, he had obtained a position as the manager of a Parisian restaurant. He then decided to start over again having secured a position as an assistant waiter at Voisin, the famous Paris restaurant. At Voisin he served some of the very best clientele in Europe. Ritz learned very quickly what pleased and what displeased them, and, more importantly, how to influence his guests. He became so professional at what he did that fashionable clients insisted that he alone should serve them.

By the age of twenty-five, he had become the manager of the Grand National Hotel in Lucerne, Switzerland; at that time the Grand National was one of the most luxurious hotels in the world. Under his direction not only did he introduce uncompromising high standards of excellence, but he also turned the faltering financial position of the hotel around. He managed the Grand National for eleven seasons.

Ritz's name and fame spread. His treatment of guests and the high-quality level of service he provided became legendary.

Richard d'Oyly Carte, the chairman and president of the Savoy Hotel Company (he was the impresario who had presented the successful Gilbert and Sullivan operettas), had become fascinated by hotels like many other successful businessmen, and he determined to build a veritable palace to outshine all the competition. The result was the London Savoy Hotel, which opened in 1889.

d'Oyly Carte sought out Cesar Ritz to manage his luxury London Savoy Hotel (the hotel was not doing well after six months of operation). At age thirty-eight, Ritz became the manager of the Savoy, with a virtually free hand to operate it on his terms. He brought the forty-three-year-old Auguste Escoffier with him to London. Escoffier was acknowledged to be *the* master chef. It was at the Savoy that Escoffier was to elevate the culinary profession to a new level. As is well known, his *Guide to Modern Cookery*, published in 1907, remains the bible of thousands of chefs all over the world to this day. His reputation with his fellow chefs at that time was illustrious.

Ritz was to become the epitome of the great hotel manager—a genuine legend in his own time. Very few men ever achieve an adjective made from their name, but "ritzy" comes from Ritz. In the *Concise Oxford Dictionary*, it means "high class and luxurious."

Cesar Ritz in charge of the front of the house and Auguste Escoffier in charge of the kitchen were a formidable team. They revolutionized dining out, and it is said they went on to change the habits of the English dining public. Escoffier created new dishes and named them for a favored few. Ritz introduced orchestras to the dining room and extended the dining period. He made evening dress compulsory and restricted unescorted women. Sunday dining became a feature of the week. The Savoy became known as the place to go and be seen. It was Edward VII (1841–1910, prince of Wales and later king of England) who remarked "Where Mr. Ritz goes, there I go." Ritz made the Savoy the center of cultural activity in London and attracted the elite of society, politics, and the arts; all became patrons of both Ritz and Escoffier. At no other time had the level of elegant dining been raised so high as under these two men.

REVIEW QUESTIONS

1. Describe the historical background to the introduction of "table etiquette."
2. Discuss the elements and incidents that were the precursors of the modern foodservice industry.
3. State the important elements relative to the introduction of tableware.
4. Explain the origins of modern table service.
5. Discuss the contribution of Cesar Ritz to elegant service.

3

Methods of Table Service

Outline

METHODS OF TABLE SERVICE

It has often been said that in all customer service operations the first thirty seconds of contact with the personnel is the period in which the customer forms lasting opinions of the business.

There are a number of styles of table service, each offering a varying degree of elegance. The common thread that links all styles of service is that guests expect courteous and knowledgeable servers who possess the skills and attitude necessary to serve and make them feel welcome and comfortable.

Regardless of the type of restaurant or method of service, there are always two requirements of good service—efficiency and courtesy. Efficient service does not necessarily mean speed. Rather, it means serving each course at the right time, with the food at the proper temperature, and with all the required accompaniments and utensils.

According to Mike Hurst: "Good service is what differentiates restaurants in today's saturated marketplace. We are not selling food in my restaurant, we are selling a pleasant experience."

In a coffee shop, efficient service is fast service. In a white-tablecloth restaurant, it is service that is timed to allow the guest to enjoy a leisurely dining experience, with each course served exactly when the guest is ready for it.

A pleasant, courteous service team can make the greatest contribution to the restaurant's image regardless of the "type" of service.

If the service team are genuinely interested in providing high quality service, guests will leave with good feelings about their dining experience.

The restaurant and foodservice industry is a people business, and running a dining room involves a lot more than just knowing the technical aspects of traditional service "types," or just bringing the food to the table and carrying dishes.

Service is a vital part of the total food service package—the food and back of the house, the ambience, and the service. Service therefore is a team effort. However, excellent service only occurs when friendliness and courtesy is combined with competence.

There are generally four distinct types of table service used in the United States. These are:

1. French
2. Russian and banquet Russian service
3. American
4. English or Family/Butler Service

Each service style should be considered by a food operation from the viewpoint of such variables as check average, skill levels of food preparation, skill levels of the service team, turnover, equipment available, and menu form. Menu construction and preparation methods may then be related to the type of service that has been selected so that maximum dining pleasure may be offered. In many cases it will be possible to achieve optimum use of team members in both the front and the back of the house if menu, preparation, and serving procedures are integrated.

Each restaurant or food service outlet, depending on its menu, decor, style, check average, and market, must design its own program to provide the service—be it French, American, Russian, English, or combinations of all, or some of these different service styles.

FRENCH SERVICE

Today French Service is characterized by the "finishing off" of the cooking, carving, and flaming of food in front of the guest.

With French service, food items are fully or partially prepared in the kitchen, placed on platters, in copper pans, or in tureens, and brought to the dining room and placed on a cart called a gueridon, which has a rechaud. (French service requires the use of a gueridon, which is a service cart or trolley).

Platters are placed on rechauds, (a rechaud is a small stove-like appliance designed to cook, flame, or to keep food warm). Food items are then finished, plated, and garnished for each guest by the service team member. Each plate is arranged and garnished on the gueridon by the server prior to presenting it to the guest at the table.

French service is the most elaborate and labor-intensive type of service.

Accompaniments for those items which are to be boned, sliced, or carved tableside, are usually plated and brought to the gueridon separately. Only those foods that can be cooked in a reasonably short time are prepared and cooked in front of the guest.

All foods are served to the left of the guest. Courses are cleared from the right. Effective service is dependent on the captain and the entire service team. Without assistance, it is virtually impossible to give full classic French service. French service has the advantage of allowing for a great deal of "showmanship" and flourish; performed correctly it is very elegant. Guests often enjoy the individual attention French service confers upon them. The potential downside to this type of service is that it is very labor intensive: it requires high technical skills to perform correctly, more space in the dining room is needed, and the room can be filled with cooking smells.

RUSSIAN SERVICE

Russian service is characterized by food being cooked and preportioned in the kitchen. All the food for a table is presented to the guests on serving platters (usually silver). The team member (server) serves the food from the platter to the guest's plate. Russian service has great elegance and requires a good deal of showmanship. It is also efficient and relatively fast, requiring less labor and skill than French service; it is also suitable for elaborate banquets.

The table setting for Russian service follows what is common for French service, but a water glass may be on the table just above the tip of the knife. A bread and butter plate and butter knife are used.

In Russian service, plates for the course to follow are put down in their proper places before the guests. If the food is to be served hot, the plates should be hot; cold foods should be served on chilled plates. Sometimes salads are brought to the table already dished onto cold plates. To put the plates down for a course, a team server uses the right hand to place the item on the right side of the guest. The movement is then to the next guest on the left, and proceeds clockwise.

When all plates are in position, the serving dish is picked up by the team member and held in the palm of the left hand, or by the left arm and palm for a tray or large platter. The right hand serves the food from the serving dish to the guest's plate. Soup may be ladled into soup dishes from a tureen, or it may be brought to the table in small, individual serving dishes on a tray.

Considerable dexterity is required to perform Russian service. The platter or silver tray on which the portions of food have been dished can be heavy and very hot. Often servers wrap a towel lightly around their left arm as protection against being burned. The serving dish must be held securely and balanced, while the right hand manipulates a large spoon and fork to grasp the portion and move it without spilling it. The right hand holds the serving spoon with its bowl facing up. Directly over this is the fork. The spoon is used to scoop up the item while the fork, with some pressure on the top, holds the item on the spoon as it is being transferred to the guest's plate. The spoon can be used to scoop up sauce from the platter and pour it over the plate.

Coffee is served after the meal. Coffee cups, saucers, cream, and sugar are not on the guest's table. Coffee may be poured from a buffet and served.

The relative advantages and disadvantages of Russian service include the following: Food is served directly from the platter to the plate, and this can be impressive when correctly performed. It is faster than traditional French service. The quality and temperature of the food can be better controlled. Some of the disadvantages with Russian service are that the server has to be skilled in serving from platter to plate, and different entrees require different platters.

BANQUET RUSSIAN SERVICE

Russian banquet service is a very elegant form of service, which is sometimes also referred to as controlled service. When performed as a controlled service it not only can be elegant, but also very efficient. When it is "controlled," each member of the service team stands at the same place at each table, or the service team can line the perimeter of the dining room. On a given signal from the maitre d' (for example, a nod of the head), the team members leave the dining room in unison and file into the kitchen, where each team member picks up the bowls or plates and the food item for the first course. The entire team returns to the dining room in a line together.

Service begins when the maitre d' again gives the signal. The presetting of china begins at each table. In a team service, for example, one server sets the soup bowl, followed by a second server who ladles the soup. Similarly another server presets plates, while a second would serve the starch and vegetable from a large platter. Still another would follow, serving the entree.

AMERICAN SERVICE

The simplest and least expensive type of service is American service. It is also fast and does not require a great amount of labor. American service is designed to give an operator the greatest control and the most efficiency.

The table setting for this service places the knife (blade side in) at the right, the soupspoon next, and the teaspoon next on the outside. Normally settings are made so that the first utensil on the outside, on either the left or right, is used first, then the next utensil to it, moving in as the courses progress, for example, placing the soupspoon on the outside, where it is used first with the first course, the teaspoon next, and the knife on the inside. The dinner fork and then the salad fork are placed on the left. In the center a service or hors d'oeuvre plate is set. The water glass is set at the tip of the knife and about an inch away. The coffee cup and saucer are usually placed on the table next to the teaspoon to speed service. The salt and pepper should be in the center of the table.

If a wineglass is to be used, it is placed to the right of the water glass. The bread and butter plate should be above the forks and to the left. The butter knife should be at a right angle to the forks on the butter plate with the blade turned toward the forks. For a normal meal, the table may be covered first with a "silencer" cloth and then a tablecloth. However, placemats alone may be used for an informal meal. Silverware and dishes should not be any closer than a half-inch from the edge of the table. Chairs should be out from the table, and away from the tablecloth.

American service, or a modified version of it, is used in operations requiring fast turnover, such as coffee shops or casual dining operations. When it is used in a fine dining operation, the coffee cup and saucer are not on the table, because hot beverages generally are served later in the meal. Procedures vary with different operations.

BASIC RULES OF AMERICAN SERVICE

- All food service is made from the left side of the guest with the left hand.
- All dishes are removed from the left side of the guest with the left hand.
- All beverages are served from the right side of the guest with the right hand.
- All beverages are removed from the right side of the guest with the right hand.
- All dishes or glasses are served and removed from the table one at a time and stacked in the other hand behind the guest. Never stack dishes on the table for removal.
- Serve cold foods cold; serve hot foods hot.

Never reach in front of a guest with elbows near their face. Use the arm farthest away. These rules give the server a graceful appearance and do not discomfort the guests by requiring them to shift their positions or lean away from flying elbows.

THE USE OF TRAYS AND AMERICAN SERVICE

One of the features of American service is the widespread use of the tray and the tray stand. There are two basic types of trays used in the restaurant industry. These are large ovals or small rectangle, round, or oval trays. With the aid of a tray stand and plate covers, large trays allow the team member to bring many items to the table at one time.

Correct loading of restaurant trays is necessary to ensure ease of handling and to reduce spillage and breakage.

1. There are two correct ways of placing dishes on tray: place heavy dishes in center of tray, and place the heavier dishes on the edge of the tray that will be placed on the shoulder.
2. For balance and stability, load the tray from the center to the outer edge.
3. Do not place cups on saucers when bringing coffee to the table.
4. Do not place appetizers on underliner plates.
5. Glasses, cups, or other containers with beverages should be placed near the center and handles turned outward to prevent spillage.

6. Fill beverages to one-half inch below lip to avoid spillage.

7. Ensure both sides of the tray are clean.

When loading trays with soiled dishes, follow the same rules. The maximum load for any tray of soiled dishes is the amount that makes sense for the person carrying the tray. It is important not to overload the tray as the damage resulting through breakage can high. If a tray of soiled dishes is to be left in the dining room, even for a moment, it should be covered with a clean cloth. Trays should be wiped clean on both sides before replacing on shelf. Remove soiled dishes from the dining room as quickly as possible. Leftovers are definitely offensive to the eyes and nose.

If the tray is heavy, slide tray from stand or counter with both hands. Put one hand under. Keep other hand on edge for balance. Bend knees, place shoulder under heavy part of tray. Keep back as straight as possible as you straighten your legs. Lift with the legs and not the back. This could help eliminate future back problems.

LEFT OR RIGHT?

It is common to serve foods to the left; wine is poured to the right, moving around the table from right to left. However, much variation occurs. All clearing may be done from the right using the right hand. The general rule in all service is that when serving at the guest's right, use the right hand; when serving at the guest's left, use the left hand. Whatever method is used, it should be based on what is easiest to do most efficiently and quickly for the guest.

It is not proper to remove dishes or to start a new course in American service, or in any other type of service, until everyone at the table has finished eating the present course.

Soiled dishes are removed from the table as follows: items to the left, from the left-hand side using the left hand, central items and items to the right, from the right-hand side using the right hand.

American service is frequently used at banquets because a large number of guests can be handled quickly by a limited number of servers.

ENGLISH/FAMILY OR BUTLER SERVICE

English service is also called formal family service or butler service. It is primarily used in family run inns and on special occasions in other foodservice establishments.

Foods are brought from the kitchen on platters and in serving dishes. The host, who remains at the table during the meal, carves the meat while the hostess (or another person) serves the vegetables, salad, dessert, and beverage. The host places the meat portion on a hot plate and then passes it to a second person who puts on the other food items and then passes it to a guest.

The host is served last, or next to last before the hostess. The meat should be in front of the host, with plates used for service immediately in front of the host. It is desirable to work out a passing pattern that requires the least handling of plates. Sometimes team members may take plates and carry them to the guests instead of having them passed. It is proper to have the first course placed on the table when guests come into the dining room. Water can be poured, and butter placed on the butter plates. Coffee cups and saucers usually are not placed on the table but brought at the conclusion of the meal or when dessert is served.

Small tables may be placed to the right and left of the host where service dishes can be placed when the service is ended.

Place settings may be similar to those used in American service, but can vary. Normally knives and spoons are to the right, and forks are to the left. The order of placement is from the outside in as the courses occur. Wineglasses are placed to the right of the water glass, which is placed just above the tip of the knife.

PRESENTING THE CHECK

At breakfast the check should be presented when the guest has finished the main course, and only when coffee or other beverage has been replenished. At lunch the check is presented when the guest has been served dessert and coffee, or when other beverages have been refilled. At dinner the check is presented when the guest has finished dessert and coffee, or when other beverages have been refilled. In those restaurants that serve alcoholic beverages, the check is presented after the guest has finished ordering.

Check presentation procedure:

1. Ensure server's name and table number are on the check.
2. Check prices have been correctly applied.
3. If the table does not order dessert or an after-dinner beverage and has indicated no more beverages, total check away from the table and present it.
4. When dessert is ordered and after it is served, refill coffee, total check away from the table, and present it.
5. If an after-dinner beverage is ordered and consumed, return to table for a second sale. If none is ordered, the check may now be presented.

How the check is handled is just as important as the greeting. The check is the guest's final interaction with the server. It must be clean, neat, readable, and correct.

FROM SOUP TO NUTS: GUIDELINES

1. **Seating guests:** Show guests to their assigned table, and give each person a menu.

2. **Take the beverage order:** Return with the cocktail or other beverage order.

3. **Explain the menu and any specials:** When the guests have had enough time to study the menu, ask them what they would like. Write the orders on the docket, using the correct abbreviations. Be sure the orders are complete, including beverages.

   Explain the specials and menu enthusiastically. Guests usually order whatever is enthusiastically suggested, so make everything sound appetizing and genuinely delicious rather than reciting the information as if by rote.

   Hold the order book in your left hand, with the side towel (if used) folded neatly and draped over your left arm if you are right handed. If left handed, reverse.

   Service team members should know the menu completely; the pronunciation and description of every dish, including ingredients; and method of preparation. Prior to service at a "pre-meal" daily, specials should be seen and tasted by the service team, so they are able to describe them accurately.

   Make suggestions according to the merchandising policy of the restaurant. Sell specials at every opportunity. If there is table-side cooking, sell table-side items if guests are not in a hurry.

4. **Serving the guest:** Serve everything with the left hand from the left side of the guest with the exception of the beverage. Beverages are served with the right hand on the right side of the guest.

5. **Service of the appetizer and or salad:** Soups are served on an underliner. Place soupspoon or cocktail fork on the right, in addition to the silver already placed. When the first course or appetizer is served, pick up the salads from the kitchen and serve. Serve bread rolls as appropriate. If a salad dressing is to be passed, bring it with you. When the guests have finished the first course or appetizer, clear the dishes. Stack dishes according to size on the tray stands. When the table has been cleared, take them to the dishwashing area.

6. **Serving the entree:** Pick up the food orders from the kitchen. Set the tray of hot food on the tray stand. Bring the dinner plates to the table. Place the first dinner plate in front of the guest with the left hand, then transfer the second dinner plate to the left hand and serve other guests.

7. **Picking up the order from the kitchen:** When picking up food from the kitchen, be as quiet as possible, talking only to the chef or expediter who is trying to get the orders out, and then only regarding the order being picked up. Remember, chefs arrange food on plates or

platters in an attractive way that is appealing to guests (we eat with our eyes first), therefore, every effort should be made by the server not only to get the food to the guest's table as quickly and as safely as possible, but also to present the food plate in the same way to the guest as the chef intended.

8. Beverage: Keep water glasses filled. Remain near the guest table as much as possible so that you will be available should the guests desire any further service. Pass bread rolls a second time while the guests are still eating the entree.

9. Clearing: Clear everything with the left hand from the left side of the guest with the exception of the beverage. When all guests at your table have finished eating, you may clear the tables. Place the dirty dishes on your tray located on the tray stand. Repeat the above process until all dishes on the table have been cleared. Clear everything except cups and saucers, water glasses, sugar bowl, creamer, and flatware for dessert. Salt and pepper shakers should also be cleared.

10. Dessert and coffee service: Pick up the dessert orders and necessary underliners. Place any necessary flatware (if there is none on the table) for dessert on the right side of the guest. When serving pie, place the plate so that the point of the slice of pie faces the guest. Serve coffee and refill as appropriate. In closing always thank the guest by name whenever possible. Inform the guest of upcoming specials or events they may look forward to. Use comment cards for guests' comments. After guests leave, clear the tables of all dishes and linens.

11. Miscellaneous instructions: When you are not busy, assist other dining room team members. Keep dining room free from soiled dishes and trays.

Follow one traffic pattern. Use one door of dining room for going into the kitchen and the other door for going out of the kitchen into the dining room whenever possible.

Always leave your station and tables clean and orderly. Return any flatware, linen, or food which has been left on the service stand to the proper place. Wipe off the top of each service stand at the end of the meal period.

DUTIES OF THE DINING ROOM TEAM

Maitre d'hotel

The maitre d'hotel is essentially the food and beverage manager. Depending on the size of the restaurant or hotel, the maitre d' may be assisted by one or more persons who would supervise various floors or rooms with the organization.

The maitre 'd has total responsibility for the dining room. He or she must be in close contact with every department and know all aspects of the business, dining room, banquet facilities, bars, kitchen, dishwashing area, and the front office.

Captain

The captain has the responsibility of supervising and organizing all aspects of a service station. This requires knowledge of the ingredients, the preparation of menu items and the correct method of service, and the meeting and greeting of guests who have been seated at tables in the service station.

A captain should have the ability to carve to remove fish bones, and to prepare and cook in front of the guest. The captain should also have the ability to merchandise the menu, and be informative, friendly, and attentive to all information concerning and explaining the menu. Generally the captain is a team leadership position.

Front Waiter

The front waiter team member assists the captain when serving food. He or she should be able to perform all duties in the absence of the captain. The responsibilities also include serving all cocktails, plated food, and cordials, as well as cleaning after each course.

Back Waiter

This team member usually brings all food ordered from the kitchen to the service area. Other responsibilities include assisting in the cleaning; providing ingredients to each table; bringing cold salad plates and hot dinner plates; serving forks, spoons, extra flatware, and doilies; possessing knowledge of ingredients, method of preparation, garnishes, and proper service of food items; being aware of each stage of service of each table; placing and picking up orders; and coordinating efforts with other team members.

Bus Person

Responsibilities include serving bread, butter, and water and replenishing these items when necessary. He or she helps to clean the table after each course.

When guests have departed from the table, the bus person cleans and resets each table, ensuring there is a supply of clean tablecloths and napkins on hand. Duties are performed that are necessary to keep the dining room in first-class order.

Sommelier (Wine Steward)

In fine establishments the sommelier is in charge of the wines—this function demands an extensive knowledge of wines. The sommelier supervises the wine inventory, and helps design and write the wine list.

ROOM SERVICE/IN-ROOM DINING

Regardless of the type or service required, efficiency and courtesy remain the norm. Efficient room service does not necessarily mean only speed; it means serving each meal at the agreed time and the food at the proper temperature, with all the required accompaniments and eating utensils.

The term room service has for some time referred to all service to hotel and guest rooms. Recently some hotels have changed the name of room service to in-room dining or private dining so as to present the service as more upscale. The intention is to bring the dining experience (high-quality food and beverage service) to the room.

Generally the larger the hotel and the higher the room rate the more likely that a hotel will offer room service. In some instances economy and midpriced hotels avoid the costs of operating room service by having vending machines on each floor and food items such as pizza or Chinese food delivered by local restaurants.

The level of service and menu prices varies from hotel to hotel. Some top-level hotels have butler service for all guest rooms without additional charge.

Some years ago room service was thought of as a necessary evil, something that guests expected but that did not produce profit for the hotel.

Room service generally operates between sixteen and twenty-four hours a day.

Some of the challenges for quality room service are delivery of orders on time (this is especially important for breakfast, which is by far the most popular room service meal) and the avoidance of complaints of excessive charges and delays for room service orders.

FORTY WAYS TO EMPTY A DINING ROOM

1. A sour greeting or none at all.
2. Not seating guests.
3. Forgetting to take guests' coats.
4. Improperly set tables.
5. Empty salt and pepper shakers.
6. Reaching in front of guests.

7. Loud talk or arguing with guests or other team members within earshot of guests.

8. Running into the dining room instead of walking.

9. Not saying "Excuse me," "Please," or "Thank you."

10. Dirty or bent flatware.

11. Dirty or chipped china or glassware.

12. Fingermarks on plates or glasses.

13. Team members in groups or lounging about—especially when guests need service.

14. Clattering dishes.

15. Littered, dirty floors.

16. Dirty, torn menu cards.

17. Forgetting items.

18. Forgetting specific instructions.

19. Bringing the wrong items.

20. Empty bread baskets.

21. Dirty ashtrays, (where smoking is permitted).

22. Reprimanding team members in front of guests.

23. Thumb in soup.

24. Shabby or stained linen.

25. Scraping crumbs onto the floor.

26. Spilling things on the table.

27. Spilling something on guest's clothes.

28. Touching food with hands.

29. Removing plates before all guests are finished.

30. Not removing dishes when all guests are finished.

31. Dirty side tables or tray stands full of dishes.

32. Ignoring guests at another server's station when called.

33. Making guests wait for a check.

34. Forgetting to assist guests who are leaving.

35. Unfriendly attitude, no smile.

36. Dirty, sloppy uniform and shoes.

37. Body odor, bad breath.

38. Uncombed hair, careless shave, unkempt makeup.

39. Dirty hands and fingernails.

40. Not saying "Good-bye."

DINING ROOM SAFETY PROCEDURES

1. Report every injury at once, regardless of severity. Avoid delay.

2. Report all unsafe conditions, such as broken or splintered chairs or tables, defective equipment, leaking radiators, torn carpeting, uneven floors, loose rails, unsafe tools or knives, broken china and glass, and so on.

3. Understand the safe way to perform any task assigned to you. If in doubt, check. If you have to move heavy objects, ask for help. When lifting any heavy object, keep your back straight, bend your knees, and use your leg muscles. The back has weak muscles and can easily be strained.

4. Aisles, passageways, and stairways must be kept clean and free from obstructions. Do not permit brooms, pails, mops, cans, boxes, and so on to remain where someone can fall over them. Wipe up any grease or wet spots from stairs or floors or ramps at once. These are serious hazards.

5. Walk, do not run, in halls, down ramps or stairs, or around work areas. Be careful when passing through swinging doors.

6. Wear safe, sensible clothes and safe, comfortable shoes, with good soles. Never wear thin-soled or broken-down shoes. Do not wear high-heeled shoes for work. Ragged or overlong sleeves or ragged clothing may result in an injury.

7. If you have to reach for a high object, use a ladder, not a chair or table or a makeshift. There is no substitute for a good ladder. Never overreach. Be careful when you have to reach high to fill coffee urns, milk tanks, and so on.

8. Keep floors clean and dry. Pick up any loose object from the floor immediately to prevent someone from falling.

9. Do not overload service trays. Trays should be loaded so as to give good balance. An improperly loaded tray can become dangerous.

10. Dispose of all broken glass and china immediately. Never serve a guest with a cracked or chipped glass or piece of china. Check all silverware to ensure it is clean.

11. Take sufficient time to serve your guests properly. Too much haste is liable to cause accidents to your guests and to yourself. Haste makes waste.

12. Remove from service any chair, table, or other equipment that is loose, broken, or splintered so as to prevent injury.

13. Cashiers should close cash registers with back of hand. Do not permit fingers to hang over edge of drawer.

14. Money is germ-laden. Keep your fingers out of your hair, eyes, and mouth after handling. Wash hands carefully. Report the slightest cut or sore at once for treatment.

IMPROVING SERVICE WITH TECHNOLOGY

The application of computers to the restaurant industry is based on the evolution of accounting of cash sales, the calculation of sales, labor costs, productivity, and the availability of statistics that enable production forecasting.

The precursor to using computers in food service operations was, first, the cash register, which was a mechanical device that determined the amount of sales and total sales and gave a visual and sometimes an auditory signal of sale amount and cash drawer position, as well as a customer receipt. This mechanical equipment was later replaced by an electronic cash register (ECR) that was more sophisticated in its ability to account for sales, both by totals, departments, and service team members. Individual keys could be preset to menu items and general keys could look up prices not carried on the keyboard, or, for example, give modifying instructions to the cooks for preparation of various menu items.

Although ECR equipment was a form of computer, its main function was to interface with the guest, place an adequate control on cash, and to provide management information. This equipment and process differs from that provided by the point-of-sale (POS) equipment, usually referred to as a terminal, which may or may not have processing capability and may either be treated as a "slave" to a central processing unit or be a central processing unit itself.

New Technology

In recent times there has been an explosion in computer technology. The processing speed, information storing capacity, and ability to communicate with other computers have increased dramatically, while at the same time, hardware costs have decreased, the physical size of computers has been greatly reduced, and most current models are capable of operating in most environments.

To compete effectively in the highly competitive markets of today, all stages of restaurant production and service must act in concert, so as to ultimately deliver quality service and products at the right prices and to the right guests. Failure to do so can result in excess inventory, poor food quality, poor guest service, underutilized capacity, and unnecessary cost. Modern computer technology helps monitor and coordinate these activities.

Computer Applications

New technology changes the way in which restaurants and hotels process and monitor transactions. More and more restaurants are choosing point-of-sale systems. A point-of-sale system can enhance decision making, operational control, guest service, and revenues. However, not all point-of-sale systems have the same capabilities and potential for improving revenue. A point-of-sale system is a network of cashier and server terminals that typically handle food and beverage orders, the transmission of orders to the kitchen and bar, the settlement of guest checks, time keeping, and interactive charge posting to guest folios. This information can also be imported to accounting and food cost inventory software packages.

Terminals

Server terminals are used by the server to enter a food or beverage order into the system and communicate the order to the kitchen or bar by means of a keyboard or touch screen. A display screen allows the server to monitor the order.

The cashier terminal includes a cash drawer, as well as a keyboard and a monitor, and is primarily used for both entering and settling guest checks.

Printers are the third essential component of the point-of-sale system and are used to print checks, orders, and reports on service areas and kitchens.

An additional feature of the point-of-sale system is the magnetic strip reader, an input device for credit-card processing. As guests settle their checks with credit cards, all the cashier has to do is "swipe" the magnetic strip of the credit card through this reader, and a credit slip is printed automatically.

If the point-of-sale system is being added to an existing system, it is important to carefully verify compatibility and interface ability. The point-of-sale system also needs to be protected by passwords and secured against power fluctuations.

The use of handheld computerized devices that allow team members to enter orders while they are at the guest table are greatly on the increase. This system uses radio signals to communicate with a base station from where the order is sent to the appropriate preparation area. This allows the servers to spend more time with guests as they do not have to go back and forth to the kitchen or the terminal. A silent paging system informs the server when the order is ready.

The Software

The hardware of the computer cannot accomplish anything by itself; it needs instructions. There must be a set of software programs directing the system in what to do, how to do it, and when to do it. Software programs not only direct internal system operations, they also maintain files and produce reports.

REVIEW QUESTIONS

1. Discuss and outline the essential elements and differences between Russian, French, and American methods of table service.
2. Describe the basic rules of American service.
3. Outline the rationale for the use of Butler/Family or English service.
4. State the steps in the presentation of guest checks.
5. Identify the all the steps of "From Soup to Nuts" in the guest service experience.
6. Explain the elements of in-room dining.
7. Outline the procedures critical to safety in the dining room.
8. Describe how technology may be used to improve dining room service.

4

Tableside Service and Buffets

Outline

TABLESIDE SERVICE

Tableside service adds an elegant touch to a dining room because it can be eye-catching and dramatic. The service skills of the dining room team member are showcased along with the food, and the drama becomes the focus of guests' attention, providing entertainment in addition to very sophisticated food presentation.

Tableside service includes making salads, carving, flaming entrees, and serving international coffees and desserts at the table. It is different from other service offered in an upscale dining room because the final product is finished off at the table. Mise-en-place (the universal foodservice term for prepreparation) and any precooking of the item takes place in the kitchen beforehand.

CARVING AND FLAMBÉING

Presenting a rack of lamb to a guest and then carving it in their presence can be very impressive. However, the prime reason for carrying this out in the dining room is to ensure that guests receive the menu item in pristine condition. Performing the task of carving tableside not only requires knowledge and skill in using a carving knife and fork, but also requires dexterity and speed on the part of the team member.

Flambeing is most impressive when conducted by experienced team members. Apart from the drama and beauty of the actual flames, there is a real purpose to it. Liqueurs are used to impart flavors to different recipe items; however, the alcohol must be "burned off" to remove impurities and reduce the alcohol content.

SAFETY MEASURES WHILE FLAMING

Flaming can be the most dramatic part of all tableside service. The real purpose of flaming foods is often overlooked. Alcohol has been added to impart flavor and character to the dish, but this occurs only after the impurities have literally been "burned off."

Safety is of paramount importance while flaming tableside. Before beginning, know the location of fire equipment and alarms, as well as the different classifications of fires.

Mishaps occur because simple, cautionary guidelines are not followed. To avoid any incident, follow these simple rules:

1. Never place the gueridon close to a guest. Position the gueridon two feet from the table, taking care that you are not under a sprinkler or smoke alarm.

2. Keep the bottled spirits on the opposite end of the gueridon from the rechaud.

3. Never leave a gueridon or a lighted rechaud unattended.

4. Never move a gueridon while the rechaud is alight.

5. Never add alcohol to a flaming pan. Take the pan away from the flame before adding the alcohol.

If a mishap occurs, remain calm. The professional behavior you demonstrate will quell any guest fears while you put out the fire.

(See Appendix 1 for dessert and international coffees recipes which are often prepared tableside.)

THE GUERIDON AND RECHAUD

A rechaud is a small stovelike appliance designed to cook, flame, or keep food warm. The heat sources that are used for this small stove are generally propane gas and denatured alcohol. A gueridon is a rolling cart used for service. It is used for all tableside preparations such as portioning, cooking, finishing, and plating and the making of salads, flaming desserts, and preparation and serving of international coffees. The gueridon is also where the preparation of food, salad making, carving, boning, or cooking take place.

The rechaud should is normally placed on the left side of the top of the gueridon, and all spirits and liqueurs for flaming should are placed at the opposite end or underneath for safety reasons.

The middle and bottom shelves are used to store underliners, napkins, condiments, service forks and spoons, other serving utensils, cutting boards, cooking pans, a fire extinguisher, and a pepper mill.

SERVING BUFFETS

A buffet may be defined as a type of service or banquet meal at which guests obtain a portion or all their food by serving themselves from a buffet table. Buffets are suitable for those clients who want their guests to have a choice of meal items. Buffets are also used for serving meals in a room which is some distance from the kitchen.

The food is placed in a line along a "serving table," which might be a straight line, a curve, a serpentine, or several smaller lines. Buffets may also be designed into separate stations using round tables or decorative carts. This is sometimes referred to as the scatter system. The guests may circle around or proceed along the buffet line or lines, first picking up a plate, then requesting portions of foods that appeal to them. A guest may try any of the selections, and return to the table for additional portions.

Chafing dishes are used to keep food hot. They consist of a frame, two pans, and a top. The top pan fits into the bottom, leaving between two to three inches of space between the two pans. The bottom pan is usually filled with hot water. Canned heat is placed underneath to maintain the water temperature.

Buffets can be deluxe, very elaborate, or as simple as the host desires, from spectacular centerpieces and carved ice displays to simple trays of hors d'oeuvres. Buffets may be of many types. Weekend brunch buffets are very popular in some areas. A commercial restaurant may offer a special buffet lunch or dinner to boost sales on low-volume days, or it may operate a buffet on a regular basis. One very popular type of service offers appetizers, salad, and breads buffet style, with the rest of the meal served at the table.

Occasionally an upscale restaurant may display menu items—usually appetizers and hors d'oeuvre—on a buffet table. The guest makes a choice, and the items selected are then plated by a service team member and served to the guest at the table. This style of service applies to the merchandising aspects of the buffet. The elegant display invites the guest to select the items.

The buffet display is generally maintained by kitchen team members throughout the meal service.

Buffet service is versatile and can lend itself to every type of meal, from breakfast to steak roasts. It is very popular for banquets, and may be used for receptions and cocktails before a table-service banquet.

It is possible for a buffet to be combined with other types of service. For example, guests may pick up only cold foods and order the remainder of the meal, or they may eat the cold and hot foods and then be served a dessert and beverage, or just a beverage.

When buffet service is used, silverware and napkins are usually preset on the table for each cover, or they may be placed on the buffet service line. Plates and other dishes needed for the buffet are set at the front of the line where guests can pick them up. When silverware, napkins, and water are to be picked up by guests, they are usually placed at the end of the line or in a separate area.

Desserts very often are set on another table. Using separate tables can speed service. It is also faster to have team members behind the buffet to serve guests than to have guests serve themselves.

Advantages of Buffet Service

1. They provide great visual impact.
2. They can speed up service.
3. Guests may eat as much or as little as they want.
4. They can be located in rooms which may be a distance from the kitchen.
5. Fewer dining room team members are required.

Some Disadvantages of Buffet Service

1. Food can become unappetizing while sitting on the buffet table.

2. Food cost can be high, as there is excessive waste when the food becomes unusable due to overexposure.

3. New laws regarding sanitation are making stringent requirements for buffet lines. All food must be covered (sneeze guards), and top and bottom heat are essential to keep food hot and out of the danger zone (40 degrees F to 140 degrees F). Sanitation codes and laws vary from state to state and community to community in this regard.

TYPES OF BUFFETS

Buffet is a fairly loose term, which is applied to many different types of occasions. At one end of the scale, it may mean no more than sandwiches and other finger food, whereas at the other end, it can mean an elaborate meal of many courses. A buffet may contain both hot and cold dishes. A buffet is not necessarily less formal than a dinner. The following outlines various types of buffets.

Smorgasbord

This is a Swedish buffet (literally translated, it means sandwich table) which includes a large assortment of cold foods after which hot foods and then a dessert and beverage are offered. A true smorgasbord must include pickled herring, rye bread, and Swedish mysost or gjestost cheese. Similarly a Russian buffet must include caviar in a beautiful glass bowl (or in a carved-ice bowl), rye bread, and sweet butter.

Breakfasts

Many hotels offer patrons a buffet breakfast, with a wide selection of dishes organized on a self-service basis. Hot beverages, which are ordered from a server, are the exception. The selection varies widely. It normally includes bread and rolls, with butter, cheeses, jams, and marmalades; cold meats and fish; hot grilled items on hot plates; fresh and stewed fruit and fruit juices; and possibly breakfast cereals.

Deluxe Decorated Buffets

A full deluxe buffet is a main meal. It is distinguished from a dinner or luncheon because the food is displayed in the dining room.

A buffet should be first a feast for the eyes; it is, however, primarily intended as a feast for the palate, and the purpose of decoration is to enhance and complement the appearance of the food, not detract from its taste.

Whenever possible, it is best if guests inspect and admire the buffet before the service begins, and are then served at their tables. This avoids the need for guests to lineup. However, this is rarely possible, and guests normally assemble their own food from the buffet table. In this case, the first course and roll and butter may be placed on the diners' table in advance.

It is traditional to have one or more of the chef team members in their whites serving behind the buffet. This has many advantages. Fewer team members are needed, and the chef can observe the speed of service and restock food as needed. Most guests like to see chefs behind the buffet table.

Almost all food items may be used for a buffet meal, although preference is usually given to dishes of an attractive appearance, because the element of display is so important. Hot dishes are frequently included and presented in chafing dishes in which case both cold and heated plates are required. It is far better to put out only a portion of each item, and replace it with a fresh supply.

FORK BUFFETS

A "fork buffet" has been defined as "a meal which can be eaten standing up, with a plate in one hand and a fork in the other." A fork buffet table should look just as attractive as that for a deluxe buffet, but the range of foodstuffs cannot be as wide. It is important to avoid sliced, roasted meats, for example, because few people can manage to eat these easily with just a fork. Salads of diced meats are the obvious alternative.

A fork buffet is less formal than a sit-down buffet, but people tend to eat less, possibly because it is less easy to manage to consume food without a table. At fork buffets it is important to provide plenty of table napkins of good quality and adequate size.

FINGER BUFFETS

As its name implies, these are simple buffets and the least formal. Similar to fork buffets, they are particularly suitable to allow guests to mingle with each other. This ability to circulate makes a finger buffet particularly suitable for many less formal gatherings or as receptions prior to some other food event. Generally finger buffets are considered snack meals.

Food should be in bite-sized pieces and finger sandwiches. With a finger buffet, large napkins are essential, along with finger bowls. Although the food can be and is generally eaten standing up, it is still advisable to have as many chairs and tables available as possible, if only for the convenience of elderly guests.

REVIEW QUESTIONS

1. Identify the important elements involved in tableside service.
2. Describe the benefits and customer "value" associated with tableside service.
3. Describe the safety steps associated with flambeing in the dining room.
4. State the uses of the gueridon and the rechaud.
5. Identify the relative advantages and disadvantages of buffet service.
6. Distinguish between the various types of buffet service.

5

Guest Relations and "People" Skill Techniques

Outline

We believe guest satisfaction is earned the old fashioned way—one day at a time. You've got to constantly listen to your guests, and demonstrate a passion to innovate and change your business to meet their evolving needs.

—John E. Martin, CEO Taco Bell

Great service means having competent and knowledgeable team members who provide customers with friendly, helpful service. It means offering quality products and services that exceed customer expectations. And, it means having a mechanism in place to be responsive to customer inquiries and concerns.

—Israel Cohen

Foodservice operations have a big advantage over many other forms of retailing in that all purchases can be influenced by direct sales personnel—front of the house team members—servers and bartenders. The service team, whether called waiters, servers, captains, busboys, or maitre d's, are the major representatives of the foodservice operator to the guest. The guest is greeted by these individuals, seated and served by them, and through them the guest expresses her or his pleasures, requests, frustrations, and problems.

Therefore, attitudes, motivation, competence, and desire to serve are the essential and important aspects of service. A service team member who feels that he or she is doing guests a favor by waiting on them or who looks at the duties as only a source of tips does a disservice to guests and the operation. Guests must be made to feel that they are welcome.

Guests who patronize foodservice operations are no different from guests throughout the ages—all want to be appreciated and pampered. The most frequent complaint of foodservice guests concerning their dining experience is the lack of friendly, competent service. Additionally guests want friendly servers who are knowledgeable about the menu without being overbearing, who are willing to provide reasonable variations in the menu, and who bring things to the table before, rather than after, they are needed.

Most guests are rational, reasonable people who make "normal" requests and meet the service team member halfway. But some will not. Certain guests will argue, have extra and special problems, and demand excessive attention. We can't please everyone, but we must continually try.

When I'm interested only in my own personal gain, I'm a peddlar. When I'm interested in serving others, I'm professional.

—Ben Johnson

There are no strangers in a good foodservice operation. Regular customers should be addressed by name, and newer customers should be addressed with the same degree of cordiality, even if their names are unknown.

Too often we become so wrapped up in the technical aspects of service that we fail to see the guest as a human being, rather they become the "New

York Strip on table ten." The foodservice and hospitality industry is a *people business*. It must satisfy our guests' needs today in order to get their business tomorrow. When team members see the guest as a hindrance to their work instead of the very reason their jobs exist, something is very wrong.

SERVICE AND PEOPLE SKILLS

People skills are about dealing with guests and providing them with a comfortable, safe, and healthy dining experience. Ultimately these skills are the ones that provide the foodservice operation with the revenue that makes it successful.

Good service is one of the primary things people consider in judging value in a restaurant. Although good service cannot overcome the problem of poor-quality food, poor service can ruin an otherwise excellent meal for the guest and cost the restaurant considerable goodwill and repeat business.

Therefore, the hospitality and foodservice industry's survival and prosperity are dependent on guest goodwill—satisfied guests generate business and profit.

What are guest expectations? They are:

1. Quality service and courtesy.
2. Good selection of menu items.
3. Efficiency, value for money, and convenience.
4. Knowledgeable, competent, and enthusiastic team members.
5. Helpfulness and clean and comfortable surroundings.
6. Entertainment.

Great guest relations are the key to transforming expectations into satisfaction. Guest relations are about people, not just guests, but also the team members. It is about all the people who have any contact with other people in the foodservice industry, whether they are guests, team members, suppliers, or competitors, and how these groups get along with each other.

People reveal their feelings in their behavior. Satisfied team members reflect their contentment to other team members and guests with whom they have contact. Satisfied guests reflect their contentment by returning to and recommending the establishment to their friends.

The needs of guests, the establishment, and team members are all different. Therefore, the more the needs of all three can be satisfied, the more effective guest relations will be.

People Skills

We all learn from an early age the principles of social interaction. However, even though the majority of people are socially competent on a personal level, some find it difficult to communicate effectively in a work or professional situation, particularly those entering the foodservice job market who may lack self-confidence and/or experience.

Foodservice and hospitality team members need to have a high level of understanding of guest relations. Guests need the help of team members and the establishment to obtain some of their basic requirements—food and beverages, comfort, and entertainment—and the foodservice establishment needs to survive financially and thrive. To do this it needs to provide a satisfactory environment for its team members, so that they can provide the satisfaction sought by its guests.

The team needs the cooperation of other team members in serving the guest. Team members need to be rewarded for their efforts, and to be recognized and appreciated for their achievements. Excellent guest relations skill is the vital ingredient that makes for a successful and thriving foodservice business. Guests benefit because they can return to an establishment they like. The establishment benefits because its reputation and profits increase. Team members benefit because they enjoy a pleasant working atmosphere. Through training, practice, and observation of other experienced team members, all can acquire the practical skills necessary for success.

Guest Needs

When serving guests, team members must take into consideration the guest's physiological needs (the need to satisfy hunger and thirst, need for shelter and rest), but also more complex psychological needs.

The psychological needs are varied but some of the most common needs are:

1. To feel a sense of belonging.
2. To be recognized; their business is valued.
3. To feel important.
4. To have satisfaction from money spent.
5. To receive attention.

Guests want to feel welcome—that they belong in the restaurant. The team must communicate the feeling that guests are very important to them and that they are glad to see them.

Michael Hurst, professor at Florida International University, owner of 15th Street Restaurant, and former president of the National Restaurant Association (NRA), initiated the phrase "We're Glad You're Here." His credo not only is applied for his restaurant guests, but also was adopted for the annual Chicago NRA restaurant show attendees and his university students. He is quite passionate about this and lives his credo everyday. His restaurant team wear large button badges proclaiming, "We're Glad You're Here," and when a guest arrives at Hurst's restaurant, the team member communicates in a sincere way, "We're Glad You're Here." Hurst believes *the guest is the most important person in any quality service environment.*

The most threatening feeling a person can have is the feeling that they don't exist, which is what the team member is saying when a guest is ignored. Each person wants to feel worthy, significant, and competent. Making guests feel important is key to high-quality guest relations.

In addition to the guests' "collection of needs," they have a set of expectations that must be fulfilled. If the needs are not met, the guests will have a poor response regardless of the quality of the food or other services. Expectations may be based on past experiences at a restaurant—recommendations of friends, advertising, or just general ideas about dining out. If these expectations are not fulfilled, guests leave dissatisfied.

Team members skilled in guest relations recognize these needs and satisfy them by making the guests feel welcome and at ease, by treating them with courtesy and respect, and by attending to their needs in an efficient and professional manner. Attentiveness to guests' psychological needs creates a climate of goodwill.

Personal contact with team members has a major influence and can determine the guests' decision to return. Most guests can assess from a team member's attitude and behavior whether the operation is efficient, professional, and customer oriented. Positive hospitality team behavior can ensure that the guest is more likely to enjoy the experience.

DEVELOPING POSITIVE ATTITUDES

Our actions and behavior are governed to a large extent by our attitudes. Our mental attitudes can either help or hinder us in our work. Therefore, to realize our full potential and to enhance our relationships with guests and other team members, a positive personal attitude is necessary.

Personal Attitude

Personal attitude is about having the best positive mental attitude toward yourself and having confidence in your own ability. You must know that what you are doing is worthwhile and that you are doing it to the best of your ability. If you believe you are a failure, you will be a failure, and your behavior will not inspire confidence on the part of guests and other team members. Success in life does not depend solely on real ability; with belief in yourself, you can make the best use of every asset you have. Quiet self-confidence is an important quality to develop and should not be confused with self-importance, which can alienate other people and make one insensitive to the feelings of others. Good positive attitudes and an enjoyment of working in the foodservice industry are key characteristics for a positive mental attitude.

There are few types of jobs that offer more opportunities to deal with people. If you have a genuine interest in, and liking for, people, being pleasant, friendly, and helpful will require little effort. However, team members who act on the assumption that most guests are unreasonable and many of them are a nuisance are doomed to failure from the start.

We should believe that the products or services we offer are worthwhile and the best. A sincere belief in our product/service will engender enthusiasm which will be transmitted to the guest. After all, how can the guest be happy with our products or services if we are not? Pride in the quality of service or product improves our performance at work because it motivates us to maintain high standards.

BODY LANGUAGE AND APPEARANCE

Communication is one of the most important parts of human behavior. Speech is just one of the many means of communication. Our facial expressions, posture, appearance, eyes, all convey messages. Smiling, frowning, and laughing are all part of an international language.

Most of us use gestures and body language without ever being conscious of them. However, it is worth examining these forms of communication so that we can gain a better understanding of how people relate to each other, and thus learn to communicate more effectively.

When we communicate with others, we use two types of language: verbal or spoken language and body language, which is a complex system of gestures, facial expressions, and postures that are often used unconsciously to express our feelings, attitudes, and personality.

When speaking, we are continuously moving our hands, body, and head. Gestures have two main purposes:

1. To emphasize or illustrate what we are saying, by using pointing gestures when giving directions to reinforce our verbal message.
2. To replace spoken language when verbal skills are inadequate.

Gestures often are unintentional and belie our real feelings, for example, nervous interviewees may often clasp their hands tightly or fiddle with small objects.

Facial Expressions

The face is the most expressive region of the body. We show how we feel mainly through our faces rather than in words or with any other part of our body. If we feel an emotion strongly enough, the emotion automatically shows itself, whether or not we want it to. In embarrassment or anger, we blush or flush; in shock or fear, we turn white; in extreme sadness, we sob; and in pleasure, we smile.

The face is the area most observed during interaction. We recognize others mainly by their faces, and we form impressions of their personalities from their faces and facial expressions.

Facial expressions can:

1. Show our emotional state (happy, sad, or angry).
2. Provide feedback during conversation on whether we understand, are surprised, or agree with what is being said.
3. Help us to interpret spoken language.

Most people look at our face at some point during a conversation. Our faces reveal feelings, our facial expressions not only show the guest how we feel, but also whether we are interested in them.

Messages transmitted by facial expressions are happiness, surprise, fear, sadness, anger, disgust, and interest.

It is important to try to avoid the following gestures because they send a negative message, and indicate that you are bored, impatient, or disinterested:

1. Fidgeting with jewelry.
2. Tapping foot/fingers.
3. Looking at watch.
4. Yawning.

The use of head nods, another common form of gesture in conversation, is very important because nods indicate agreement with what the other person is saying or doing; and they encourage the other person to continue talking while reassuring them of your attention. Once we learn to avoid the gestures that convey negative attitudes, we can use other gestures which signal interest, alertness, and cooperation to our advantage in guest situations.

The main facial expression we should use is a smile. It can be the biggest icebreaker of all. If we smile at the guest, it is most likely that he or she will smile back. If we have developed positive mental attitudes to other people, ourselves, our service team and our employers, they will be reflected in our facial expressions.

Eye Contact

We convey sincerity with our eyes. It is the only way to convey sincerity, therefore, eye contact is one of the most important aspects of body language. When engaged in conversation, most people look in each other's eyes for one-third of the time or more, and this maintains a mutual attention. When listening, we watch the other person most of the time to take in as much information as possible and because it is a basic courtesy to pay attention in this way.

Eye contact sends the following messages to the guest: "I'm awake," "I'm alert," "I'm interested in what you are saying." It also underlines honesty, confidence, and sincerity.

A smile costs nothing—and in the hospitality industry, it means everything.
—Bryan D. Langthon, CEO, Holiday Inn Worldwide

Remember it takes seventy-two muscles to frown but only fourteen to smile!

It takes 14 facial muscles to smile   It takes 72 facial muscles to frown

THE MEANING OF A SMILE

It costs nothing but creates much.

It happens in a flash, but the memory of it sometimes lasts forever.

There are none so rich that they can get along without it, and none so poor but are richer from its benefits.

It brings rest to the weary, comfort to the sad, hope to the discouraged, and is the countersign of friends.

It fosters goodwill in business and happiness in the home.

It is something that cannot be begged, bought, borrowed, or stolen, but is of no earthly good to anyone until it is given away.

So if in the course of your day your friends are too tired to give you a smile, why don't you give them one of yours.

—Anon

Appearance

Being professional means having absolute confidence in your ability to deliver superb food and high-quality service. Professionalism begins with an individual's appearance. This includes grooming, personal hygiene, appropriateness of dress, hair length, style, makeup, and jewelry. A team member's appearance reflects his or her self-regard. Clothes, facial features, hair, hands, and physique are the main components of physical appearance that convey much information about us, such as social status, occupation, age, ethnicity, and personality traits.

Choice of clothes and the way in which they are worn reflect our personalities. Team members should pay special attention to how they dress, because it only takes a few seconds to make a visual impact on a guest. Before guests have time to react to personality, they will have formed an opinion based on dress, and it is difficult to remedy a bad first impression.

Remember: You don't get a second chance to make a first impression.

NONVERBAL MESSAGES

As noted earlier, nonverbal communication is just as important and, at times, even more important than verbal communication. Gestures include nodding of the head, use of hands, and facial expressions. All these body signals send messages. Smiling and frowning convey emotion as does voice intonation or loudness. Ideally the right nonverbal cues will always accompany the verbal communication. Nonverbal communication may influence the impact of a message more than verbal communication alone.

Some of the more important signals we send to others are conveyed in the following:

1. Leaning forward is a positive gesture. The person is listening and wishes to hear what is said. It also suggests acceptance and willingness to take action.

2. Direct eye contact is a positive gesture. Lack of contact despite sincere words can be interpreted as untrustworthiness.

3. Open hands are a sign of agreement and careful listening, while crossed arms and legs or leaning backward are considered to represent defensiveness, resistance, and rejection.

4. Arms folded over the chest with fists clenched is usually a negative sign. It suggests that communication is one-way. This gesture is

usually indicative of people who are nervous, anxious, uptight, and are holding in their emotions.

5. Leaning away in a chair may indicate disinterest in what is being said.

6. Leaning far forward with a defiant posture, hands spread on table, is indicative of a person with a volatile personality who may be frustrated, angry, and explosive.

7. Backing away or avoidance is generally a sign of disagreement with what is being said.

8. Shoulders hunched forward and down with arms extended and hands overlapped in front of the body usually indicates shyness.

Nervousness, embarrassment, anxiety, and guilt, to name a few, are conveyed through different elements of body language:

Talking while moving the hands

Playing with finger ring

Moving restlessly

Sighing heavily

Blushing

Not being able to look someone directly in the eyes

Biting knuckles or nails

Perspiring

Hands gripping arms of chair or seat

Defensiveness

Arms folded across chest

Legs tightly crossed

Rationalization actions

Defending actions

Frustration

Excessively jerky movements

Anger

Mouth tightened, eyes squinted

Clenching and unclenching fists

Holding onto doubled-up fists

Loud, threatening voice
Threatening voice

Apathy

Drooping, monotone voice
Slow movements
Individual ceases to care for himself or herself physically
Individual ceases productive work

Disgust

Disrespect in voice
Sneer on face

Withdrawn

Vacant look in eyes
Body turned to one side
Not really hearing what is being said
Expressionless face and voice

Exclusion

Turning away from speaker
Crossed legs
Folded arms

Receptiveness

Listening attentively
Facing speaker
Arms and legs uncrossed

Boredom

Tilted head
Doodling fingers
Vacant look

Reflectiveness

Intensity of gaze
Wrinkled forehead
Downcast look

These nonverbal communication signs are keys to whether communication is taking place with understanding. Understanding body language and how to use it as a tool can be extremely valuable.

"PEOPLE" DISTANCE

Relationships between people can also be reflected in the way they position or orient themselves. American culture is becoming increasingly diverse. It is no longer a melting pot, where new ethnic groups attempt to leave their original cultures behind them. A more accurate image is a tossed salad, where various ingredients remain distinct even as they are mixed together.

Embracing cultural diversity involves issues and mannerisms which are sensitive to valuing the differences within the team. A big consideration in nonverbal communication is distance. Close physical contact is normally reserved for our immediate family and special friends.

In the hospitality industry, handshaking is the most usual form of bodily contact. When the situation arises, it is important to offer a firm handshake; a limp handshake denotes a weak or insincere character. Offering a good handshake can help to project a warm and sincere personality, which is so important when dealing with guests.

There is a limit to how far two people can be apart and yet hear and see each other. Within that limit, their distance from each other will vary depending on their relationship. We each have a kind of personal space around us into which only certain people are allowed, usually close family or young children.

The distance that people maintain when communicating has been determined as follows:

Personal Distance

Close phase:
One and one-half to two and one-half feet, comfortable if the people know one another.

Far phase:
Two and one-half to four feet, arms' length.

Social Distance

Close phase:
Four to seven feet, impersonal business.

Far phase:
Seven to twelve feet, more formal communication.

Public Distance

Close phase:
Twelve to twenty-five feet, can get away.

Far phase:
Twenty-five feet or more, set around important public figures. Most social interaction, however, takes place between four to nine feet. Standing
too close to guests will cause them embarrassment and discomfort. Yet
standing too far away can imply to the guest that you are unhelpful or
disinterested.

Obviously the team member should not approach a guest's table to take
the order and call out from a distance: "Would you like to order?"

COMMUNICATION

Barriers to effective communication become obvious during the first few
minutes of interaction when attention span is at its highest; the eyes and ears
focus on the sender and the brain receives what it sees and hears. We tend to
focus on what we see first, and the order in which we process information
about others is their skin color, gender, age, appearance, facial expressions,
eye contact, movement, personal space, and touch.

It only takes two to four minutes to create a positive or negative impression. Success as a communicator is measured by the impressions you create.
The four key questions that need to be addressed to overcome perception barriers are:

1. How am I perceived by others?
2. How do I "sound" to others?
3. What do I say to others?
4. How well do I listen to others?

Significance may be applied to a part of you that has little to do with
your skills, for example, the nonverbal messages sent by your body language,
how quickly you speak, your handshake, and how well you maintain eye contact. Knowing what you sound like tells a lot about your personality, attitude,
and anxiety level. Being aware of how you sound can help to correct and improve your communication skills. It is possible to learn to recognize signs of
tension and stress in your voice and the voices of others. Verbal skills should
support and balance the nonverbal and verbal messages sent. What you say is
reflected by how you say it. Balance between language and delivery is critical
in removing barriers.

Communication Barriers

The fundamental communication barrier between people stems from differences in backgrounds, personalities, beliefs, education, religion, life experiences, and professional outlook. Our ability to receive messages is limited by

our tendency to hear only what we want or expect to hear. It is a normal human phenomenon that the mind resists what it does not expect or want to perceive. We have a natural tendency to judge or evaluate statements and to reach hasty conclusions. We evaluate messages from our own frame of reference instead of understanding the sender's point of view. In general, senders are consciously attentive only to their spoken word.

Words and Communication

The word "talk" is not the same as "communicate." Communicate is fuller, more accurate. When people talk, they are constricted by the limitations of words. True communication is more about translation and transmission of feelings. Communication uses thought; however, thought and feelings are not the same. When one communicates with thought, images and pictures can be used—therefore, they can be more effective than words alone.

When feelings, thoughts, and experiences fail, words are all that are left. Words are the least effective communication vehicle. Words are always open to misinterpretation, as well as misunderstanding. The problem with words is they are only symbols. Two of the most powerful words are "thank you." Don't just say the words. Communicate them.

LISTENING

Communication is always a two-way process. One person says something and another person hears what was said. Because each person comes to the listening situation with different fields of experience, there is often a gap between the speaker's intention and the listener's interpretation. Listening is the complex and selective process of receiving, focusing, deciphering, accepting, and storing what we hear. Listening does not occur without these five interrelated, yet distinct, processes. Hearing is the absorption of sound. Listening is something quite different. Ineffective listening can be a major communication problem. Poor listening habits may result in costly errors and inefficiency. Being an active and effective listener has important benefits

Ways to Improve Listening Skills

Avoid distractions. Focus and concentrate. Don't let your mind wander. Most people think at the rate of 500 words per minute. People talk at the rate of 150 words per minute. Stay focused on what is being said, or you will risk missing key points.

Listen for main ideas. Guests sometimes formulate ideas as the conversation develops. These ideas and comments may be vague. Individuals may have trouble coming to the point. Restate the guests' requests in your own words and ask if you have understood them correctly. Ask questions. If something is unclear or seems to contradict your own personal sense of logic, seek clarity. This encourages the guest, and shows that you are listening and are interested in what they have to say.

Concentrate and don't let your mind wander. Stay focused. This shows respect for the guest. Refrain from fidgeting, squirming, scribbling, or twiddling your thumbs. Give the guest your undivided attention. Most of us can do only one thing well at one time. Looking away during conversation communicates indifference to what the guest is saying. Show the guest the interest and attention that you yourself would like to receive. Listen for the rationale behind what the guest is saying. This is important, if what they are saying does not make sense to you. Respond to nonverbal cues. This clarifies the meaning of a bodily reaction; it ensures that behavior and words convey the same message, and it shows understanding. If we are poor listeners, our inclination is to stop listening.

As much as 85 percent of a server's working day is spent in some form of communication. Effective and quality service relies on the ability of the server to transfer information in such a way that it is understood by the kitchen in the way that the guest intended.

Speech

We use our voice in subtle ways to express feelings and attitudes. The volume and tone of our voices vary to allow others to interpret what we are saying. In many cases it is not what we say but how we say it that is important. Most research has shown that a louder voice is used by more aggressive people and expresses strong feelings such as anger, surprise, and fear. Softer volume is adopted by shy or warm people. We use volume to emphasize what we are saying. Our tone of voice injects meaning into what we say; it shows whether our comments are intended to be serious, funny, or sarcastic. Our tone of voice also conveys attitudes or disposition—whether we are friendly or hostile, cheerful or downcast. We do not speak at a constant speed. We talk faster when excited or nervous; we pause for emphasis and talk slowly when making a serious or profound statement. We also use pauses as a type of auditory punctuation—a short pause for a comma, a longer one for a period. Also we need to maintain eye contact and leave time for questions and answers.

It is always helpful to personalize what you are saying. Use the right tone of voice and body language. Sounding bored or looking disinterested relays to the guest that what you are saying is unimportant. Speak clearly and loudly enough to be heard. Using the guest's name once or twice during the transaction is also helpful; it shows friendliness, which makes the guest feel at home, and it also demonstrates recognition, which makes the guest feel secure, and boosts the ego, making the guest feel important.

The quality of our personal communication depends on listening. We should listen actively by focusing our full attention on the guest and what he or she has to say. We should avoid talking too much about ourselves and interrupting the guest while he or she is speaking.

A good listener also provides feedback during conversation by being alert, by looking at the speaker, and intermittently nodding, smiling, and making various comments.

There are ten commandments for good listening:

1. **Stop talking!**
   You cannot listen if you are talking.

2. **Put the guest at ease.**
   Help the guest feel free to talk.
   This is often called a permissive environment.

3. **Show the guest you want to listen.**
   Look and act interested. Do not read while the guest talks.
   Listen to understand rather than to oppose.

4. **Remove distractions.**
   Don't doodle, tap, or shuffle papers.
   Would it be better if you come back later?

5. **Empathize with the guest.**
   Try to put yourself in the guest's place so that you can see their point of view.

6. **Be patient.**
   Allow plenty of time. Do not interrupt.
   Don't start for the door or walk away.

7. **Hold your anger.**
   An angry person gets the wrong meaning from words.

8. **Avoid arguments and criticism.**
   This puts the guest on the defensive. He or she may "clam up" or get angry. Do not argue: even if you win, you lose.

9. **Ask questions.**
   This encourages the guest, and shows you are listening.
   It helps to develop points further.

10. **Stop talking.**
    This is the first and last, because all other commandments depend on it.
    You can't do a good listening job while you are talking.
    Nature gave us two ears but only one tongue, which is a gentle hint that we should listen more than we talk.

INITIATING INTERACTIONS

There are a multitude of ways for team members to initiate conversations which can make a guest's time at your establishment more memorable. The following are suggestions for initiating conversations.

1. Be yourself—use techniques that allow you to draw upon personal strengths.

2. Suggest before guests ask, for example, beverages, foods, menu items, or house specials.

3. Read your guests—asking them a question can open up numerous topics of conversation. Sports, traveling, and the weather are other areas of interest to most people.

4. Try different approaches such as anecdotes and stories.

5. Make your time and your guests' time fun and festive.

6. Some guests only desire "quality service" so provide it and leave it at that.

7. Get to know guests' names, it makes conversation more comfortable.

8. Introduce guests to other team members.

9. Knowing your guests can help when changes in behavior may indicate that one or more guests approach their limit of alcohol consumption.

10. Always invite your guests back. This leaves a positive lasting impression in their minds, and it works.

Above all else, enjoy doing your job because if you are displaying a positive and cheerful disposition, chances are guests will too!

COURTESY

How many times have you entered a restaurant to be greeted by the hostess with a cold and uncourteous disposition who says, "How Many?" or "Smoking or Non-smoking," or some other comment such as "The waiting time is thirty minutes" or "Please have a seat at the bar."

The word courtesy once referred to certain behaviors that were required in royal courts to show respect for royalty and the "upper social classes." Later behavior became identified with manners and good "breeding."

It is almost certain that we have all experienced discourteous or at least apathetic service at some time. When the pace of business is hectic, sometimes courtesy can be forgotten. There are times when perhaps a team member may consider courtesy demeaning or a bunch of meaningless words or believe that there is not enough time to be courteous.

For high-quality guest relations, courtesy is not something to do only when there is time for it. Courtesy is the underlying principle of giving service. If one cannot show respect for those who patronize your business, then you are undeserving of that business.

Courteous behavior does more than show respect; it has been described as the "lubricant of guest relations." It reduces the frictions that can arise in any interaction, and it helps to keep actions and behaviors on a level at which they can be managed and often predicted. In simple terms, courteous behavior yields courteous reactions.

Courtesy should not be limited to guest interaction alone. Courteous behavior toward other team members also produces courtesy in return, which makes the job a lot more pleasant. It is also much easier to be courteous to the guests in an atmosphere of all-around courtesy.

Courtesy is more than words and phrases, although the words and phrases are important. Courtesy is expressed through informal communication channels. Courtesy is also action. It is doing something a little extra—being helpful, not just checking back to see if "everything is all right."

Guests are pleasantly surprised when they get pleasant, courteous service and recognition. That positive experience builds both repeat and new business.

TELEPHONE ANSWERING SKILLS

When answering the telephone in your establishment always:

1. Answer promptly.

2. Your opening words should include:
Identification: Hotel/Dining Room or Kitchen
Greeting: Good morning/afternoon/evening
Offer of Help: May I help you?

3. When you have found out the caller's name, use it.

4. Repeat the message to check accuracy. If you are unclear on a point, don't be afraid to ask questions.

5. Let the caller hang up first in case there's an afterthought.

6. Take notes—don't trust your memory!

Answering the telephone also provides other opportunities for quality guest relations.

Ask yourself the following:

Question: How can I make this guest relations opportunity more welcoming?

Response: The tone of voice of the person answering the telephone can signal to the caller how welcome the call itself is.

Question: How can I provide as much information as possible to the caller?

Response: Consistently answering the phone with the name of the establishment helps to create a more informative environment.

Question: How can I make this call more entertaining?

Response: Cheerfully respond, explaining outstanding features of the menu.

Question: How can I make this call more caring and "hassle-free"?

Response: Avoid transferring the call to other departments or placing callers on hold.

Remember the value of the call to the business! Potential guests who have to wait too long before their call is answered may just hang up and call a competing establishment to reserve their meal, thereby resulting in lost revenue for your establishment.

"PEOPLE" SKILLS SUMMARY

> The atmosphere and service in the establishment is what determines the guest satisfaction level. It's really the total atmosphere that we give to people in restaurants—that we are there to help them and serve them...once that is executed and executed well, nobody can take that away from you. It's your total personality that counts and that total execution that makes your establishment unique.
>
> —Gordon I. Segal, CEO, Crate & Barrel

Guest relations is one of those aspects of the foodservice and hospitality industry that makes it so interesting—and so frustrating. It is a continuing challenge. A sense of humor and a lively intelligence are decided assets. A desire to please and to serve are even more valuable.

Service and servitude are sometimes confused. Leadership is defined as service—doctors, lawyers, and accountants all provide service. Hospitality service is one of the most difficult services to provide; it is a highly personal service. Quality service is defined differently by each guest. High-quality service is sometimes hard to quantify; however, when it is not present it sticks out like a sore thumb. On the other hand, servitude is clear: it is the indentured position of a person in the dark ages and has no place in today's modern world.

Many foodservice people are skilled performers. With their guests, they radiate, and guests often feedback similar feelings. Both are actors in the play; both knowingly engage in the drama. The guest gets feelings of warmth and friendship. The reward for the team member not only is a tip but also the excitement of participation in this little drama.

When our technical and social skills are working effectively, the feedback from others is very rewarding. If we approach others with a genuine, friendly smile, backed by a friendly and enthusiastic manner, 99 percent of the people with whom we come in contact will respond in a friendly, cooperative, and appreciative way. This goodwill generates a very pleasant working atmosphere and greatly increases job satisfaction.

WHAT IS A CUSTOMER?

A Customer...

Is the most important person in any business.

A Customer...

Is not dependent on us—we are dependent on the Customer.

A Customer...

Is not an interruption of our work but the purpose of it.

A Customer...

Does us a favor by being a Customer—we do not do the Customer a favor.

A Customer...

Is part of our business, not an outsider.

A Customer...

Is not a cold statistic, but a flesh and blood human being with feelings and emotions just like our own.

A Customer...

Is not someone to argue with or match wits with.

A Customer...

Is the lifeblood of this and every other business.

A Customer...

Is a person who brings us his or her wants—it is our job to fill these wants.

A Customer...

Is deserving of the most courteous and attentive treatment possible.

A Customer...

Is the person who makes it possible to pay your salary whether you are a chef, server, front office employee, salesperson, or manager.

"No Customer can be worse than no customer" (Leopold Fechtner)

REVIEW QUESTIONS

1. Describe the critical elements relative to effective guest relations.
2. Explain the connection between quality service and the effective use of "people skills."
3. Indicate the necessity of positive personal attitudes.
4. State the elements associated with gestures, facial expressions, and nonverbal messages.
5. Outline communication barriers and the important steps in listening.
6. Describe how team members may initiate conversations with guests.
7. Identify and discuss the importance of courtesy in the foodservice industry.
8. List and review the steps used for effective telephone skills.

6

Suggestive Selling and Merchandising

Outline

Merchandising food and beverages is simply another term for selling. One of the primary steps in suggestive selling is for the guest to like and trust the server.

There are two main purposes of suggestive selling; these are (1) to enhance the dining experience for guests, and (2) to create a higher check average by suggesting accompaniments a guest may otherwise skip, and to improve the profit opportunity for the establishment.

The establishment should become well known for its great food, beverages, and good value. The team member contributes to this recognition by being a great salesperson who helps guests to find and to enjoy the right menu selection. It takes a great salesperson, not an order taker, to do this consistently. However, guests should not be pressured to order something they do not want. Gentle guidance is usually all it takes to help guests make a great choice.

Essentially each team member should:

1. Have an in-depth knowledge of the food menu and the beverage and wine list.

2. Sell the menu. Always suggest an appetizer. Many guests are visiting for the first time and might not be familiar with the establishment. They are open to suggestions. Team members have the ability to dramatically increase the guests' satisfaction if guidance is offered. Do not say, "How about an appetizer to start with?" Say something like, "Would you like our special house platter or some of our delicious buffalo wings?"

SUGGESTIVE SELLING TECHNIQUES

1. Talk about products by name, particularly featured food items, their ingredients, and the methods of cooking. Discuss your favorite items.

2. Suggest specific menu items or signature specials when asking guests for their orders.

3. Do not say, "May I get you a cocktail this evening?" Instead say, "Would you like to start with [server's suggestion] this evening? It is one of our house specialties."

4. If the guest orders a beer without naming a specific brand, do not say, "What kind would you like?" Say something along the lines of: "Would you like a Guinness? It's very popular." Or, "Try one of our great Martinis."

5. If a guest orders a gin and tonic, give suggestions on a specific brand. Say, "Would you like Beefeater's or Tanqueray?" If they say

the house brand will be just fine, do not suggest anything further. You do not want to be pushy, just helpful. In order to do this well, you should know the in-house alcohol brands. Effective selling helps guests to enjoy their visit and will also increase revenue.

IMPORTANT SALES POINTS

1. Sell yourself by using your social skills effectively to convey to the guests your willingness to serve them.
2. Sell your establishment by being enthusiastic about your work and show that you are proud to be associated with the business. Your enthusiasm will be infectious.
3. Sell the product and services by being fully informed and by suggesting and recommending what services are available to guests.

Personal recommendations are the best form of advertising. Making suggestions will help the guests because they may not know what is available. They may be indecisive or simply too shy to ask. When making suggestions, it is important not to press the guests. Let them make the final decision. However, by not making suggestions you can lose potential business. For example, when leaving a restaurant, have you ever noticed another guest eating a delicious-appearing piece of cake and thought to yourself, "If I had known that was available, I would have ordered it"?

MENU AND WINE LISTS

Keep menus and wine lists clean. Grubby, dog-eared menus do not help sales. Also make certain that there is an adequate supply of menus. A menu serves as a "silent salesperson" for the establishment. It is important to realize that your menu sells your food. Many of the people that come into your restaurant are indecisive—they're hungry, they want to eat, but they are not sure what they want or how they want it prepared. Therefore, the menu must help make the final decision.

To accomplish this task, the menu must stir pleasant taste memories, and descriptions of the items must arouse desire for the food. Here are some other areas you can describe:

1. Method of cooking, that is, roast, braised, grilled.
2. Cut of meat, that is, shoulder, loin, rib, and so on.
3. Form: rolled, boned, sliced, diced, and so on.

4. Essential ingredients such as sauteed chicken breast with mushroom sauce.

5. Method of serving, for example, in a casserole, on a skewer, and
so on.

It is important that the guest gets exactly what is read on the menu and
that the food reaches the customer in the way it was described. The same
principle applies to mouth-watering descriptions of items. These prepare the
guest for a promise of eating pleasure, and the actual presentation of the meal
must fulfill that promise.

The proper size plate plays a big part in visual presentation, as does the
color combination of the items served. For example, imagine a six-ounce filet
mignon with four mushrooms and a baked potato on an eleven-inch plate. It
would look lost. Or consider a T-Bone steak on an eight-inch plate, which
would not show its value. It does not matter what the customer pays for the
item, the first impression is going to be that there is not value for the money
spent.

USEFUL HINTS REGARDING MENU MERCHANDIZING

Include interesting little news items to encourage a greater interest in food.
Notes about the romantic background of familiar items may be included. Because there are probably places of interest in your area that you can feature
as well, such local history is appreciated by guests. Use the menu to provide
guests with interesting information about your restaurant. Feature a famous
local dish with a history. If the restaurant or foodservice establishment is
famous for something, or if the building has some historical significance, relate that to your customers through your menu. Remember that although
promotion, decor, and reputation can bring customers in the door, it's up to
the menu to sell the food, and up to the food you serve to bring them back.

MENU PRESENTATION

1. Be sure to inform guests, when presenting the menu, if any items
are unavailable. It is aggravating to make a choice only to discover
that it is not available.

2. Suggest such side orders as salads, vegetables, french fries, or rice or
baked potatoes with main courses.

3. If guests request an item that is not on the menu, check with the
kitchen to see if it can be served rather than simply assuming that it
is not available.

4. If your restaurant has a specialty, be sure to inform the guest about it.

5. If the dining room is full and more guests arrive, do not simply turn them away. Find out when a table will become available. Be as accurate as possible, and let the guests decide if they wish to wait. If they decide to wait, suggest they wait somewhere comfortable—the lobby or bar—and give them a menu. This helps speed up service.

6. Know cooking times. If the guests' orders will take some time to prepare, tell them in case they are in a hurry.

7. Accommodate guests' needs such as preparing separate checks if asked, permitting substitutes on menus, or serving sandwiches or smaller snacks during the period when full meals are normally served. Avoid negative announcements or notices such as "no substitutions" or "no sharing."

8. Display an attitude in appearance, voice, tone of voice, or body language, indicating that the guest is welcome and the server is ready to serve.

THE CULINARIAN'S ROLE IN MERCHANDISING

Obviously chefs make a very important contribution to the establishment's sales turnover. A reputation for great cuisine is a tremendous sales attraction. Chefs can improve sales and increase profits by:

1. Ensuring that all food is well prepared and properly cooked.

2. Presenting food in an appetizing and attractive way.

3. Maintaining high standards of cleanliness and sanitization.

4. Minimizing wastage.

5. Serving correct portions. Portion control is important and should be consistent. Guests will feel cheated if they receive very small portions. By contrast, overgenerous portions are wasteful, as much of the food will be returned uneaten.

6. Planning the work of the kitchen well to avoid long delays.

7. Checking the quality of food supplies regularly.

8. Cooperating with dining room team members, and if guests request something that is not actually on the menu, making every attempt to make it available.

9. Preparing dishes to guest specifications and satisfaction.

HANDLING GUEST COMPLAINTS

Guest expectations should be met and exceeded whenever possible. If a guest receives food or beverage or service that is not to his or her liking, team members should take steps to rectify the situation immediately. Enlightened employers empower team members to take any reasonable action they think necessary. Guests should be satisfied, and team members should be able to correct situations quickly and efficiently.

The most important method for handling complaints is to see that you have the right attitude about the complaints. Team members should be pleased when a guest has a complaint because the complaint presents an opportunity to turn a dissatisfied guest into a satisfied one, and to repair the damage done.

Many dissatisfied guests do not complain but simply never return. Therefore, every complaint should be thoroughly investigated as it may serve as an example of others that are not reported. Within certain limits, complaints are to be expected as mistakes do happen. Therefore, you should not feel personally guilty or required to defend yourself. Never show resentment, annoyance, or fear to a guest who comes to you with a complaint. Do, however, greet the guest with a friendly smile and impress the guest with your sincerity, your desire to help, and your ability to listen attentively to what they have to say.

Procedures for Handling Complaints

1. Thank the guest for bringing the complaint to your attention.
2. Apologize for the inconvenience caused.
3. Don't join with the guest in abuse of your service, establishment, or other team members. Comments such as "We're very understaffed"; "He's new here"; "I keep telling her not to do that"; or "It's chaotic here most of the time" don't pacify the guest. They only add fuel to the fire!
4. Let the guest tell their full story without interruption. Listen attentively.
5. Note the facts that will help to classify the problem and decide where the fault lies.
6. Try to remain as objective as possible in order to see the problem from a number of viewpoints. Jumping to conclusions can be dangerous.
7. Avoid guest confrontations in public. Politely draw the guest aside.
8. When the guest has finished speaking, rephrase the complaint in your own words to make sure that you both have the same understanding of the nature of the complaint.

As soon as action is taken, tell your guest about it and explain the reasons for the action. Make sure the guest understands and accepts the reasons concerned and that the action has the desired result of retaining the guest's goodwill.

The opinions or attitudes that guests have toward the company may be determined by the actions of one team member. It is sometimes easy to take a guest for granted, but when you do, you not only run the risk of losing that guest, but also his or her associates, friends, or family, who may also be guests or prospective guests. Each team member must be sensitive to the importance of providing courteous treatment in all working relationships.

Become a Psychologist

Try to identify your guests' needs and gauge their mood so as to be as helpful as possible. This requires sensitivity and the realization that guests are individuals and not a homogeneous mass with identical needs.

Although guests may share certain common needs, try to give a personal touch, tailored, as far as possible, to the needs of each guest. Your efforts in this area will be greatly appreciated by guests who will feel flattered and grateful that you have taken the trouble to do something special for them. For instance, remembering that a regular guest has a special dish or likes to sit at a special table requires little effort on your part, but your thoughtfulness will be greatly appreciated.

Your role as a psychologist is central to the quality of your performance as a diplomat, a salesperson, and a source of information. You need to be able to identify the clues in the guest's behavior and personality in order to deal with them diplomatically, to sell them what they actually want, and to give them the type of information they require. Remember guests are not always right, but they are always our guests.

Key points in handling complaints:

1. Always be polite when dealing with an irate guest.
2. When a guest complains about food or a beverage, offer to replace it. If that is not acceptable, remove the "offending" item from the bill and make management aware of the situation.
3. Sometimes it is not possible to appease a dissatisfied guest. Alert the manager to this situation as soon as possible.

The language and positive behavior displayed by the team member receiving the complaint can inspire confidence that the guest's complaint will be satisfactorily resolved. Use language that will inspire confidence and the sincerity of your intention to remedy the guest's dissatisfaction.

Inspires No Confidence	*Inspires Confidence*
Okay, I've got that.	Let me read this back to be sure I've got it right.
That's a common problem.	I'll give this my immediate attention.
We've had a lot of trouble with that.	I'll bring you a fresh one right away.
I don't know if I can help you with that.	Thank you for calling. Let me transfer you to Mr. Smith who can help you with that.
Don't worry about it.	I'll call back within an hour and tell you how it will be handled

Most guest complaints can be resolved with an apology and corrective action, and most guests generally will be understanding if the situation is handled politely, promptly, and professionally.

Never argue with an angry guest. Arguments accomplish nothing but irritation. Tact, courtesy, and a quiet tone of voice reduce the guest's anger and can open a way toward a satisfactory settlement.

Finally, report the complaint to the supervisor or manager. This will help to prevent future complaints of a similar nature.

STEPS IN SUCCESSFUL GUEST RELATIONS

1. Obey two rules. Rule number one: The guest may not always be right, but he or she is always the guest. Rule number two: If you ever have any doubts, go back to rule number one.

2. Attitude toward the guest must be pleasant, caring, attentive, thoughtful, courteous, service oriented, positive, helpful, and friendly with a smile.

3. Be knowledgeable of the establishment's products and services, and believe in them.

4. Greet guests with a warm welcome and smile. Use their names whenever possible.

5. Give guests a warm good-bye and invite them back.

6. Present a professional image. Wear an immaculate uniform, including footwear and name tag. Maintain first-class personal grooming standards.

7. Resolve guest complaints before they leave the establishment. Find solutions, not excuses. Listen to the guest and have an empathetic attitude.

8. Telephones should be answered promptly, courteously, and accurately.

9. See the good in people and try to develop those qualities. A positive and productive mind-set results in a positive and productive performance.

10. There is never an excuse to be rude to a guest.

11. Teamwork and respect for each other is important. Be a team player, and be open and honest with each other. The level of teamwork present in the establishment is usually reflected in great guest service.

12. Quality of the product and service with a consistency is a must. Do not compromise when it comes to standards. Consistency is essential and provides an assurance of quality, which results in unshakable guest loyalty.

13. Have confidence and believe in yourself without being arrogant.

14. Think objectively and maintain a sense of humor. Make the business fun for you and others.

15. Service is not a luxury, but it is an essential ingredient for the success of the hospitality and foodservice industry.

16. Pay attention to details. What makes the difference is doing little things right.

17. Be loyal to guests, fellow team members, the employer, and the establishment.

18. Be creative. Keep learning and growing—change with the times. Change not only helps us professionally, but also in our total life.

19. Our health comes first, family second, and our job comes third. When the first two are well taken care of, then our performance at work will be excellent.

20. Quality guest service can be best described as an opportunity—a chance to evoke positive change through cooperation and teamwork.

Business goes where it's asked and stays where it's appreciated.

REVIEW QUESTIONS

1. Outline suggestive selling and merchandising and describe its associated elements.

2. Outline how menus and wine lists can be used as merchandising tools.

3. Describe how chefs can contribute to merchandising in the foodservice industry.

4. Indicate the crucial steps and elements involved in handling guest complaints successfully.

5. List and review the steps involved in successful guest relations.

7

Legal Issues and Dining Room Service

Outline

TRUTH IN MENUS

Although the first reference to truth in menu by the National Restaurant Association occurred in 1923, much more attention has recently been given to this concept. The Federal Trade Commission has been involved with proposals for nutritional disclosure and labeling requirements which would be comparable to that required on container labeling by the Food and Drug Administration.

This truth-in-menu movement is not new to the foodservice industry. Some agricultural states have always been interested in assuring that their butter production was protected, thus requiring a menu notification when margarine is served. Interest and activity in the area of menu control has become more widespread with consumer movements.

When research showed a relationship between cholesterol consumption and coronary heart disease, many guests became interested in what saturated fats were included in the foods they were eating. Others were interested in knowing the geographic source of the product, if frozen food had been used, if meat substitutes were added, or the nutritional components of the menu being offered. Almost all consumers and many state governments became concerned about substitutions in food, reductions in quality, changes in methods of preparation, and the amount of food being served.

The menu serves as a form of contract between the foodservice establishment and the guest. It is important, therefore, that it properly reflects the type, form, style, amount, condition, and method of preparation of the food item that is being offered. Consumer groups, governmental regulatory bodies, and even industry self-regulating bodies are ready to ensure that what the customer sees on the menu is what he or she gets on the plate.

Truth-in-menu legislation is a major piece of guest protection legislation that directly affects restaurant service operations. Giving misleading names to menu items is unfair to the guest and is illegal where truth-in-menu legislation has been enacted. In general this law requires that the menu accurately describe the foods to be served.

Truth in menu should be standard operating procedure for any foodservice business, regardless of whether it is required by law. It makes no sense to falsely promote an item. Saying that fish is fresh when it is frozen or that meat is prime when it is not only raises false expectations in the guest. Unfulfilled expectations cause guest dissatisfaction. Furthermore, some restaurants that falsely claimed to be serving branded food products have been sued by the manufacturers, who have become quite protective of their trademarks.

Truth-in-menu legislation generally deals with the following types of misrepresentations:

1. The point of origin of the product is not as advertised.
2. The size, weight, or portion is not as advertised.

3. The quality or grade of the product is not as advertised.

4. The product is adulterated in one of the following ways:

    a. A valuable component has been omitted from the product, either in whole or in part.

    b. A substance is used to replace the product, either in whole or in part.

    c. The product is damaged or inferior, and this fact has been concealed.

    d. A substance (other than seasoning) has been added or mixed so as to increase the weight, diminish the quality, or make the product appear better than it is.

For example, "Fresh Shrimp Cocktail" is probably a violation of truth-in-menu laws, because virtually all shrimp is marketed frozen; "Camembert Dressing" had better be made with Camembert cheese; and "Coke" had better be the real thing, that is, Coca-Cola. "Maine Baked Potato" must come from Maine and "Whipped Cream" had better be the real thing and not an artificial substitute.

Descriptive words do enhance the menus and, if accurate, may influence the guest's selections. The menu therefore, should not include recipe items or products unfamiliar to the guest, or descriptions of recipes that do not indicate the contents.

Truth in menu is not limited to what is printed on the menu card. It can also apply to oral representations made by the dining room team.

THE AMERICANS WITH DISABILITIES ACT AND ISSUES OF SERVICE

The Americans with Disabilities Act of 1990 is one of the most important and far-reaching pieces of legislation that applies to both team members and guests. It forbids discrimination against those who have mental or physical disabilities in hiring, supervising, or serving and requires companies to provide "reasonable accommodations" to help workers cope by scheduling, providing adequate workstations, special tools, and so on. It also requires that guests with disabilities be provided with such items as wheelchair access, adequate parking, and large print menus. Title III of the Act became effective in 1992.

Title III requires that there be an accessible route of travel to get into the dining room. There are specific guidelines for both new and existing restaurants.

As a result of this Act, many disabled Americans are now afforded equal treatment in and accessibility to restaurants.

GUESTS WITH DISABILITIES

The biggest barrier to physically disabled guests is not the physical environment, it is social acceptance. The goal should always be to provide service to disabled persons just in the same way that we provide service to the able-bodied person.

People with disabilities also have abilities, and that is what many people tend to ignore. We sometimes assume that because a person has limited vision, they must also have a limited mind, or that a person with limited mobility is dependent and must be treated as a child.

Dining room team members should use the same degree of empathy with guests who have disabilities as they use with other guests. The problem is that it is very difficult for someone who has never experienced a disability to really know how to be empathetic toward someone with one. This is especially true for a young, healthy team member, who has never had to depend on others for certain basic needs.

Service team members should relate to the disabled person in a humane way, using all the skills of empathy they know. This means recognizing the individual and greeting him or her directly, making eye contact—and especially refraining from asking others in the party for information about the disabled guest and then talking as if that person were not there.

Special assistance should be provided by the team member only to the extent that it is warranted. When unsure about any assistance or if any is required, you should ask if any special assistance is wanted. In many cases the individual is quite capable of taking care of his or her own special needs and does not want help. If help is wanted, you should ask how the individual wants to be assisted.

Often intervention by others, even though well meaning, can be worse than no help at all.

GUEST FRAUD AND THE POTENTIAL OF CIVIL LAWSUITS

The primary type of guest fraud is when guests walk out without paying their checks. However, guests may also cheat an establishment by a number of other methods. They may, for instance, claim that the food was unsatisfactory and indicate they have no intention of paying for it. Another possibility that occurs frequently is for guests to suggest that their food contained some foreign matter, such as glass or china, or even an insect (possibly even brought in by the guest).

Because there is always a possibility that certain events may be fabricated, the normal policy in most establishments is to offer complimentary drinks or dinner to the guest in order to avoid embarrassment, or to prevent possible lawsuits, and, of course, to encourage the guest to return. In most cases of guest fraud, the guest will not return to perform the same type of fraud nor will they return merely to buy dinner.

In the case of falsified complaints, the establishment has no recourse except to treat the affair as a normal business expense. In cases of walkouts, the establishment may have legal recourse. The main course of action usually is to set up procedures that minimize this type of theft. The best type of prevention is vigilance which also contributes to first class service.

Guests normally cannot perpetrate any other type of theft, because they do not have access to food or beverages. Disputes may arise on an issue such as how many drinks were served. In cases of parties where payment is based on head counts, lower figures may be presented by the guests. However, generally verification can readily be made by team members. Credit cards and bad checks are another issue.

CREDIT CARD FRAUD

Credit cards are used extensively in today's restaurant and hotel industry. Most establishments honor them. The following is the recommended procedure for handling these transactions professionally:

1. Check the expiration date to see if the card is still valid. If it is an Amex, Visa, MasterCard, Diner's, or Carte Blanche card, run it through the credit card approval machine—magnetic stripe on the bottom, on the right-hand side, for most machines.

2. Wait for the approval code.

3. Compare the signature on the charge ticket with that on the card to see if they are the same.

4. Card companies publish lists of stolen, lost, or canceled cards. Check to establish if the card is on the current list. If it is and you accept the charge anyway, you can be stuck for the total amount on the bill.

5. Card companies also place limits on certain cards. All transactions above this limit must be cleared by a telephone call with the card company, even if the card number is not on the blacklist.

6. If there is any doubt about the validity of the credit card or if it appears to have been altered or defaced, ask for additional identification.

7. Choose the appropriate credit card slip for the credit card. Transfer the check number to the upper right-hand corner of the voucher slip.

8. Allow the guest to complete the voucher, adding a tip, if he or she so desires. The completed voucher is returned to the guest on a plate (if that is the house policy) with a pen.

9. If there is any indication of illegality, detain the guest and seek help.

Credit card companies can now check card validity when the card is "swiped" on the terminal. Nevertheless, industrious and clever thieves are ingenious at finding ways to beat any system.

CASHING CHECKS

Payment by check is not as common in restaurants as payment with credit cards. However, as a last resort restaurants will accept a check to collect a bill from a guest. To reduce the exposure to risk, the following procedure is recommended:

1. Read the check face and back. It should look like a check.

2. A check must be made out properly. If a personal check is made out to the restaurant, it should bear the current date, and should be cashed within two or three days. The writer's name and address should be imprinted on the face of the check. It should be made out to the restaurant or hotel cashing it. The amount in numbers should be identical to the spelled out numbers. The bank's name and address should be imprinted on the check. The signature of the maker should be legible, as should all writing on the check.

3. The check should not show signs of erasures or alterations; if either is present, the check should not be cashed.

4. Identification should be required. Certain types of identification that are hard to steal or duplicate are those that bear the name and description of the person to whom they are issued, or demonstrate that the individual's credit-worthiness has been previously determined.

Only certain forms of identification should be used to determine whether to cash a check or not, but even then it is best to ask for two or three. Examples of proper identification include a valid driver's license, an employee I.D. card bearing a picture, or a valid major credit card if it bears a signature. The type of I.D. presented by the person cashing the check should be noted on the back of the check.

5. The check should be reendorsed in the cashier's presence especially if there is doubt that the guest is the original signer of the check. Often a forger may not be able to spell the name of the payee or to duplicate the previous endorsement.

6. Remember, check cashing is a courtesy. There is no obligation to cash any check.

POTENTIAL OF CIVIL LAWSUITS IN FOODSERVICE

Although the typical freestanding restaurant (because it does not furnish lodging) is distinguished from an inn and the laws relating to innkeepers, the owner is still required under common law to protect his or her guests. The term "to exhibit reasonable care" so that the guest will not be injured in a manner that "the prudent person" could prevent serves as the basis for any claim of negligence on the part of a hotel operator or a restaurant or foodservice operator which might result in a liability judgment. The failure of the operator or a team member to do something such as wipe up spilled water or to post a sign indicating a wet floor or to replace a burned-out light bulb in a darkened area might result in a judgment according to the laws of torts.

WHAT IS A TORT?

A tort is any wrongful conduct that does harm. Tort law provides punishment for those who do wrong and compensates those who are harmed (sometimes, it appears, excessively). At times this tort award, despite the degree of negligence (if in fact two or more people or organizations are considered to be jointly liable but in different degrees), goes to what is known as the "deep pockets" principle and attacks the one who has the most money and the ability to pay the full judgment.

There are, of course, hundreds of potential actions, activities, and conditions within foodservice operations that could cause potential problems in relationships with guests and visitors. Of these, the two most important are the dispensing of alcoholic beverages and the serving of food.

It has been said that the American public sue more than any other population in the world. Anyone can file a lawsuit against another person or against a business or organization for any cause, and the party sued must then be prepared to defend itself against the suit. The best defense is to minimize the chance of being sued by striving to ensure that no one is wronged or injured. The next best defense is to keep very careful records of incidents which occur in the dining room or bar areas that might result in a lawsuit.

Prevention of accidents that could lead to lawsuits and negligence claims require proactive actions. Another type of claim is for physical assault or verbal abuse by a team member or another person. The courts have held that a restaurateur has a duty to provide protection to patrons from insult or annoyance. They may eject a guest guilty of this offense. As for protection from assaults, the courts have required that all reasonable care be taken to prevent such assaults. Certainly this includes careful screening of potential team members.

Dealing with a guest suspected of stealing is very touchy. Do not make accusations. Raise questions until you are absolutely sure and have the proof required to press charges.

In any case, whether it be an accident or other type of incident, be sure to record all the details in a logbook. Be very specific as to who was involved, who said what to whom, when and where it happened, and what conditions existed at the time. Such a record could be invaluable in the event of a lawsuit.

REVIEW QUESTIONS

1. Explain the necessity for a "truth-in-menu" philosophy.

2. Discuss the Americans with Disabilities Act. Review the requirements placed on the foodservice establishment as a result of this Act.

3. Describe and discuss the primary types of guest fraud.

4. Outline the recommended procedures for handling credit card transactions in the foodservice industry.

5. Describe the steps involved in cashing checks.

6. Identify and review the potential for civil lawsuits in the foodservice industry.

Part Two

Fundamentals of Wine Production

An Overview of:

The History, Origin, and Methods
of Wine Production

Wine Tasting and Appreciation

Wine Service Methods

8

Wine Making
and the Major Varietals

Outline

The subject of wine is vast. To treat it in detail would comprise many more pages than those available in this section of the text. This section is intended only as an introductory primer to this vast and fascinating subject.

It is believed that wine probably dates from prehistoric times when a cave dweller accidentally left some crushed grapes behind. There are no less than 521 references to wine in the Bible, including Noah's unfortunate experience when he drank unwisely. Louis Pasteur once remarked, "Wine is the healthiest and cleanest of drinks." Since ancient times wine has been thought of as a food. It is one of the three great gifts of yeast: wine, cheese, and bread.

Archaeologists maintain that grape wine was made 10,000 years ago, and it is possible that honey was fermented even earlier.

There are indications that the grapevine was cultivated about 6000 B.C. in Mesopotamia and Asia. By 3000 B.C. the vine was being cultivated in Egypt and Phoenicia, and there is some evidence of wine in China at about the same period. The art of making wine reached Greece by 2000 B.C., and the Greeks were probably the first to practice the aging of wines. They stored wine in airtight clay cylinders called amphoras. Wine ages and improves under these conditions. The secret of aging wine was later lost, and some 1,500 years passed before the bottle and cork were used for the same purpose.

Wine, both American and imported, basically falls into two distinct categories—generic and varietal. Generic wine is a designation of a particular class or type of wine, but such designations also may have geographic significance (the name of a district, commune, or region from where the wine originates). A simpler definition would be a "place-name"—wines that are named after European wine-producing districts such as Burgundy, Chablis, Champagne, Port, Rhine, Sauternes, Sherry, and so forth. Varietal is a wine made wholly or predominantly from a single grape variety, named on the label (for example, Cabernet Sauvignon, Chardonnay, Pinot Noir, Zinfandel).

SO WHAT IS WINE: THE BASIC ELEMENTS

Wine is an alcoholic drink produced by the fermentation of grapes, but wine is much more than an alcoholic drink. Wine contains many components which give interesting and enjoyable taste sensations. It has what is called character, and is ideally appreciated when accompanied by food and shared with others.

Essentially there are four components that determine the eventual quality of a wine. They are soil, climate, vine type, and the skill of the winemaker. Any variation of these will affect the taste and aroma of the grape, and, consequently, through to the wine.

The marriage of vine and soil, complemented by the weather—rain, sun, wind—and the skill of the winemaker, must all come together to make good wine.

In simple terms wine is the fermented juice of freshly gathered grapes. How the juice is converted into wine can best be described by the following process. (There are, of course, special procedures in various fields, but these general methods are broadly similar.)

The gathered grapes are taken to the winery, loaded into receptacles, and either crushed by mechanical crushing or from the grapes' own weight. The juice is then run off, with the skins and pips (which must never be broken) placed into the fermenting vats. Vats are traditionally made of oak, but glass, stainless steel, and concrete are now also used.

The bunches of grapes may be partially or totally destemmed by machine, according to the tannin content of the grapes, or the type of wine to be made and the individual technique of the winegrower.

In the vats, under suitable temperature, fermentation begins spontaneously by the action on the juice of the yeasts carried by the skins. This is sometimes aided by the addition of cultured yeasts.

Fermentation

Fermentation is the chemical process in which yeast acts on sugar or sugar-containing substances, such as grain or fruit, to produce alcohol or carbon dioxide. Fermentation converts the natural sugar of the grapes into alcohol and carbonic gas. It produces a bubbling activity in the must, and a rise in temperature (must is the term used to indicate the juice of the crushed grapes). The skins, pips, and stalks (if they have been retained) are forced up by the gas to form a floating cap. Sometimes the cap is kept partially submerged by means of a grill.

Under or around the cap, the fermenting grape juice develops a number of subtle chemical by-products, including glycerine, which gives the wine its taste and bouquet. The color comes from the contact with the skins—for grape juice is colorless. Sulphating is now carried out (sulphur is an ingredient in most wines which prevents refermentation) to neutralize bacteria, to assist with certain desirable chemical processes, and to intensify the color.

Almost every label on every bottle of wine sold in the United States has the statement "Contains Sulfites." This does not mean that winegrowers add chemicals to wine with no concern for the customer or the environment. Sulfur dioxide is a basic compound found naturally in many foods. It has also been used in many food processes (such as drying fruit, packing seafood, and bottling fruit juice), because sulfur dioxide is a major antioxidant. Sulfur dioxide also blocks the metabolic process of many bacteria, thus preventing their development and spread. In addition, in wine production, sulfur dioxide renders inactive the naturally occurring yeasts and other microorganisms that collect on the skin of the grape before harvest. Most winegrowers would point out that sulfur dioxide is a naturally occurring by-product of the fermentation process.

Sulphur dioxide checks premature fermentation in the harvested grapes. It also destroys undesirable yeasts, eliminates microbes and bacteria, protects against oxidation, and is used to prevent sweet white wines from fermenting in the bottle.

Chaptalisation

In unfavorable wine years, the addition of sugar, called chaptalisation, is necessary (chapalisation is the French term for the addition of sugar to the fermenting must in order to build up the alcoholic content of the wine). The degree to which it is permitted is strictly controlled for fine wines.

CHARACTER OF A WINE

When, in the judgment of the winegrower, fermentation has reached its desired point, the freely running juice is runoff into a large vat, where it is blended with wine extracted by pressure from the remaining must.

The quality of the wine and 90 percent of its character depend on the variety, selection, planting, and cultivation of the grape from which it is made. Learning about a grape's various characteristics and knowledge about wine making and the more common grapes can provide clues to determine a wine's probable taste.

Modern systems of temperature regulation in the vatting rooms have greatly facilitated the control of fermentation. It is impossible to give an average time for this process; in some areas it is done in three days, in others—according to local techniques—it goes on for weeks and even months.

GROWING THE GRAPES

As previously outlined, making great wine is very much dependent on the soil and microclimate of each grape-growing region and, in the case of the great limited-production wines, the exact location of the vineyard, in addition to the traditional cultivation methods of the winegrower.

Cultivation of the vine bearing the grapes influences the yield of wine and the quality of the product—the greater the yield per acre, the less flavor in each grape and a "lesser" or more diluted wine. With great wines the growers limit the yield per acre, usually by pruning the vines. In some places the maximum yield per acre is dictated by law.

The age of the vine also influences the quality of the grapes. Very young vines do not have a well-developed root system reaching down into the soil for the nutrients and minerals that give the grapes their wonderful, full-bodied taste. Consequently grapes from very young vines (under four years old generally, up to ten years in some instances) will not be as flavorful as grapes from older vines—even if grown in the same vineyard.

The wine's essential character is attributable to the marriage of vine and soil, complemented by the weather—rain, sun, and wind. Replenishment of nutrients to the soil is essential, which explains why portions of some vineyards lie fallow some years, being fertilized and nourished, then are planted with young vines the following year. This begins the five-year (or more) wait until the vine produces flavorful grapes.

WHY IS WINE AGED?

Wines are aged to increase their complexity. The aging of wine distinguishes wine from almost every other drink and most food products.

The chemical reactions that occur during aging add new aromas, flavors, and textures to the wine. The primary fruit compounds are gradually transformed into their developed forms, and as these reactions occur, the number of chemical compounds increase. The complexity of the wine grows as the aromas and flavors of youth intermingle with those that form with the progress of age. If the wine is aged for too long and all the reactions progress through to their final steps, there will be fewer chemical compounds in the wine, and these are likely to smell and taste very similar. The wine will have lost its complexity and in wine terms, "be over the hill."

Reactions other than those that lead to changes in the color and flavor profile also take place; for example, some of the acids and alcohol present can react to form volatile compounds, but the impact of these changes on the character of the wine is generally regarded as minimal. However, the acid may appear to soften as complexity increases.

After the second fermentation, the wine is placed in storage casks or vats to age or mature. The extent of aging is determined by the particular qualities of the grapes of that season. It may be a matter of a few weeks for some wines, or many years for others. At this point the wine is left alone and checked occasionally to judge when it is ready for bottling. The most radical and distinctive changes occur during this storage period—not, as many individuals imagine, during further maturation in the bottle.

When the wine in the cask is ready for bottling, having developed flavor, brilliance, and clarity, it is filtered and bottled.

Prolonging the aging does not necessarily result in a continued improvement of every wine. Each wine has a definite peak noted by balance in acidity and fruit flavors, after which the wine declines—usually the fruit flavor decreases and the acidity goes up. Age as a standard of evaluation has meaning only in comparing bottles from the same vineyard, of the same production batch, of the same production year, but tasted in different years.

Once bottled most wines are ready for drinking. However, some require further aging, especially red wines from "hearty" grapes such as Cabernet Sauvignon or Pinot Noir. Depending on the wine and how it is handled and stored, a year, a decade, or a half century may be the "right" amount of time to age the wine in the bottle.

A note on tannins: There are many different types of tannin, found in nuts, wood bark, berries, and, of course, grapes. The stalks, skins, and pips contain tannins which are released during pressing and fermentation, giving the wine its character and contributing to its capacity for aging. Storing the wine in new wood allows the addition of tannin from the wood.

STORING WINE

Wine must be stored correctly to preserve its quality and to promote further moderate maturation. Wine is a living substance and is very sensitive to any stimulus. Therefore the following conditions must be maintained in the wine cellar.

Temperature

The wine cellar temperature must remain fixed year round. The standard temperature is a bit lower than room temperature, about 55° F. The ideal temperature is 53° F. If the temperature changes rapidly, the wine ages prematurely.

Light

It should be almost dark in the wine cellar. Intense light such as fluorescent will go through a bottle of wine, causing it to age prematurely and to develop an unpleasant taste. Generally an underground cellar is ideal.

Humidity

The wine cellar should be maintained at a humidity level of 65 to 70 percent. If it is too dry inside the cellar, the cork will dry. This will allow the wine to come into contact with the air, causing a deterioration in the quality of the wine. If it is too humid, the wine itself will not be affected; however, the label or the cork will become moldy. If it is too dry in the cellar, place a humidifier inside or water the sand that is spread on the floor of the cellar.

Vibration

Because wine is a living substance, it is important to keep it free from vibration. A very slight vibration will not affect the wine, but a strong one will disturb the sediment that has settled in the bottle. Once a bottle of wine has been placed in the cellar, it is best not to move it until it is time to serve the wine.

Smell

Wine easily absorbs odors; therefore, it is important that nothing but wine be kept in the wine cellar.

Laying the Bottles

Corks should remain in contact with the wine inside the bottle so it does not become dry. Therefore, the bottle should always be stored horizontally.

THE MAJOR VARIETALS

The Vitis

The Vitis Vinifera is considered to be the wine vine. There are as many as 5,000 types named, but only fifty are of concern to the winegrower. Within each grape type, there are further separations of style. For example, there are about 150 clones logged of the Pinot Noir alone. The grape is the common denominator among the wines of the world. To recognize the grape is to know the general characteristic of the wine.

A Varietal wine is made completely or predominantly from a single grape, for example, Chardonnay or Cabernet Sauvignon. Varietal is a term describing wines made chiefly from one variety of grape. Such wines portray the dominant characteristics of the primary grape used.

RED WINE VARIETALS

Cabernet Franc

Related to the Cabernet Sauvignon, Cabernet Franc is also a small grape with high acidity, but it has a less-intense flavor profile and a distinctive mineral, ashlike aroma. It has been produced for decades in the Loire Valley in France, where it has been a single variety wine. Cabernet Franc is most often used to blend with Cabernet Sauvignon and Merlot. It is prized for its acidity, distinctive aroma, and strawberrylike fruit qualities.

Cabernet Sauvignon

Red wines from this most revered of Varietals, native to Bordeaux, offer great richness of body, numerous flavors, and a nature that lends itself to long cellaring. The wines are deep colored with aromas suggesting black currant, black cherry, plum, and other fragrances determined by cultivation areas. It is one of the world's most complex wines.

Gamay

Gamay makes the wines of Beaujolais. It is light, delicate, fruity, and some sugar may be noticeable. It is best consumed young (one to seven years). Because it is delicate, it can be slightly chilled. Gamay is best adapted to a soil with a high-granite concentration.

Grenache

Dark reddish-purple grapes make a light red wine from the Provence region of France and Spain. The wine produced is medium bodied with slightly noticeable acidity and a subtler character. It is used as a blending wine and for rosé wines. It is deliciously fruity and fresh, dry rather than sweet. It is a high sugar grape with character, but not much color, and is used in a blend to make Chateauneuf-du-Pape. It ages somewhat.

Merlot

A red-wine grape widely grown in France's Pomerol and Saint-Emilion districts of Bordeaux and, to a lesser extent, in California and the Pacific Northwest. The wine it produces is similar in flavor to Cabernet Sauvignon, but tends to be softer and more mellow. It also matures sooner than Cabernet. Though the Merlot grape has been principally used for blending in the United States, it's now beginning to be appreciated on its own. The French have long known its value as is indicated by the great Chateau Petrus of Pomerol, which is often 100 percent Merlot. The wines of St. Emilion and Pomerol, among the most treasured of Bordeaux reds, use a large amount of this grape. For the most part, Merlot wines may be consumed at a youthful stage. They tend to meld their tannins into other sensor components within two years.

Muscat

Muscat is the name of the most highly scented variety of Vitis Vinifera, the wine-making parent grape. It is popular both as a dessert grape and for making sweet dessert wine. There are many types of Muscat wines, and most of them are sold under the name of their place of origin, such as Muscat de Frontignan and Muscat de Samos.

Nebbiolo

Most at home in central Piedmont, the Valtellina of Lombardy and the Val d'Aosta, this marvelous variety is responsible for Italy's grand Barolos, Barbarescos, Spannas, Gattinaras, and the more gentle Grumello and Sassella. Barolo is a wine of underlying power moderated by a "ripe-raspberry" and spice aroma.

Pinot Noir

Pinot Noir is the foundation of nearly all the grand red Burgundies of France. Its character, elusive as it can be to the winegrower, is an incomparable "cherry-spice" aroma; soft, velvety consistency; and a lasting aftertaste of fruit. This is one of the most challenging varieties for the winegrower. This single red grape of the Cote d'Or area of Burgundy, France, produces some of the best wine in the world if planted in the right area. Wines such as

Chambertin are world renowned for being elegant, soft, and smooth. They also command tremendous prices. Pinot Noir is also used as the primary grape to produce the Standard Cuvee (blend) of the great champagnes and in making sparkling wines. The American Pinot Noirs are less expensive and some—particularly those from California and Oregon—are rapidly gaining in excellence and popularity.

Sangiovese

Sharing the spotlight with the great wines of Bordeaux, the Sangiovese is a wine grape that can best be described as refined. It is medium bodied in nature. The fragrance is one of raisiny, earthy ripeness and is easily identifiable and lingering. Although it forms the basis of all the Chianti and Brunello di Montalcino, it is commonly blended with other varieties much as the Cabernet Sauvignon is married with several grapes in Bordeaux to develop scents and flavors.

Sirah, Shiraz

This is a high-quality red wine grape that gained its reputation in France's Rhône region. In the northern Rhône, Syrah is the principal grape of the esteemed wines from Cornas, Côte-Rotie, Crozes-Hermitage, Hermitage, and Saint-Joseph. In the southern Rhône, Syrah is used to contribute flavor and structure to the multivariety wines from Chateauneuf-du-Pape and Côtes-du-Rhône. Dark, rich, and tannic, with a fragrance of smoky-fruit, Syrah may be found in the form of Côte Rotie and as Shiraz from Australian producers. The fountain of culture and civilization claims the distinction of having given wine to the world. The Shiraz or Sirah vine had been planted and prospered in different parts of the world. Shiraz red or white has a pungent, spicy, and perfumed flavor. When young, Syrah wines are deep-colored and tannic, with spicy and peppery qualities. Mature Syrahs show characteristics of sweet blackberries, black currants, and plums. In Australia, Syrah is called Shiraz. Wines are also made from the Shiraz vine in Australia and South Africa.

Tempranillo

Rioja is the most widely known Tempranillo-based wine. The grape is not the only one used, but the better Rioja is more likely to have a majority of Tempranillo in the blend. Tempranillo grapes ripen early, making it suitable for the high, cool areas, such as Rioja and Ribera del Duero. It also suits the limestone soils of these regions. Tempranillo produces wine of good color, which is relatively low in acidity and ages well in oak. The Tempranillo is low in tannin, so other grapes such as Manzuelo and Cabernet Sauvignon are sometimes added to the blend to compensate.

Tokay

Tokay is a sweet white wine from the Tokay region of Hungary; it is made primarily from the Furmint grape. Botrytis Cinerea-infected grapes from the better vintages produce marvelous dessert wines which rival the best from France and Germany.

Zinfandel

Although indigenous to the California coastal areas, Zinfandel is a true "Vinifera" or Old World variety. It is among the most versatile of wine grapes and offers styles ranging from "fresh," light-bodied red to powerful, highly tannic wine suitable for many years of aging.

Legend has it that the Shah Djemsheed always kept a dish of grapes by his bedside. One day he noticed that some of them had become overripe and had begun to ferment. Believing that the fruit had turned rotten and therefore poisonous, he ordered it to be thrown away. Hearing of this, a discarded mistress ate the "poisonous" grapes as a means of committing suicide and ending her sorrows. The Shah was surprised to find her suddenly gay and happy. When questioned, she confessed about the grapes. The shah discovered the secret of the grapes, the wine industry began, and the discarded mistress was reinstated in the royal affection.

WHITE WINE VARIETALS

Aligote

This variety of central France yields a rather ordinary white table wine. It is found mostly in the Challonais district of the Burgundy region.

Chardonnay

American wine lovers have experienced at least several wines from this pre-eminent variety. Solid, "fat," buttery, alcoholic, and perfumed, Chardonnay is native to Burgundy, France. When you buy Chablis, Pouilly-Fuisse, Meursault, Puligny, or Chassagne-Montrachet, you are drinking Chardonnay.

Chenin Blanc

The white grape of Anjou and Touraine on the Loire. Gives intense wine. Honeylike when very ripe but always high in acidity. Its finest wines are Vouvray. It is fruity with sugar and acidity, sometimes slightly or half sparkling.

Cortese

An old classic vine, Cortese is again in the limelight because of the remarkable popularity building for wines from this variety grown in the now famous Gavi district in the Piedmont region of Northern Italy. New wine-making techniques have succeeded in extracting more of its delicate stony-almond flavor and taming its biting acidity.

Gewurztraminer

Gewurz means "spicy," and this white wine is known for its crisp, spicy characteristics. It's a specialty of the French region Alsace—the area that buffers Germany and France—and is also produced in Germany and California. Gewurztraminer has a distinctively pungent, perfumy, yet clean flavor. It's available in varying degrees of sweetness; the drier versions complement fish and poultry, the slightly sweeter styles are perfect for summer spritzers, and the sweet late harvest version make excellent dessert wines. Gewurztraminer is best when drunk fairly young because even the vintage versions won't usually age well over five years.

Malvasia

Malvasia is quite a vigorous grape and is sometimes blended with the more acidic Viura to produce the best, rare Spanish riserva white wines of Rioja. This grape does well in oak-aged white wines.

Muller-Thurgau

This German grape produces a pleasing low acid white wine. It is highly aromatic, rather soft, lacks acidity, and is a cross between the Riesling and the Sylvaner.

Muscat de Frontignan

One of many Muscat grape varieties that are prized for their bold, powerful fig-guava flavor, Muscat de Frontignan is widely cultivated in southern France. A close relative, Moscato, is grown in northern Italy for the famed Asti Spumante sparkling wines. Muscat de Frontignan produces elliptically shaped berries in compact medium-sized clusters.

Palomino

This variety is often incorrectly referred to as "Golden Chasselas" in some winegrowing regions. Palomino is the principal grape grown in Spain for the production of the finest sherry dessert and cocktail wines. It is a vigorous, productive vine, maturing its fruit in late midseason to large, frequently shouldered, clusters of greenish-yellow oblong berries.

Pinot Blanc

A variety of white grape that is used in some white Alsatian wines and bottled as a Varietal by a few California wineries. Pinot Blanc wine is crisp and dry but has less intensity and flavor than Chardonnay. Its price is also considerably lower.

Pinot Grigio

This is one of the most widely cultivated vines across the northern sectors of Italy, and as "Pinot Gris" can be found in many other European countries. It is known as "Rutlander" in Germany, as "Szurkebarat" in the Tokay region of Hungary, and as "Tokay d'Alsace" in the Alsace region of France. Its rich golden color and bold fig-almond flavor have prompted the establishment of many new vineyards of Pinot Gris in North America.

Resling

Riesling is considered one of the world's great white wine grapes and produces some of the very best white wines. It's a native of Germany, where it's believed to have been cultivated for at least 500 (possibly as long as 2,000) years. Riesling wines are delicate but complex, and characterized by a spicy, fruit flavor; flower-scented bouquet; and long finish. Riesling is vinified in a variety of styles, ranging from dry to very sweet. In Germany, these sweet wines—which are usually affected by Botrytis Cinerea—are graded in ascending order of sweetness as auslese, beerenauslese, and trockenbeerenauslese. German Rieslings from the Mosel and Rhinelands are glorious, piquant models of the word elegant. They are normally low alcohol but high in acidity. Ironically it was France's Alsace region that brought it to a high level of recognition. In this region the grapes have a grapefruity perfume, and dry, generous body. It is a totally unique experience in the world of wine.

Sauvignon Blanc (Fume Blanc)

The chief white Bordeaux grapes blend with Semillon to make dry Graves with an earthy, gravely characteristic. In the Loire Valley, it makes a clean, lighter wine where it is used alone. May have a smoky or flinty taste. What often prevents this variety from being as broadly accepted as Chardonnay and Riesling is its gripping acidity. A Sancerre or Pouilly Fume from the Loire Valley provides the true taste of this grape varietal. The green-apple soul of Sauvignon Blanc is quickly apparent in aroma and flavor.

Semillon

An excellent white grape used to blend with Sauvignon Blanc to make the great, lusciously sweet wines. Fruity, often has an aroma of ripe figs. When mixed with Sauvignon, makes a top sweet Sauterne, and a Barsac with a sweet botrytis style; it is smooth, noble, and ages well.

Silvaner

A white-wine grape of German origin. Long popular in Germany and surrounding areas of Europe, this white-wine grape has been transplanted to California and Chile. Although the wine produced from Sylvaner grapes is light and pleasant, it's not as flavorful or fruity as Germany's Johannisberg Riesling.

Trebbiano

Known as Ugni Blanc in France, the Trebbiano variety takes its name from the Trebbia Valley in central Italy, where many acres are planted.

SPARKLING WINES

Sparkling wines are usually white or rose in color. Carbon dioxide gas is captured during secondary fermentation in a closed container. The traditional French method of bottle-fermentation is called "Methode Champenoise." The bulk or tank method is called the "Charmat" process. Sparkling wines are those bottled with dissolved carbon dioxide, which forms bubbles when the wine is opened.

The first sparkling wines may have been made in France in the 1600s by a monk named Dom Perignon who is thought to have been blind. The invention and the use of plugs made from tree bark to use as bottle stoppers have been attributed to Dom Perignon. Apparently the seal was so good that wine bottled in the autumn, before it was completely finished fermenting, built up some carbon dioxide gas pressure inside the bottle during storage. When the cork was released, sparkling bubbles were produced.

Nowadays many people use the terms "champagne" and "sparkling wine" interchangeably. However, Champagne is a sparkling wine–producing region in France; therefore, the term is generic.

Other countries produce sparkling wines by the "bottle fermentation" method. According to European regulations, sparkling wine produced in Germany must be labeled as *Sect*, whereas in Italy it is referred to as *Spumante*, and in Spain as *Cava*.

Much to the dismay of the French Champagne vintners, American regulations permit the use of the word champagne on labels on sparkling wines produced in the United States. However, the word champagne must be preceded with an approved designation, such as "California Champagne" or "Napa Valley Champagne."

METHODE CHAMPENOISE

Champagne is one of the most legendary wine regions of all France. It is located about 100 miles northeast of Paris in the department of the Marne. Although some bordeaux and burgundy selections are priced much higher, champagne is still considered to be the most luxurious of wines. By national decree, a wine labeled "champagne" can only be sparkling wine.

Champagne is that sparking bubbly wine that everyone drinks on New Year's Eve. But it is more than that. Champagne is a region in France, the northernmost wine-making region, northeast of Paris.

The location of the Champagne region has an effect on the taste of the wine. In this region, the growing season is shorter, therefore the grapes are picked with higher acidity than in most other regions, thus producing a high-acid sparkling wine.

The Champagne region is divided into three main areas: (1) Valley of the Marne, (2) Mountain of Reims, and (3) Cote des Blancs. Three grapes can be used to produce champagne. These are Pinot Noir (red) which accounts for 37 percent of all grapes planted, Pinot Meunier (red) which accounts for 32 percent of all grapes planted, and Chardonnay (white) which accounts for 31 percent of all grapes planted.

HOW IS CHAMPAGNE MADE?

Harvest

The normal harvest usually takes place in late September or early October.

Pressing the Grapes

Only three pressings of the grapes are permitted. The first pressing produces high-quality champagne, whereas the second and third pressings are either made into inexpensive champagne or sold to other winegrowers.

Fermentation

All Champagnes undergo a first fermentation when the grape juice is converted into wine. The formula is Sugar + Yeast = Alcohol + CO_2. The carbon dioxide dissipates. The first fermentation takes two or three weeks.

Blending

Blending is the most important step in Champagne production. The winegrower has to make a lot of decisions here. Three of the more important ones are:

1. What grapes to blend—how much Chardonnay, Pinot Noir, and Pinot Meunier?
2. From which vineyards should the grapes come?
3. What years or vintages should be blended?

Liqueur de Tirage

After the blending process, the wine is placed in its permanent bottle. At this point the winegrower adds Liqueur de Tirage—a blend of sugar and yeast—which will begin the wine's second fermentation.

Second Fermentation

During this fermentation, the carbon dioxide stays in the bottle. This is where the bubbles come from. The second fermentation also leaves a natural sediment in the bottle. Now the problems begin: How to get rid of the sediment without loosing the carbon dioxide?

Riddling

The wine bottles are now placed in A-frame racks, neck down. The riddler goes through the racks of Champagne bottles and gives each one a slight turn while gradually tipping the bottle further downward. After six to eight weeks, the bottle stands almost completely upside down with the sediment resting in the neck of the bottle.

THE CHARMAT METHOD

This method of making sparkling wine is also known as "cuve close." When sugar and yeast are placed in a large vat to allow for secondary fermentation, the wine is chilled, filtered, and transferred under pressure to a second tank, where it is sweetened and bottled. This is the bulk method of making champagne; it is simple, direct, and inexpensive.

In the United States, if a sparkling wine is produced in this fashion, the wine must be labeled as either "Bulk Method" or "Charmat Method."

OPENING AND SERVING A BOTTLE OF CHAMPAGNE

Champagne corks are wired on to hold the cork in the bottle under tremendous pressure. Bottles must be handled gently to reduce the danger of fast flying corks, to prevent the waste of spouting wine, and to retain the "bubbly" quality longer.

Remove the foil covering the cork to expose the base of the wire, hold the bottle at a 45-degree angle, pointed away from any vulnerable targets, including the windows. Ease the bottle from the cork with a whisper, without a pop, resulting in more wine to drink and less foaming out of the bottle.

If the mushroom cap of cork on a bottle of sparkling wine should break off, the bottle must be opened with a regular corkscrew. Unfortunately, this is a difficult procedure as such corks are highly compressed and of excellent quality so it will be difficult to get the worm into the cork. Also the pressure of the wine will prevent a controlled release of the cork. This is a dangerous procedure and should only be done in the service bar area or in the kitchen, not in the dining room or a public space area, and certainly not in front of any guests.

When pouring, start each glass with about one inch of champagne, and then take the bottle around again after it has settled down. This gets the bubbles into the glasses quickly, without rising foam and spilled wine.

FORTIFIED WINES

This generally means that alcohol spirit is added to certain wines. The three main types of fortified wine are port, madeira, and sherry. Fermentation for port starts in a way similar to red wine. Fermentation removes the natural sugars from the grape juice. Port wine will be dry if it is permitted to reach its natural end. For port fermentation is stopped at the halfway stage, when the juice is poured into casks containing grape brandy. The addition of the yeast ceases, the sugar is retained, and the alcoholic strength is increased by the spirit.

Madeira is made similarly to port, except that the spirit is made from sugarcane. This is added at different stages. Madeira then receives a unique treatment. It is made in an "estufa" (large heating chamber). Heat is gradually applied, and the wine is brought up in temperature. (See *About Wines*, pp. 285–295.) This method provides madeira with its slightly burnt flavor, and enables this naturally strong wine to last indefinitely without loss of quality.

Sherry is naturally a dry wine. Sweetness is derived after fermentation by blending with wine made from exceptionally sweet grapes, whose sugar is sufficient to resist the effect of fermentation. Thus the fermentation of sherry is allowed to proceed to its end, and the brandy is added later, to act as a strengthener and preservative.

BLUSH (OR ROSÉ) WINES

Blush (or rosé) wines are either made like red wine, with only slight maceration (soaking) permitted between juice and skins to minimize coloration, or by mixtures of other white grapes in the fermenting process.

The color of the grape is not necessarily the color of the wine. Both white and rosé wines may be made from red or black grapes. The taste of the wine is usually a better indicator of the grape variety than the color.

REVIEW QUESTIONS

1. Restate the origins and history of wine making.
2. Describe the basics of wine making.
3. Outline the elements that make up the character of different wines.
4. Describe the critical elements associated with grape growing.
5. Explain why some wines are aged. Describe the steps associated with storing and aging wines.
6. List and review the major wine Varietals.
7. Describe and explain what sparkling wines are, their methods of production, and the difference between "Methode Champenoise" and the "Charmat method."
8. Outline what fortified wines are—their methods of production and their uniqueness.

9
Major Wine-Producing Countries

Outline

EUROPE

Most countries produce good wine, and many countries produce superior wines. No one country produces the best wines.

Germany, Italy, Spain, Portugal, and France are the main European wine-producing countries. Germany is noted for the outstanding Riesling wines from the Rhine and Mosel River Valleys. Italy produces the world famous Chianti. Spain makes good wine but is best known for sherry. Portugal also makes good wines but is best known for its port. France is the most notable of European wine-producing countries.

FRANCE

The French regard wine as a national possession all their very own, just like their 360 varieties of cheese and their culture.

Roland Barthes

France is the wine center of the world. The two most famous wine-producing areas in France are the Bordeaux and Burgundy provinces. The Bordeaux wine region supplies the finest assortment of quality wines of any country. Most of these fine wines come from different varieties of the Cabernet vine, influenced by the humidity and the mild climate of the area. In addition, their majestic clarets; fine, medium dry grapes; and incomparable sauternes are world renowned.

The Burgundy province is a most important wine center, producing sparkling Burgundy, Côte d' Or, Chablis, and Beaujolais. These wines come primarily from two types of grapes—Pinot Noir for red and Chardonnay for white. Chablis, when referred to correctly, is a rare wine and is made from grapes grown in the Burgundian town of Chablis.

Burgundy

Most of Burgundy is situated in a narrow ninety-mile strip of land between the cities of Dijon and Lyons. The entire region cultivates approximately 100,000 acres of vineyard, amounting to 4 percent or so of total French wine-growing. Burgundy consists of five regions. These are:

1. Chablis, often referred to as the "Yonne" or "Auxerrios" centered on the village of Chablis. This area is also sometimes referred to as "Lower Burgundy."

2. Côte d'Or, the magnificent "Slope of Gold"; its capital city is Beaune. This district is subdivided into Côtes de Nuits, the northern portion, and Côte de Beaune, the southern portion.

3. Chalonnais, centered on the city of Chalon.

4. Maconnaise, centered on the city of Macon.

5. Beaujolais, the largest district in Burgundy. There are thirty-nine "villages" in the district from which wine production may be labeled "Beaujolais Villages." In each township surrounding a village in Burgundy, the vineyards are divided into small parcels known as *climats*. As a rule, Beaujolais Villages are blends crafted from wines grown in several villages.

Bordeaux

Of the more than 2,000 Chateaux in the Bordaeux region, 200 of the best are classified. The official classification made in 1865 still holds good, with the Chateau Lafite, Latour, Margaux, and Haut Brion. It was only in 1973 that Chateau Mouton-Rothschild joined the select band, owing to the untiring efforts of Baron Phillipe de Rothschild over many years.

The seaport city of Bordeaux is built along the Garonne river, some sixty miles southwest from the Atlantic coast. Bordeaux has approximately 250,000 acres of vines that yield 100 million gallons of wine in an average vintage. It is the largest "fine wine" viticultural region in France and in the world. About 60 percent of this production is white, but most of the highly classified vineyards are red, with only a few exceptions. Bordeaux is typified by an aristocracy of individual owners operating large wine estates or chateaux.

The important subdistricts of Bordeaux include the following:

Medoc, the higher portion of the "Haut Medoc," is the single most important subdistrict of the Medoc. Its four principal villages are Margaux, St-Julien, Pauillac, and St. Estephe. Each village has classic chateau estates which are known worldwide. From the Bordeaux region also comes the incomparable earthy "Graves" and sauternes, where grapes are harvested radically overripened to produce the delicate, sweet-tasting superior wine.

Entre-Deux-Mers, translated literally, means "between two seas." It is truly between two rivers, the Garonne and the Dordogne. Within Bordeaux is the medieval village of St. Emillion, which provides some of the finest red wines of France.

Pomeral is characterized by ironstone subsoil beneath its clay-gravel topsoil. This soil combination produces some of the world's best grapes, which in turn produce some of the most mouth-filling, full-bodied, intensely complex red wines found anywhere. Also found within this region are the important subdistricts of Fronsac and Canon-Fronsac, Bourg and Blaye, and the historic Bergerac.

The Loire Valley

The Loire, more than 600 miles in length, is the longest river in France. It originates in the central highlands west of Lyons and gathers the tributary rivers of Cher, Indre, Layon, Loir, Sevre, Vienne, and others on its way toward the Atlantic seaport of Nantes. This region has many fine districts and individual estates within its borders. The Central Vineyards, which is also referred to as "The Nivernais," is famous for its "Blanc Fume." Tournaine is the largest district of the Loire Valley. Vouvray is one of the most notable wine subdistricts in the Tournaine. The other important areas of this region include Anjou-Saumur and Nantais.

The Rhône Valley

The Rhône Valley has a rich heritage. Most Rhône wines are marketed in similar fashion to those of Burgundy. Côte Rotie is the area's best red. This district is divided into two subdistricts, Côte Brunette and Cote Blonde. Legend has it that these subdivisions were so named because a medieval winegrower had two daughters, one blonde and one brunette. Also from the Rhône come the famous Syrah vineyards of Hermitage, and the jewel of the Rhône, Chateauneuf-du-Pape, the "new home of the pope."

Alsace

The white wines of Alsace are made from the grapes grown in the vineyards at the foothills of the Vosges Mountains, facing the Rhine and in the plains of the Rhine. They are dry wines, with a fair bouquet and body, which are sold under the name of the particular species of grape used for each. Slyvaner Varietal is light, whereas Riesling, the White Pinot, Traminer, and Gewurztraminer are better and more costly wines.

ITALY

Italy is one vast vineyard, from its snow-covered mountains to the north to its southern volcanic tip. It is one of the world's largest producers of wine. From the Piedmont district in the north come the classic red wines—Barolo and Barbera, and Nebiolo, medium sweet wines, and perhaps Italy's best-known white sparkling wine, Asti Spumante.

The wines from Umbria, Trentino Alto-Adige, Veneto, Friuli-Venezia Giulia, Lombardia, Marche, and Campania can also be excellent. These wines represent a small fraction of Italy's prodigious output. The actual number of wines available can be staggering.

The diversity of Italy's climate is unmatched; soil types differ from one region to another. The end result is a range of distinctive wine types, with variation within individual regions. The comprehensive scope of Italian winegrowing is expanded further by the seemingly endless number of vine varieties cultivated across the nation. Some varieties, such as Nebbiolo, Barbera, Dolcetto, and Freisa, are limited to cooler climates. Others, including Trebbiano, Sangiovese, Malvasia, Moscato, and Verdicchio, are cultivates in warmer climates. There are nearly 200 different types of Italian wine recognized officially by controlled classification.

From Tuscany comes the famous Chianti. Sicily's hot climate and volcanic soil produces sweet, fortified wines. The most notable are Marsala and some rich Muscatels. The wines of Italy are full of regional and local personality and spirit.

GERMANY

Germany's cold climate makes it a difficult country for growing grapes. However, with skill and tenacity, the winegrowers in the Rhine and Mosel river valley districts do produce fine white wines which are celebrated all around the world. Most of the wines are produced from the Riesling grape, and they have a very pleasant, flowery bouquet. Mosels are light, delicate, and generally dry to slightly off-dry.

Despite the inconsistent weather patterns, Germany's winegrowers produce white wines with high acidity and a crisp, fresh fruit character. Sometimes extraordinary wines are produced in what appears to be unfavorable wine-making conditions. For the true wine lover, the wines of Germany hold a long-lasting attraction.

AUSTRIA

Grapes have been grown in Austria since the days of the Romans, but with only a few exceptions, the quality of the wines has remained unrecognized outside Austria itself. Austria's wine regions are highly distinctive. Long experience and local tradition have shown them as particularly suited to certain styles of wine or certain grapes, and this has led to a tremendous variety among Austrian wines.

Benedictine monasteries were responsible for the development of many vineyards in Austria. The Riesling grape, originally cultivated in Germany, was introduced to Austria, and by the early fifteenth century, Trockenbeerenauslese wines were being produced in some of the present-day Austrians vineyards. Trockenbeerenauslese, "shriveled hand-picked selected harvest" wines are made from noble-rot grapes, harvested individually, which have been allowed to dry on the vine, shriveling and appearing like raisins, concentrating the sweet grape juice and flavor.

Another important development in Austrian wine technology was the development of the system of trellising vines vertically. This system allowed for the mechanical harvesting of grapes. To this day, 75 percent of Austria's vineyards employ this trellising system.

SPAIN

Spain produces some of the world's most highly esteemed wines, especially the classic red wines of Rioja. Rioja is known throughout the world for the quality of its red wines. The climate is regulated by Rioja's position, which is halfway between the Atlantic Ocean and the Mediterranean. The Atlantic provides cool breezes; the Mediterranean's breezes are warmer—a combination that ultimately gives strength and body to the wines.

Rioja has produced quality wines in the bottle for more than 100 years, primarily relying on the Varietals Tempranilla and Garnacha, and, secondarily, Mazuelo and Graciano grapes. Some of the wines are from lesser known wine growing areas such as Albarino from Rias Baixas, the red wines of Ribeira del Duero, and the whites of Rueda and Ribiero. These show real promise for the future.

Spain is also world renowned for its sherry, produced in Jerez de la Frontera in southern Andulusia. Amontillado and cream sherries are of superior quality and are among the best known of the sherries produced from grapes grown in this region.

PORTUGAL

Portugal is famous for its ports. Ruby is a young, fresh, fruity port; tawny port is matured in wooden casks, during which time its color changes; and white port has a straw-gold hue.

Vintage ports may require ten to fifteen years of aging in the bottle before they reach the point of perfection. They must be decanted very carefully so as not to disturb the heavy crust in the wine.

Port comes from the Douro region in Northern Portugal. True port is named Porto or Oporto, from the name of the port through which it is shipped. For centuries port was the preferred after-dinner drink of the British.

The Portuguese island of Madeira has produced the longest lived wines. These wines are fortified with an alcohol content of about 20 percent. Madeira is made in a similar way to port, except that the spirit is made from sugarcane, which is added at different periods during the fermentation process. However, Madeira then receives a unique treatment. When the wine has fermented enough, the heating process follows. This process is unique in wine making. The duration of the heat treatment is not less than six weeks. The wine in a large tank or in a heated chamber, and the temperature of the wine is gradually raised to about 140 degrees F. The temperature is held for a further six weeks and then slowly reduced to normal. The chamber or tank in which the wine is heated is known as the estufa, and the wine is said to be "estufado" when the heating process is complete. It is said that the estufa is a device for reproducing the effects of a slow journey through the tropics.

In the days of sail, it was found that the Madeira wines which were transported through the tropics in the sun-baked hold of a ship were greatly improved. As a result of this, the estufa was born. The effect of this heating is to give the wine its caramel-like flavor and its unmistakable tang. It also gives it longevity, for it seems that the wines of Madeira live forever. Many people claim to have tasted wine made in the eighteenth century, and a Madeira wine over one hundred years old is quite common.

HUNGARY

The pride of Hungarian wines is Tokay. Tokay Aszu and Tokay Szamorodni are the most popular. The greatest glory of Hungarian wine making is the famous product of the twenty-five villages of the Tokaji district. This great wine is made of a blend of three grapes. The superb flavor is due to very late harvesting after a hot, sunny autumn, when the grapes have shriveled and the juice becomes concentrated in sugar and flavor through the action of the "noble rot." Known as the famous "Bull's Blood" of Eger (Egir Bikaver), it is made of kadarka and other vines imported from France. It is a deep red, full, serious wine with a fragrance of its own which develops by long, slow maturing. It is mildly dry.

The climate and soil in Hungary are ideal for viticulture. Generally there is plenty of sunshine, and the prolonged fine autumn weather is conducive to the making of Hungary's best wines which depend on late harvesting. In some areas, local geographic conditions assist the winegrowing. Along the northern shores of Balaton, the vast inland lake, the hillside receives the benefits of reflected heat and moisture rising from the water.

The best wines include those produced on the shores of Balaton Lake, mainly from an Italian variety of Riesling grapes, which thrive in this particular type of soil and situation.

GREECE

Greece has been producing wine since prebiblical times. Its rich, volcanic soil produces the very sweet Malvasias and Muscats. The most popular Greek table wine is Restsina, which is the most controversial of the Greek wines. Although Restsina is drunk throughout the country, it is drunk only locally, as it does not travel well. A resina is a wine (either red or white but usually white) which has been deliberately and heavily resinated. To those who acquire a taste for it, it can be an agreeable wine.

In the days before casks, the Greeks kept their wine in goatskins and then poured pitch pine on the top for preservation. Critics of the wine say that resin spoils it. It depends. However, the fragrant scent of pine needles mingles with the taste of the wine and does enhance it.

Resina wines belong to the tavernas of the towns and villages, and it is on the quality of its resina that the reputation of a taverna is made or lost. If the resina is good, the word flies swiftly throughout the district, and word flies with equal speed if the wine is bad.

SOUTH AFRICA

When they landed at the Cape, the Dutch recognized a land and a climate that were ideal for the growing of grapes. Within three years the first vines were planted, just over three hundred years ago. Another four years passed and the first wine flowed. After a further thirty years, French Huguenots seeking religious freedom settled there; many of them brought French winegrowing skills with them. By the early nineteenth century, South African wines were known throughout Europe, although Britain was the main customer.

The wine country is concentrated mostly in the western region of Cape Province, within 150 miles of Cape Town. The best red wine comes from the Constantia district close to Cape Town.

The climate and soil conditions in South Africa gives their wines a special character. These wines, after many years of isolation, are now reestablishing themselves among some of the best in the world. South African wines have an unusual spiciness, and these special flavors also are reflected in South Africa's fine brandies.

AUSTRALIA

Australia is producing some of the finest red Varietals to be found anywhere in the world. The birth of Australian wine goes back to a spring day in 1778 when Captain Arthur Phillip, the first governor of New South Wales, thrust a spade into the earth. This earth had just been cleared of eucalyptus trees and dense growth; Phillip planted grapevines brought in his flagship *Sirius* from Rio de Janeiro and the Cape of Good Hope. Until then the whole continent had not nourished a single vine.

It was not until 1854 that Australia's first commercial shipment of wine arrived in England. Although this was a small shipment, wine production continued to increase.

With its great expanse of suitable land, its variable climate, access to water, and highly skilled work force, Australia has many natural advantages as a wine-producing nation. In many aspects of wine making, it leads the world in technology and innovation. The diversity of soil types, climate, and wine-making skills allows for a full range of wines, from very high-quality sparkling wines using traditional methods, through a complete range of table wines using the classic grape varieties, to some of the greatest fortified dessert wines in the world.

Since the first vines were planted at Farm Cove in Sydney in 1788 by Captain Phillip, the vine has been planted to many regions in all states of Australia, from the irrigated areas where citrus crops were grown. Much has been learned in Australia's relatively recent wine industry about the importance of site selection, viticulture, selecting the appropriate varieties, studying climatic conditions, new and improved vineyard management, new trellising systems, improved methods of irrigation, harvesting, pruning, and then the techniques of handling the fruit, attention to hygiene, controlled fermentation, refrigeration, stabilization, filtering, and the importance of oak maturation.

The distinctive Australian wine style emphasizes brightness, freshness, and retention of the primary fruit flavor.

Viticulture continues to expand, and many high-quality white wines with a light dry taste are produced. Unquestionably Australian wines will continue to make an impact on the world's wine stage.

ARGENTINA

Argentina has the third highest per capita consumption of wine in the world (after Italy and France). Therefore little of its wine finds its way to foreign markets, even though the country produces a prodigious amount! Despite its internal marketplace, new vineyards are constantly being planted, and Argentina is now emerging as an important international player. Warm climate grapes such as Cabernet Sauvignon and Sauvignon Blanc do particularly well.

Wines were first produced there in 1556 from European vines brought there via Chile, but a large Italian immigration in the 1880s brought new life to wine production. The great majority of Argentina's wines are red table wines, but there are also many other wines made, including sparkling and dessert wines, vermouths, and brandies.

CHILE

Vinifera vines were introduced to Chile by the Spanish explorer Cortez, and there has been continuous wine production in Chile for at least four centuries. Spain, in an attempt to protect its export market, tried to ban new vineyards in Chile during the late seventeenth century. Despite this action, Chile developed a reputation for producing large quantities of inexpensive but drinkable wines by the early eighteenth century.

As a result of Chile's Spanish cultural roots and ancestry, red wine is the primary product. Chile's Merlot and Cabernet Sauvignon wines are extremely popular in the United States. However, they lack the complexity of the finer wines of Bordeaux and California's North Coast. Chilean white and red wines are excellent and tend to be inexpensive. The Chilean government restricts wine consumption and exports its surplus.

Est Est Est (It Is, It Is, It Is)
A story often told but worth repeating. In 1110 the German Bishop Johann Fuggar was on his way to Rome for the coronation of the Emperor Henry V. Loving wine as he did, he sent his servant a day's journey ahead, with orders to write on the door of any inn where the wine was good the simple word "est."

How many inns the servant classified for the Bishop history does not record. But in Montefiascone, a small hill town some sixty miles from Rome, the wine was so good that the enthusiastic servant wrote "Est! Est!! Est!!!"—

and stayed. The Bishop went no farther. The other members of his group continued on to Rome but he (and his wine-loving servant) stayed behind tasting and drinking. The Bishop drank himself into his grave. However, before he died the bishop willed that the town of Montefiascone should be his heir, on the condition that they pour a barrel of the local wine over his grave every year. And this was done, until a Cardinal ruled this to be a waste and that the wine should go to the local seminary for the benefit of the young clerics.

REVIEW QUESTIONS

1. Outline the major wine producing countries of the world.
2. Identify the unique features and the historical background to the wine regions of France.
3. Describe the special features of wines from South Africa, Australia, Argentina, and Chile.

10

Wine and the United States

Outline

In the extreme northern parts of America and on the Canadian coast, the wild grape was so prolific that the early Viking explorers, who preceded Columbus, named it "Vineland."

In precolonist America, the wild grape was widely distributed over the entire country, a type of fermentation was known, and Indians did use the grape as fresh fruit, in cooking, and in the preparation of dried foods.

The early Spanish settlements in the New World took root in the beginning of the sixteenth century. By the end of the first quarter-century, comparatively large towns had sprung up, complex fortifications were built, and trade was established with the Indians in the interior. Saint Augustine, in Florida, was an important port and bastion of the Spanish. Fort Marion, which exists today, rivaled in size and complexity those forts of the Old World. History records the "Dons" took wine with their meals, and brandy was stored in the cellars of Fort Marion. But who furnished the wine? Was it all imported? There are no records to supply these answers, yet Florida did and still does abound in the native grape.

When colonists came to America, many of them settled in New England. They were very pleased to find vines already growing wild, so they did not have to worry about importing their own. The first thing they did was prune the existing vines and plant more of the same. Within three years (the length of time it takes before a mature grape crop can produce wine), they had harvested the grapes and made the wine. When they tasted their first vintage, they were disappointed to discover that the wine did not taste the same as European wine.

They soon discovered that to make their own style of wine, they would have to bring cuttings of their own grapevines to the new land. Once again ships from Europe landed on the East Coast where the colonists took the Vitis Vinefera vines and planted them. The vines, however, did not grow. The cold was blamed, but actually the European vines lacked immunity to local plant diseases and pests.

PHYLLOXERA AND AMERICAN VINES

Phylloxera are beetlelike plant lice which brought devastation to the European vineyards. A native of the eastern United States, it long prevented the growing of grapes within its originating territory. No one understood what was happening—only that all the European vines planted withered and died.

There was, however, a vine native to the United States which gave bad wine but was immune from these attacks. The plant lice found their way to Europe, probably on an experimental vine, and the progeny swept through the vineyards doing terrible damage.

It was eventually realized that the roots of the despised American vine were immune, and after much argument, millions of American vines were grafted onto the surviving European stock. The new roots resisted the scourge, and although there have been endless arguments since as to whether the prephylloxera wines were better than those produced after the disaster, everyone acknowledges that but for the American vines there would have been no wine—and, but for the American "beetle," there would have been no phylloxera.

By the time of the American Revolution, there is evidence of attempts at more sophisticated vine crossbreeding and improvements to make production of wines more marketable. Both George Washington and Thomas Jefferson produced wine in reasonable quantities on their farms. Indeed, Thomas Jefferson, an ardent wine lover, spoke in support of wine as a national beverage of moderation. Jefferson said: "No nation is drunken where wine is cheap, and none sober, where the dearness of wine substitutes ardent spirits as the common beverage. It is, in truth, the only antidote to the bane of whiskey."

In the west (what is now California), Spanish settlers had imposed law and some order. As the area became more settled, roads and religious missions were built, and Spanish monks began to produce wine at these missions. The wine produced was from transplanted Spanish vines. The Spanish purple grape was for many years the standard American wine grape.

IN THE BEGINNING

Father Junipero Serra, a Spanish priest, built a total of seventeen missions; most had vineyards attached to them, and some wine production at these vineyards was good enough to ship to Mexico.

What has been referred to as a turning point in American wine making occurred in New York State in 1830. Viticulture became a thriving industry. Many improvements in crossbreeding were achieved, and different hybrids were grown. Wine production was further developed, and at the vineyards of the Finger Lakes District, new vines were developed. These new vines were based on the native Labrusca and new categories of such wine-making grapes as Concord, Catawba, Elvira, Duchess, and Delaware were introduced.

Most Americans are surprised to learn that Ohio also has had a long tradition of wine making and has in excess of thirty wineries, where a full range of white, red, fortified, and sparkling wines are produced.

It is in California that the full potential of American wine making has yet to be realized. It is difficult to imagine at this time, but until a relatively short time ago, Californian wine producers marketed their wines under European generic terms and descriptions. However, this is no longer the case. The confidence in Californian wines is immense. California now enjoys a reputation for the production of some of the best high-quality wines in the world, and Californians are now judged to be major quality players. California wine makers are very much members in the arena of the world's excellent wine production.

WINEGROWING REGIONS OF THE UNITED STATES

California

Viticulture began in California in 1769 when Junipero Serra, a Spanish friar, began to produce wine for the missions he started. At one time the French considered California wines to be inferior. However, California is blessed with a great vine growing climate and excellent soil.

There are five principal wine-producing districts in California. These are:

1. Napa Valley: well-balanced reds and fine whites.
2. Sonoma Valley: full-bodied red wine.
3. Livermore Valley: soft red wine, superior whites.
4. Central Valley: sweet dark wines.
5. Southern Coastal: dessert and table wines and sparkling wines.

The North and Central Coastal region produces the best wines of California. A high degree of mechanization allows for efficient, large-scale production of quality wines. The two best-known areas in this region are the Napa and Sonoma valleys. The wines of the Napa and Sonoma valleys resemble those of Bordeaux and Burgundy. It has been said that the wines now produced in California rival and, in some instances, surpass those of France.

Eastern United States

The white wines of New York and Ohio are generally felt to be better than the reds. Many of the white wines are preferred over similarly priced wines from California. In fact many people feel that California makes better red wine than white. Eastern white wines are bettered received than reds because the must is not fermented on the grape skins, where most of the foxy odor resides. Eastern generic wines are sometimes called "The Swiss Wines of America."

Oregon

The first known wineries in Oregon were established in the 1850s, followed by Ernst Reuter's in 1880, and Adolph Doerner's wineries in 1890. Prior to Prohibition, grape growing was sparse and haphazard, with little documentation on the type of variety of grapes grown and no information on the quality of wine produced. Following Prohibition, small wineries, often family owned, started to sprout, encouraging further planting and the start of Oregon's wine industry.

Oregon is noted for the quality of many of its wines, including Pinot Noir, Chardonnay, Pinot Gris, Muller-Thurgau, Riesling, and Gewuztraminer.

Washington

Washington is the second-largest producing state (after California) of Vitis vinifera grapes. Its vineyards lie just north of the 46-degree latitude, which is the same as that of the Bordeaux and Burgundy regions of France. The grapevine growth pattern is also similar to that of the French regions because of the long summer days (averaging approximately seventeen hours of daylight in June) and crisp, cool nights. This favorable combination in the annual growing cycle provides additional light for photosynthesis. The day and night temperature difference in Washington helps to produce balanced grapes—ideal sugar and fruit levels, good natural acidity, and distinctive Varietal character.

The first vineyards were planted in 1872 in the southern part of the Puget Sound area. Plantings throughout the area continued until the early 1900s. When Prohibition arrived, Washington ceased production of commercial wine, although some sacramental wine was still available.

Washington's wineries center on the Columbia, Yakima, and Snake rivers in the east and Spokane to the northeast.

Primary American Grapes

Vitus Labrusca is the vine most associated with the distinctly American so-called fox grape. Some people contend that the essential character of Labrusca is related to an odor associated with foxes. Although this association takes some imagination, a more plausible legend tells of foxes being attracted by the intense flavor often associated with grapes.

VITIS LABRUSCA: WHITE WINE

Catawba

Catawba is a vine found growing in the wild near the Catawba River in North Carolina. It was discovered to be disease resistant, as well as being productive and hardy. It was introduced commercially in the District of Columbia in 1823 and in Cincinnati in 1925. It is pale in color. The juice developed adequate sugar content and high acid in favorable locations and seasons. Unfortunately it ripens late. When well made, the wine has a clean taste and a rather flowery bouquet.

Delaware

Delaware County, Ohio, is the origin of the Delaware grape, a native American variety discovered during the early 1800s. An early hybrid, it is about the best of the native white wine grapes, considered by many the standard against which other native producers should be judged. The vine is a light, regular bearer of fruit with high sugar content and moderate acidity. The grape produces a Mosel-like wine which needs some aging to develop a fine, distinct bouquet and delicate flavor.

Niagara

The Niagara is a vine developed by researchers in Niagara County, New York, during the 1860s. It is a Vitis Labrusca hybrid with the parentage of Concord crossed with Cassady. In preferred locations Niagara is a vigorous and productive vine, its heavily scented flavor being the standard for rich, fruity, native American white wines.

Emerald Riesling

A variety of grapes developed at the University of California at Davis; not a true Riesling, it is developed from Johannisberg Riesling parentage. However, it is crisp and clean, and it produces a refreshing, inexpensive white wine with a touch of sweetness.

VITIS LABRUSCA: RED WINE

Concord

The most widely grown of all American grapes, it is responsible for at least 75 percent of the grape production of the eastern United States. This "foxy" grape produces a wine of moderate quality, lacking in delicacy and richness. It can be profitably grown in any grape-growing soil or climate for it bears well and long, blossoms late, and thus avoids late frosts, ripens fairly quickly, and withstands insects and fungi.

Isabella

First introduced in 1816, by the 1850s it became the mainstay of America's viticulture. The Isabella is thought to have originated from the garden of Isabella Gibbs in South Carolina. Successfully grown for Episcopal Communion Wine in Hammondsport, New York, during the 1840s, it became widely planted in the Finger Lakes district. Although it ripens early, it is a poor producer, and today is not grown extensively.

Norton

Introduced commercially in 1830, it is the best red-wine grape of the east. Though the wine is hardy, unfortunately the grapes need a long time to mature properly, so that production is spotty.

Barbera

Barbera is a California grape of northern Italian descent. It makes a robust deep, deep red, Italian-style wine with a fresh, quite tart, and fruity taste. When aged, it is very mellow but puckers the taste buds.

Carignane

Carignane is a red-wine grape with no distinctive flavor of its own. In addition to California, it is extensively grown in Spain and Southern France. It is primarily used to stretch the wine yield from scarcer grapes. It has a dry taste and is slightly fruity, and the addition of Merlot gives it an interesting flavor.

Zinfandel

A California red-wine grape that produces wine in at least three ways: as a fresh, young wine; as a wine to be aged for several years for complexity of flavor; and as a late-harvest wine for meal time. Young and fruity, it has a berrylike flavor and aroma. When aged, the bouquet is complex and suggests spices.

REVIEW QUESTIONS

1. Discuss and review the background and origins of wine growing in the United States.
2. Describe Phylloxera and its effects on wine making.
3. Outline the principal wine-growing regions of the United States.
4. Explain the principal varieties of grapes used in wine making in the United States.

11

Tasting, Evaluating, Appreciating, and Cooking with Wine

Outline

> The true amateur sips his wine; as he lingers over each separate mouthful, he obtains from each the total pleasure which he would have experienced had he emptied his glass at a single draught.
>
> —Brillat-Savarin

There is much mystique in the production and enjoyment of wine. Each individual who drinks a glass of wine tastes something different in it, and what pleases one may not please another.

How often do you recall foods that tasted terrible as a child that now are favored fare? The appreciation of various food groups broadens as we get older. This will never end. In a similar way, a comfort with different wine styles evolves.

Different wines made from the same grape variety will not share the identical taste but should be in the same taste family. For example, a person with a good taste memory can remember the taste of Pinot Noir grapes and will be able to identify the Pinot Noir grape taste in wines, even though each wine tastes slightly different. Because wine-making grapes are grown in many climates and soils in both hemispheres, natural differences emerge.

The wine growing areas of California, the Rhône Valley of France, much of Italy, and Australia with their unbridled heat provide wines of ripe, pungent, and lasting flavors. Wines of New York State, the Pacific Northwest, Burgundy, Bordeaux, and the Loire Valley are, as a rule, more restrained, although no less characteristic or unique.

There are wines that taste youthful, grapey, and fresh and those that project a more aged, earthy, or nutty taste. One can find a white wine that captures the same crisp, cutting acid of a Granny Smith apple or a wine like the Gewurztraminer, which is the epitome of spice and overripe grapefruit.

The real test of the wine is your final judgment after drinking it. Was its consumption a pleasant experience that left you wanting more? The subjective answer is always the right one. What you need to understand is that your answer, favorable or not, is no more than a personal reaction, one that may very well change with the passage of time as your tastes become more acute and adventurous.

So when knowledge improves, don't take offense if someone calls you an oenophile. It simply describes someone who enjoys wine.

TASTING AND EVALUATING WINE

> Wine was given by God, not that we might be drunken, but that we might be sober. It is the best medicine when it has moderation to direct it.
>
> —St. John Chrysostom

Sensory evaluation of wine is an appraisal of wine by the action of observing, smelling, and tasting. The terms "tasting wine" and to "taste wine" are used in a broad sense to describe the actions of sensory evaluation and to make an appraisal of the color and clarity, the aromas and flavors, and the basic taste experience of a mouth feel of the wine.

The prime components of character, the sugars, acids, aromas, flavors, and phenolic compounds, are present in the grape at harvest. These provide the foundation of character, which in turn evolves with time. The sensory characters that come from wine making complement the inherent qualities of the grape to create the total sensory experience.

The sensory experience is sensed through the eyes, nose, and mouth. The sensory signals are registered and interpreted in the brain, and we form an overall impression of the characters of the wine and whether we enjoy it.

The assessing of wine works best if the taster is well rested, and the taste sensors are free of strong substances such as coffee or tobacco. The taster should follow the same routine each time wine is seriously assessed. There are essentially three main steps to evaluating and tasting wine.

1. The wine is scrutinized in the glass by holding the wineglass by the stem, tilting it slightly, and observing it against light.

2. The aroma and bouquet of the wine is evaluated by nosing (smelling).

3. Tasting the wine to evaluate its qualities.

STEP ONE: APPEARANCE

1. Before starting, make sure that the wineglasses are clean and suitable and the lighting is adequate.

2. Use a normal tulip-shaped all-purpose wineglass. Pour a measure of wine in the glass so that the depth of hue can be seen at a glance. Do not fill the glass more than half full as it is easier to tilt the glass to observe the wine closely.

3. Pick up the glass by the stem, not the bowl. This makes it easier to examine the wine. It also reduces the possibility of sticky finger marks on the glass.

4. Daylight is best. Artificial lighting can affect both the hue and tone of the wine. Avoid blue fluorescent lighting, it makes red wine look unhealthy, dark, and blue tinged. Candlelight is often mentioned in the context of wine tasting, but a candle's use is usually confined to the glamorous ritual of decanting wine.

Color

All table wines fall into one of three basic categories: red, white, or blush.

Red Wines.   Red wine varies in color from deep purple through different shades of red, mahogany, or even amber, depending mainly on the state of maturity, the varietal, the vintage, and the district that the wine comes from. The aging process—the length of time the wine has been kept in a cask—directly affects color.

1. Purple
   Purple indicates youth or immaturity. Almost all red wines in casks will be this color. It begins to lose the strong purple tinge in the bottle; the time this takes depends on the initial depth of color of the wine.

2. Ruby
   Ruby is self-descriptive; it is the color of a young port, a full claret, or a burgundy wine.

3. Red
   In wine terms this is the color nearest to "claret," which indicates the period between youth and maturity and bottle age.

4. Red-Brown
   This color indicates maturity. A brown tinge to the wine can be the result from baked vines in a hot vintage, or artificially heated and baked wine (during fermentation), or from aeration and oxidation due to overexposure to air in a cask.

5. Mahogany
   Mahogany is a more mellow red-brown, indicating maturity.

6. Amber-Brown
   Amber-brown usually indicates a wine of considerable age, or one that is prematurely old and/or oxidized.

White Wines.   All white wines contain some degree of yellow pigment, but in some instances, the concentration is low. They vary, therefore, from almost colorless, through the palest yellow-green and deeper shades of yellow to gold and deep amber-brown.

Dry white wines usually start with little color, and, unlike red wines, they gain color with age. Sweet wines generally start at a fuller shade of yellow then turn to gold, and then take on a brown tinge with age. Sherry is basically a pale straw-yellow. Some of the deeper shades are the result of aging and blending. Practically all the dark wines gain their color from other wines which are added.

1. Pale Yellow Green
   A distinct green tinge is quite common in youthful white wines and is a particular characteristic of a Chablis or a young Moselle. It is rarely seen in the white wines of hot climates.

2. Straw-Yellow

This is a pleasant and lively color common to the majority of white wines.

3. Yellow-Gold

Yellow-gold is a normal color for any white wine, but most frequently seen in the sweeter varieties such as sauterne.

4. Gold

Gold generally indicates either a very sweet wine or one with bottle age (for example, a white Burgundy, usually pale straw when young, will develop a golden sheen after about six years in bottle).

5. Yellow-Brown or Old Gold

Many dessert wines and some fortified wines are yellow-brown or old gold in color. A brown or orange tinge in a white wine indicates bottle age over maturity or even oxidation. Many white Burgundies usually take on an unhealthy brown tinge after about twelve years in bottle, yet a fine sauterne may not develop it for thirty years or more.

6. Maderised

A maderised white wine will be dull with a pallid brown color. The word is used to describe the appearance of maturity and/or oxidation.

7. Brown

Brown suggests that a wine is probably well past drinking (unless it is a sherry of that name or the tawny brown of an old port).

Blush (Rosé) Wines.   Wine described as blush or rosé can vary enormously in color and depth. Each wine district has its own style, depending on the type of grape used and on the method used by the winegrower. The better blush wines are made from black grapes, but the juice has had a very brief contact with the grape skins. This produces wines that can range in color from pink to pale orange to barely red. Blush wines can range from dry to sweet and may be light- to medium-bodied. Generally they are served chilled, but not icy.

The term "Blush Wine" has all but replaced the more dated term "Rosé" in the United States.

A blush wine is normally drunk young. If it is allowed to age, it loses its freshness of color and distinctive taste. Blush wine should not look like a watered-down red wine. It should be clear and appealing.

1. Orange

Some grape varieties produce a distinct orange tint. Pure orange is not a desirable wine color. A pleasant orange/pink is normal and characteristic of many blushes from the Loire Valley in France.

2. Pink

The color pink is self-descriptive. However, any indication of a blue tinge suggests unhealthiness, probably from bad finishing or metallic contamination.

Depth or Tone

1. Although the basic fullness or paleness of any wine depends on its origin, the depth of color will give a good indication of its quality.

2. A very full, almost clear red or purple will almost certainly have more tannins and other natural component parts. This level of color is seen in a well-made wine of a fine vintage; its properties come from rich, fully ripe grapes with sun-baked skins.

3. The opposite is equally true. For example, a pale red wine results from a weak and watery year in which the grapes have failed to mature, and the skins are thin and lacking in pigment.

4. It is sometimes difficult to judge depth of color of two matching wines. One method is to fill two wineglasses to the same height, and place them side by side. Another method is to arrange a light behind the glasses and compare the depth of color of the shadow cast by each wine. In association with color, depth gives an indication of the maturity of the wine.

Clarity

Clarity is an essential element in the various stages of development of all wines from the time of fermentation, life in the cask, through to the time of bottling. White wines should be star bright. Only red wines normally have sediment in the bottle.

A dull cloudiness or haze in a wine bottle is a bad sign. In normal circumstances such wine should always be returned to the supplier.

Old vintage port usually has a heavy sediment and even when carefully decanted may still have sediment or what is known as beeswing in it. This is normal and can be ignored. (Beeswing settles on the glass of the bottle like crust; it is quite tasteless and harmless.) Tiny pieces of floating cork are harmless, and so are most forms of sediment that settle in the bottle easily. Bits of cork in the wine are attributed to the careless use of a corkscrew. Wine with cork floating on it is not "corked," a misunderstanding that often leads to complaints in restaurants.

The term "corked" is used to describe a wine that is not fit to drink because it has acquired the smell of a musty or otherwise faulty cork. A beautiful limpid color often indicates a great or fine wine, and a dull blended wine will often have a nondescript color.

STEP TWO: NOSE

A great deal of information can be gathered from "nosing" a wine. The first impression is generally the most telling.

It is difficult to analyze and describe most common smells, and it is even more difficult to describe a complex wine bouquet. It is also difficult to convey the complexity of these smells to another person, but wine tasters do learn to make analogies to other wines. "Nosing" is the term used to describe the process of assessing the aroma and pronouncing the bouquet of the wine.

The elements of "nosing" are best examined in the following order.

Cleanliness

Quickly assess whether the wine is free of any of the obvious flaws mentioned earlier, for example, mustiness, dirty smells from microbial infection, or mildew aromas from an infected cork. In other words, first judge whether the wine is sound. If so, proceed to the Varietal character.

Grape Variety

After overall cleanliness, the taster should search for the characteristics of the grape Varietal from which the wine was made. The classic or noble vines produce their own individual aromas. Grapes such as Cabernet-Sauvignon, Pinot Noir, Riesling, Chardonnay, and others, all have distinct varietal aromas. For instance, Cabernet Sauvignon has an array of typical aromas, including blackberries and fresh ground coffee. Pinot Noir is described as earthy, and its aromas resemble mushrooms, or freshly turned soil. Riesling's aromas are fruity, most often green apple. Chardonnay can include hazelnuts, pineapple, or figs among other aromas. Sauvignon Blanc's aromas are herbal or grassy.

Maturity

The age of a wine can be judged by an experienced taster. The comparison of good wines of different ages is the best way to acquire this skill. The physical components of young wine tend to be raw as they have had little time to settle down and blend. Youthful acidity has a mouth-watering effect. An excess of malic acid is frequently found in young white wines. Malic acid gives an applelike aroma to the wines made from insufficiently ripened grapes.

As wine mellows with age, its bouquet becomes softer. It is almost impossible to describe what is called "bottle age." On most white wines, this shows up as a "honeyed" quality; red wines become richer and deeper with bottle age. A wine with too much bottle age will be flat and dull, and have a toffeelike smell or what is known as a bottle stink.

Fruit

Fruit is a desirable quality; however, some wines can be described as fruity without having any trace of grape. A distinctly grapey bouquet is generally only found in wines made from certain unmistakable grape varieties.

Bouquet

A bouquet can be described as light or deep, superficial, full or rounded, depending on the development of the wine. Do not to be misled by the "full" bouquet of a ripe but poor quality wine, or by the undeveloped bouquet of a very fine but immature wine.

STEP THREE: TASTE

Before tasting, the wine should be swirled in the glass, especially a red wine, to give it some oxidation and assist in releasing flavor and bouquet. The taste of the wine should confirm the conclusions drawn from the other elements of evaluation—appearance and bouquet.

There are several points of mouth feel or contact that reveal different taste characteristics. One tiny sip is usually inadequate, swirl it round the mouth, spit it out and repeat the process if necessary.

The mouth processes taste in the following order:

1. Tip of tongue—sweet.
2. Under the front side of the mouth—salt.
3. Sides of the mouth (acids)—sour.
4. Back of the mouth (tannins)—bitter or astringent.

Dryness or Sweetness

Dryness or sweetness is a basic element, which is particularly important in white wines. Thinness or excessive acidity in wines often mislead the taste buds.

Body

The "weight" of wine in the mouth is basically due to alcohol content.

Flavor

Flavor is most important. Even if it is impossible to describe, at least decide whether it was agreeable to your taste.

Acidity

After dryness and flavor, acid is the most important and noticeable element. It gives a wine purpose and finishing. Extremes of acidity are undesirable. Excess sugar, natural or otherwise, tends to mask the true degree of acidity.

Tannin Content

Although it is harsh and dry in the mouth, it is a vital part of any young red wine. Tannin acts as a general preservative, and it is essential for the long life of certain wines. Tannin is a natural compound that comes from the skins, stems, and pips of the grapes and also from the wood that wine is aged in.

Quality

Quality can be judged by the length of time the flavor lingers in the mouth, by its richness and subtlety, and by its aftertaste, and not by its price.

SUMMARY OF WINE EVALUATION

Grading for Clarity

1. Good: Bright, sparkling, very clear.
2. Bad: Dusty, filmy, cloudy.

Grading for Color

1. Good: Bright-colored, paper-white, straw-colored, greenish white, golden yellow, amber, tawny, cherry, claret, and ruby red.
2. Bad: Faded, dull, too deeply colored, brownish yellow, dirty yellow, too tawny, deep purplish red, purplish, gray.

Grading for Clarity and Color

1. Good: Elegant, of good appearance.
2. Bad: Cloudy or grainy appearance.

Grading for Sweetness

Dry: (Without sugar), semidry (with little sugar), medium (the sweetness is perceptible), semisweet (the sweetness is more perceptible), sweet.

Grading for Acidity

1. Good: Palatable, fresh, tart, neutral.
2. Bad: Weak, flat, lifeless (progressive lack of acidity), green, sour, harsh (progressive excess of acidity).

Grading for Alcoholic Content

1. Good: (Decreasing alcohol), light, warm, rich.
2. Bad: Fiery (increasing quantity of alcohol), cold, poor, weak.

Grading for Texture

1. Good: Smooth, velvety.
2. Bad: Harsh, rough.

Grading for Taste

1. Good: Perfumed, tasty, palatable, reminiscent of raspberries, peaches, hazelnuts, violets, Blushes, cherries, fruity taste, and bouquet of grapes. Madeira wine has a bright, marked, bitter, prickly taste.
2. Bad: Weak, insipid, lifeless, lacking in personality, stale, earthy, or having other disagreeable smells or tastes.

Grading of Body, Refinement, and General Quality

1. Good: Complete, full-bodied, strong, powerful, rounded, well balanced, fine, delicate, elegant, palatable.
2. Bad: Heavy, coarse, bodiless, too light, weak, empty, thin, lacking in balance, sickly.

Although it is not necessary to describe or record your impressions of the wine to fully enjoy its sensory experience, a few words about its flavor, balance, mouth feel, structure, and interest can readily convey your impressions of the wine. Simply expressing an appreciation of the quality and interest of the wine may be all that is necessary.

FUNDAMENTALS OF MATCHING FOOD WITH WINE

It is important to know the traditional rules (sprinkled with elements of common sense) regarding the matching of foods with wines, even if those rules are ignored because of a personal taste.

1. For the full value of the wines to be appreciated when several wines are served during a meal, they must be ordered so that the palate is not prejudiced by the first wines drunk:
   - Dry before sweet.
   - White before red, unless the serving order violates the dry-before-sweet rule.
   - Young before old.
   - Light before full bodied.

- Modest before great.
- Table wines before fortified wines.

2. If champagne or another sparkling wine is used as a table wine, its service should be continued throughout the meal.

3. Dishes that contain vinegar, or any other foods that contain it, do not go well with wine, for example, pickles, mustard, ketchup, and salad dressings.

4. Madeira and sherries are preferred with soup, unless the soup contains wine, in which case no wine is served.

5. Once a person has developed a palate for fine wines, a few very good wines are more enjoyable than a lot of inexpensive poor wines.

6. Delicate wines should be served with delicate dishes.

7. Robust foods need robust wines to "stand up" to them.

8. Sweet wines should be served with sweet fruits and no wine with citrus fruits.

9. Very sweet wines are usually used for dessert courses.

Lamb dishes blend well with most red wines. The richer red wines such as Cabernet Sauvignon and Zinfandel go well with braised beef dishes and "Entrecote Sautes." Game such as venison and boar are suited to full-bodied, robust reds. Poultry works well with both red and white wines. Fish requires a young dry white Chablis or Graves. Dry white wine can also be a pleasant addition to legumes.

More can be learned about wine and food pairing via the "hit-and-miss" process than from any book. In the end you will have experienced and gained respect for the world's most "diverse" and civilized beverage.

GUIDE TO WINE CATEGORIES AND FOOD PAIRING

The author is indebted to Dellie Rex for her insights and notes on the food and wine pairing categories.

Sparkling Wines

The most versatile of all wines, and the most festive, "sparklers" can function as aperitifs and as accompaniment to a wide range of foods from brunch through dinner, from soup through dessert.

- Champagne
- Asti Spumante
- Cava from Spain
- Californian and Oregonian sparkling wines made in the champagne method

White Wines—Light and Crisp

Fresh, lively wines can serve as aperitifs, or as accompaniment to certain simple luncheon dishes and to lighter dinner fare. These wines show good acidity, and are light in body. Most are straightforward and lack complexity. They are excellent with many seafood dishes, light poultry creations, or pasta with white or oil-based sauces.

- Bordeaux, excluding Graves
- Most Italian wines
- Muscadet from the Loire Valley
- Sauvignon Blanc from California and Chile
- Pinot Blanc and Riesling from Alsace and the United States
- German Kabinett
- Burgundies from a lesser appellations like Macon, also A.C. Chablis
- Pinot Gris from Oregon
- Spanish and Portuguese wines

White Wines—Full and Fruity

These are more substantial and full-flavored wines, with greater elegance and style, in which the balance is more toward fruit than acid, and oak aging is often evident. These wines are heavier in body and more complex than Category 2 wines. These are formal dinner wines to serve with roasted poultry, fancy seafood dishes, and some veal preparations.

- Burgundy, especially Meursault and Montrachet
- Vouvray and Pouilly-Fume from the Loire Valley
- German Spatlese and Auslese
- American Chardonnays, as well as those from Australia
- Graves whites from Bordeaux
- Alsace Gewurztraminer

Red Wines—Light and Fresh

Described as young and friendly with vivacious fruitiness, these wines are easy to drink, light wines with minimal tannins. They are the perfect complement for luncheons of salads and sandwiches, or light, informal suppers, such as quiche or pizza. They are light enough to match to some seafood preparations as well as duck and some game birds. With ham and other salty meats, they are ideal. This is especially true of rosés, which are included in this category.

- Tavel, Rosé d'Anjou and all other rosés, and blush wines
- Beaujolais
- Bardolino and Valpolicella
- Gamay-based California wines
- Loire Valley reds
- Cabernet Franc from California

Red Wines—Medium Body and Flavor

The diverse wines in this broad category fall midway between the light, easy quaffers and the big, intense reds. The medium reds, fairly complex, somewhat aggressive but often graceful, and usually warmly flavorful, work well with stews and casseroles, chops, roast veal, game birds, and many pasta dishes.

- Chianti, Barbera, and Gattinara
- California and Washington Merlot
- Most California Zinfandel
- Many Cotes du Rhône, as well as French country wines from the South
- Lesser appellation Bordeaux, such as Fronsac and Cote du Bourg
- Lesser appellation Burgundies, especially from Chalonnais
- Spanish reds from Rioja and Penedes, Portuguese Dao wines

Red Wines—Full and Complex

Characterized by complexity of aromas, intensity of flavors and firmness of structure, these wines often show power coupled with finesse. These are the wines to serve alongside the most elegant meat dishes of beef, lamb, or game, or show them off accompanied simply by full-flavored, ripe cheeses.

- Bordeaux from the Medoc, Graves and St. Emilion and Pomerol
- Burgundy from the Cote d'Or
- Piedmont's Nebbiolo-based reds, such as Barolo and Barberesco
- Cote Roti from Cotes du Rhône
- Cabernet Sauvignon from California, Washington State, and Australia
- Pinot Noir from Oregon and parts of California
- Some California Zinfandels

Dessert Wines and After-Dinner Liqueurs

Offered by the glass, these are the ideal way to cap off a fine meal. Luscious late-harvest wines, such as Germany's Trockenbeerenauslese or Bordeaux's Sauternes; rich old ports, especially a well-aged vintage from, say, 1963; or soothing, mellow liqueurs are the comforting way to prolong a pleasant evening.

Remember, these categories and the suggested food matches are just that: suggestions! The only firm "rule" is that if you are planning a multi-course meal, with a different wine to be served at each course, serve the wine categories in the same order in which they are presented here. Other than that, be creative! The ultimate rule in matching food and wine is to trust yourself. The first instinct you have about a wine to serve with a certain dish is usually the best one.

FOODS RARELY SERVED WITH WINE

Chocolate

Chocolate coats the tongue; its powerful aroma drowns the subtleties of most wines, and it can impart a metallic flavor to tannic wines. However, at times a strong, sweet wine, and some reds, are delicious with chocolate.

Eggs

Eggs also can coat the tongue and seal the taste buds.

Smoked Food

All smoked foods have a strong flavor, but they can work well with some aromatic or oak-aged wines.

COOKING WITH WINE

> Wine is the intellectual part of the meal, meats are merely the material part.
> —Alexander Dumas

> Good wine cries out for good food, and sauces have an age-old affinity with the vintner's art.
> —G. Roupnel

Since ancient times, wine has been seen as a food. It is one of the three great gifts from yeast; wine, cheese, and bread. Cooking with wine is therefore as old as wine itself.

There is much to be said about this renewed interest in the kitchen and the companionship of wine. Logic will tell you that pungent seasoning or a healthy dose of lemon juice will be strong contenders for the wine to deal with and that your choice should be a wine of equally "hearty" nature.

Extremely delicate seafood, freshwater fish, and mildly seasoned meats benefit from a light dry to semidry white wine. Wine should never overpower the flavor of the dish. It should be subtle and mysterious with a flavor that simply makes one want more of whatever dish it complements.

Fortified wines such as Madeira, port, and sherry may have very strong flavors so caution is the byword when adding them to food.

WINE AS AN ESSENTIAL BASIC

Wine is meant to accompany food. Whether working acts of magic in the cooking process or serving as an accompanying beverage, it can bring out the flavor of foods and aid in digestion. In cooking, wine may be classified as an essential basic. Used correctly and wisely, it can raise the normal dish to an exceptional level. Wine cuts down the desire for salt and enhances the appetite.

Additionally wine contains glycerine which helps to bind sauces so less fat can be used. As a cooking liquid, wine adds flavor and necessary moisture. It is ideal as part of the poaching process in court bouillions for fish, excellent in braising chicken and meats, and wonderful for poaching fruits and making syrups for cakes. Braising with wine has the additional benefit of tenderizing tough cuts of meat while enhancing the braising sauce.

WINE AND CLASSICAL CUISINE

Cooking with wine is deeply embedded in the rich traditions of classical cuisine. The tradition of including wine as part of the cooking medium is mainly associated with French cuisine, which of course most self-respecting Italian chefs will immediately point out is really Italian cuisine, thanks mainly to Catherine de Medici.

Master Chef Antoine Careme, in his early writings on food, includes wine as part of his cooking preparations. Later, the "Emperor," Escoffier, had truly systemized the use of wine in cooking, laying down simple yet logical rules for its use which still hold true to this day. However, not all ingredients have an affinity with wine. High-acid liquids such as vinegar and citrus juice can give wine an "off" flavor. Other enemies of wine include artichokes, asparagus, chocolate, pineapples, and tomatoes. Although the alcohol in wine cooks off quickly, the acid does not.

The great Escoffier was particularly supportive of the use of wine in marinades. He believed passionately that when wine was included, they contributed flavor and tenderness, particularly with meat and poultry. As well as adding flavor of its own, wine also assists food in absorbing the flavors of herbs, vegetables, and spices. According to Escoffier, marinades have two primary purposes: first to act as a flavor giver and tenderizer for tough cuts of meat, poultry, and game; and second to act as a preservative, which was a necessity in the days prior to modern refrigeration. Wine is also used to macerate fruit for desserts.

The Saucier

The true majesty of cooking with wine lies in the sophisticated skills of sauce making. Simple logic is associated with the principle of saute, that is, the use of first-quality meat, fish, poultry, and vegetables cooked quickly and separate from the sauce, then the recovery of the solidified food on the bottom of the pan to the sauce through the process of deglazing and reduction with wine. This simple step contributes enormously to the quality and flavor of the resulting sauce. A good sauce cannot be made from a poor wine.

When wine is heated, the alcohol evaporates, so a poor wine only leaves acidity behind, whereas a more complex wine leaves those elements that add flavor. It makes little or no sense to use a "great" wine for cooking. The properties that make wine exceptional will be lost once it is heated. How suitable the wine is depends on how it is going to be used. If it is to be reduced to almost nothing in the pan with shallots, an inexpensive but good wine can be used. If the recipe calls for reduction by half, a better quality wine would then be preferable.

REVIEW QUESTIONS

1. Describe the steps in tasting and evaluating wines.
2. Outline the critical elements in wine tasting, particularly as it relates to appearance and color, depth or tone, clarity, nose, grape variety, maturity, and bouquet.
3. Identify the points of mouth feel relative to wine tasting.
4. Explain the fundamentals of matching food with wines.
5. Outline the basics of food pairing.
6. Outline the benefits of and use of wine in cooking.

12

Wine Styles: Highly Rated Wines of the World and Quality Controls

Outline

131

STYLES: WINES OF THE WORLD

White Wines—Dry, Light Bodied

Beaujolais Blanc
Cotes du Rhone Blanc
Frascati
Galestro
Gruner Veltliner
Macon-Village
Orvieto

Pino Bianco
Riesling (Kabinett)
Rioja Blanco
Soave
Trebbiano
Vinho Verde

Dry, Medium Bodied

Fiano di Avellino
Fume Blanc
Gavi
Graves (White)
Pouilly-Fuisse
Pouilly-Fume

Riesling (Alsace)
Sancerre
Sauvignon Blanc
Sylvaner (Alsace)
Vouvray Sec
Pinot Blanc

Off Dry—A Touch of Sweetness

California Chablis
Chenin Blanc
French Colombard
Gewurztraminer
Johannesberg Riesling

Pinot Noir Blanc
Sylvaner
Vouvray Demi-sec
White Zinfandel

Full Bodied, Complex

French Chablis
Chardonnay
Chassagne-Montrachet
Puligny-Montrachet

Hermitage Blanc
Meursault
Gewurztraminer (Alsace)

Sweet

Asti Spumante
Barsac
Eiswein
Gewurztraminer (Late Harvest)
Muscat Beaume-de-Venise
Muscat Canelli
Riesling (Late Harvest)

Auslese
Beerenauslese
Spatlese
Trockbeerenauslese
Sauternes
Tokay Aszu

Blush (Rosé) Wines, Dry

Cabernet d'Anjou
Castel del Monte
Chiaretto del Garda
Côtes-de-Provence Rosé

Sancerre Rosé
Tavel
Vin Gris

Off Dry or Lightly Sweet

Grenach Rosé
Rosé d'Anjou

Pinot Noir
Vin Rosé

Red Wines—Light, Fruity

Nouveau-style reds
Beaujolais
Bergerac
Blauburgunder
Bordeaux Superieur
Brouilly
Cabernet del Fruili
Chinon
Corbieres

Côtes de Baune-Villages
Côtes du Ventoux
Gamay
Italian Merlot
Napa Gamay
Saint-Amour
Sancerre Rouge
Valpolicella

Rich, Classic, Full-Bodied

Barbaresco
Beaune
Bordeaux (Chateaux)
Cabernet Sauvignon
Chambolle-Musigny
Echezaeux
Fixin
Fosne-Romanee

Gevrey-Chambertin
Nuit-Saint-Georges
Pernand-Vergelesses
Pommard
Syrah
Tignalello
Volnay

Robust, Very Full Bodied

Barblo
Bruhello di Montalcino
Chambertin
Chateauneuf-du-Pape
Clos Vougeot
Cornas
Côte Rotie
Gigondas
Hermitage

La Romanee Conti
La Tache
Merlot
Musigny
Petit Sirah
Richebourg
Romanee-Conti
Shiraz

Fortified Wines/Dessert Reds

Commanderia   Port
Madeira   Oloroso Sherry
Marsala   Late-Harvest Zinfandel

THE RAREST OF WINES

Michael Broadbent, a leading wine expert, outlines and describes the following rare wines, using all the wonderful and colorful descriptive language of the wine connoisseur. Five stars is his best rating, representing an outstanding wine.

Lafite-Rothschild (Bordeaux)

1865.   Four stars. Still remarkably youthful, with deep vinosity and fruit . . . amazingly good on the palate.

1874.   Four stars. Rich and interesting, medium body, firm, gentle flavor. Of all old wines this seems to benefit most from long exposure to air.

1899.   Five stars. Delicate, slightly smoky; incredibly beautiful bouquet and flavor. Dryish, clean as a whistle, exquisite.

1929.   Five stars. The best vintage since 1900, soft, elegant wines of great finesse, and delicacy, old but exquisite.

1953.   Five stars. The epitome of elegance, an open, relaxed, fully developed bouquet, sweet cedar, fragrant, delicate yet generous.

1961.   Five stars. Undoubtedly the greatest postwar vintage and one of the four best of the century, subdued, restrained but rich and elegant nose, a very fry, even austere wine, full bodied, concentrated.

Mouton-Rothschild (Pauillac)

1945.   One of the greatest of all vintages, for me certainly one of the top three of this century. Five stars, fabulous and, I like to think, totally unmistakable bouquet—highly concentrated, intense black currant Cabernet-Sauvignon aroma, touch of cinnamon flavor to match. Ripe, rich.

1952.   Three stars. Deep, fine, flavor with silk/leathery texture.

1955.   Four stars. A beautiful, calm, dignified Pauillac bouquet, delicate flavor, nice balance, very attractive.

1959.   Five stars. Masculine and magnificent, wonderfully concentrated Cabernet-Sauvignon aroma, cedar and black-currants; fairly dry, full bodied, massive yet soft, velvety, packed with flavor.

1961. Five stars. A stunning wine, amazing richness and ripeness of grape, concentrated Cabernet-Sauvignon bouquet, flavor; magnificent, balanced.

1966. Five stars. Plummy color, magnificently pointed Cabernet-Sauvignon aroma; dry stylish, it should be excellent.

Latour (Pauillac)

1945. Five stars. Magnificently huge, opaque in appearance, a bouquet like gnarled old cedar; rich yet dry, massive, intense.

1949. Four stars. Deep, sweet—almost honeyed, cedary bouquet; on the palate full and rich, soft yet firm and perfectly balanced. Great depth, length of flavor and marvelous aftertaste.

1953. Five stars. Perhaps the most attractive of all the postwar vintages and, for me, a personification of claret at its most charming and elegant best.

1961. Five stars. An enormous wine, deep alcoholic, port-like nose; still peppery; medium dry, very full bodied, packed, beefy but beautiful balance.

1962. Four stars. A rich, soft, cedary, classic Cabernet nose; fullish, excellent flavor and balance. A fine classic wine.

1966. Five stars. Magnificent color; bouquet and flavor packed and closed in, but an enormous, rich wine. Dry, yet velvet-lined.

Pichon-Baron (Pauillac)

1955. Three stars. A good but under-appreciated vintage, has quietly blossomed in recent years.

1961. Five stars. Undoubtedly the greatest postwar vintage and one of the four best of the century.

Margaux (Margaux)

1945. Five stars. Intensely rich and fragrant bouquet, classic cedar-pencil/cigar-box character, velvet textured and magnificent.

1947. Four stars. Still magnificently deep, a big ripe hot-vintage color; bouquet to match, very mature but no signs of decay, velvety, towering yet delicate, rich yet dry.

1952. Four stars. A fairly massive wine, velvety with, seemingly, a whole cask of bouquet and flavor waiting to burst out.

1953. Five stars. Margaux at its best, magnificent bouquet; rich, waxy, elegant, soft and silky, excellent balance, long fragrant aftertaste.

1959. Four stars. rich, cedary scented bouquet, fairly full bodied, rich, velvety, certainly no lack of acidity.

1961. Five stars. Intense fragrance, the bouquet is extraordinary—rich, singed creosote, intense, lovely; rich, silky, elegant, long flavor, very dry finish.

1962.   Four stars. Somewhat delicate wine, fragrant, smoky, very fine bouquet and flavor. Richness and delicacy.

1966.   Five stars. Rich, fruity, elegant bouquet and flavor, some plumpness but slim, elegant yet with fine structure.

Leoville-Las-Cases (St. Julien)

1962.   Four stars. Almost opaque color; fine, iron-tinged, sweet bouquet and flavor. Most attractive.

Gruad-Larose (St. Julien)

1959.   Four stars. Fine, deep, mature color, heavy bead (legs); rich, meaty flavor.

Cos d'Etournel (St. Estephe)

1959.   Four stars. Beautifully made, well-balanced. A full, firm, beefy wine.

1961.   Four stars. Magnificent depth of color, bouquet, and flavor. Very tannic.

1966.   Four stars. Deep, tannic.

Haut Brion (Graves)

1934.   Three stars. Undoubtedly the best vintage of the 1930's.

1945.   Five stars. Absolute perfection, fine, rich, fragrant and complex bouquet; slight sweetness of wine made from fully ripe grapes, magnificent, chewy, chunky yet smooth. Magnificent aftertaste.

1949.   Four stars. Elegant and rich, deeper than Latour; sweet, rich, velvety nose; very rich, complex earthy wine, sound, characterful.

1953.   Five stars. Lovely rich Graves-earthy aroma and flavor; great depth, richness, vinosity.

1955.   Four stars. Soft gentle bouquet; Graves earthy, slightly charred flavor with typical Haut Brion elegance.

1959.   Five stars. Deep, magnificent tobacco-like bouquet; excellent earthy heavyweight with a dry tannic finish.

1961.   Five stars. Characteristics hot, earthy/pebbly bouquet, ripe, lovely texture understated.

Cheval Blanc (St. Emilion)

1947.   Five stars. A complacent, abundantly confident bouquet, calm, rich distinguished, slightly sweet, plump, almost fat, ripe, incredibly rich, a magnificent wine, almost port-like.

1959. Four stars. Sweet and fruity bouquet, ripe, full, rich, soft. Dry finish. Fully developed.

1961. Four stars. Mulberry aroma, rich port-like (reminiscent of the '47); distinct sweetness of fully ripe grapes, soft, open, gentle but firm finish.

1966. Four stars. Extremely vintage. Stylish, elegant, well-balanced. Lean rather than plump, though with good firm flesh, Bordeaux at its most elegant.

Petrus (Pomerol)

1961. Five stars. Extremely deep colored, magnificent bouquet, amazing fruit; a lovely, rich, velvety wine.

Romanee-Conti (Côtes du Nuits, Burgundy)

1952. Five stars. Very rich, complex, excellent pinot bouquet; rich, fine flavor and balance. Real Romance quality. Holding well.

1959. Five stars. Nose slightly aloof and withdrawn, excellent but still hard; a huge, dry tannic and alcoholic wine, almost Latour massiveness.

1966. Five stars. Very rich bouquet; ripe and rich on the palate, firm, even a little austere, with a dry finish. Clearly years of development ahead.

La Tache (Côtes du Nuits)

1970. Three stars. Light aroma and sugary aroma; slightly sweet, soft yet come acidity. But flavor as always.

Grands Echezeaux Lebegue-Bichet (Côtes du Nuits)

1959. Five stars. A great vintage and, in my opinion, one of the last classic heavyweights made in Burgundy.

Chateau d'Yquem (Sauternes, Bordeaux)

1784. According to the Wine Spectator, a bottle of 1784 Yquem was believed to have been ordered by Thomas Jefferson. It sold (1989) for $56,000—highest price ever paid for a white wine.

1811. Bottle of excellent condition wine sold for $30,500 at Christie's per the Wine Spectator. The bottle was from the "comet vintage," named for the Napoleon comet. Considered to be the finest d'Yquem of the 19th century. Recorked at the chateau in 1987; label and capsule in excellent condition.

1967.   Five stars. Pure amber gold, honeyed, overripe, botrytis grape
smell; holding its sugar, fairly full-bodied, rich pronounced
flavor.

CONTROLS AND QUALITY GUARANTEES

Some wines have a potential market that far exceeds the production capacities of the region producing the wine. To guarantee that the wine in the bottle
is as it is represented, the governments of several countries, notably France,
Germany, and Italy, authenticate the origin of the wine.

French Controls

To some extent, they also guarantee that the wine meets certain standards of
excellence. For example, in France, where regulations are strict and well en-
forced, there are three Appellations d'Origine, which, in addition to guaran-
teeing origin, are tantamount to broad ratings. Appellation Controlée is the
highest grade, to which almost all great French wines belong. The others are
Vins Delimites de Qualités Supérieure (V.D.Q.S.) and Appellation Simple
wines which are seldom exported.

On a wine label, the name of the wine may be followed by the words Appellation Controlée, or by a phrase with these words bracketing a geographic
name, for example, Appellation Pauillac Controlée. The smaller the region
named in the middle, the better the control, and often the wine.

Italian Controls

The Italian wine law is similar. When the words Denominazione di Origine
Controllata appear on a wine label, the wine is certified as to place of origin,
grapes used, planting of vines, and so on. There is also a category above this
one, Denominazione di Origine Controllata Garantia, which is a quality standard given to selected wines that already merit Denominazione di Origine
Controllata.

German Controls

German wine law is relatively recent. The 1971 bottles, which arrived in the
United States in 1972, were the first to use the new labeling system. There are
three categories of "quality" German wines of varying quality.

Deutcher Tafelwein ("German table wine") must be produced from approved grape varieties in one of five major table wine regions: Moselle, Rhein,
Main, Neckar, or Oberheim. No vineyard name appears on these bottles.

Deutscher Qualitatswein Bestimmter Anbaugebiete (QBA; "German
quality wine of designated regions"), which must be made of approved grape

varieties, have at least 7 percent alcohol, and come exclusively from one of the eleven quality German wine regions. Every bottle carries a control number showing that it has been tasted and analyzed to ensure that it is worthy of the label. It can be labeled by the region, subregion, or vineyard in connection with the name of a village. To use its name on a label, a vineyard must be at least 2.5 acres in size; this eliminates 23,000 to 24,000 vineyards and simplifies the understanding of German wine labels.

Deutscher Qualitatswein mit Pradikat (QMP; "German quality wine with special attributes") is the highest category of German wine. It is made from approved grape varieties and contains at least 9 to 10 percent alcohol without sugar added. Within the category, several subcategories—the attributes (Pradikäts)—are indicated on the wine labels.

American Wines: Federal Laws and Controls

Federal laws differentiate between the grape varieties used in the wines, but otherwise they are fairly standard.

If a wine is labeled as a Vitis Vinifera Varietal (e.g., Chardonnay, Pinot Noir, Cabernet Sauvignon, Sauvignon Blanc, Pinot Blanc, Semillion, Chenin Blanc, Gewurztraminer), then 75 percent of the grapes used to make that wine must be the grape stated on the label.

If a specific geographic area is specified on the label, for example, Napa Valley, then 75 percent of the grape juice used to make the wine must be from the area.

If a specific viticultural area (e.g., American Vintners Association area) is specified on the label, such as Caymus, Oakville, Alexander Valley, or Carneros, then 85 percent of the grape juice used to make the wine must be from that area.

If a specific viticultural area and vintage year are stated on the label, for example, Diamond Creek Vineyards 1997, then 95 percent of the grape juice used to make the wine must come from the specified area and the specified year.

If a label states "Estate Bottled," then 100 percent of the grapes used to make that wine must have been grown on the winery's premises.

If a label states "Produced and Bottled by ?," then 75 percent of the grapes used for that wine must have been crushed and fermented at the winery, but not necessarily grown there.

READING A WINE LABEL

The brand name tells you the name of the produce.

The vintage year cited on the label tells you that 95 percent or more of the wine is produced from grapes grown during that year. An appellation of origin other than the country will also be shown if the vintage date appears on the label.

Varietal designations tell you the names of the dominant grapes used to produce the wine.

Alcohol content tells you the percentage of alcohol by volume.

Appellation of origin tells you where the dominant grapes used in the wine are grown.

Viticultural areas are grape-growing regions defined by their soil, climate, and geographic features. Should such an appellation appear on a label, it tells you that 85 percent or more of the wine is produced from grapes in that area.

If the label reads, "Estate Bottled," it tells you that 100 percent of the wine is from grapes grown on the land owned or controlled by the winery in a given viticultural area. The entire operation, from crushing the grapes to bottling the wine, takes place there.

REVIEW QUESTIONS

1. Review and describe the various styles and properties of wines of the world.

2. Indicate the style of language used to describe the quality points of rare wines.

3. Discuss and describe the controls and quality guarantees associated with French, Italian, and German wines.

4. Distinguish the elements that make up the descriptions on American wine bottle labels.

5. Indicate the fundamental information generally described on a wine label.

13

The Service of Wine and the Wine List

Outline

In selecting wine, two elements must be considered, first, what will the guest demand, and second, can a profit be made on it. Most guests don't want to be educated on wine, they want to drink what they like.

Most professionals agree that if a wine list is well compiled, twenty-four to thirty wines should satisfy even the most discerning guests in their selection of wine with food. A rule-of-thumb relative to the number of wines on a list is balance and variety. If the restaurant is small, this figure may seem high, but consider that wines are divided among aperitifs, champagnes, sparkling wines, white, red, blush, and dessert wines from different regions or countries.

The size of the wine list is in part determined by the size of the storeroom. Wine requires specific storage conditions and storing it improperly jeopardizes the wine investment. Capital investment also figures prominently in determining the size of the wine list. The basic reason for a short list could be a matter of dollars and cents, or limited storage space. A distinct advantage of a small list is that it is flexible enough to go with changing menus.

Some establishments believe that when guests are presented with a list containing 200 or more wines, they tend to order with more frequency. It is felt that this communicates the idea that the restaurant specializes in wine, the service team members are knowledgeable, and the wines will be of excellent quality. Perhaps when guests view this type of list, they will purchase an even better quality (usually higher priced) wine.

WINE SERVICE

Wine orders may be taken and served by an experienced member of the service team, or by a wine steward or sommelier. Servers should know all of the establishment's wines and which wines might be suitable with certain foods in order to make sensible suggestions.

Both sommelier and servers should be able to present a good reason for a wine suggestion. For instance, if lamb and beef make up the entree orders, a red Bordeaux or Burgundy will have the requisite flavor qualities. If the selection is seafood, a Chablis, Chenin Blanc, or German Reisling will bring out the best flavor qualities of the seafood. However, individual tastes vary, and servers should be prepared to make secondary suggestions.

It is also necessary to enhance wine selection with the correct service procedures. Some wines should be served at specific temperatures. However, some guests often desire wine at different temperatures, and servers may ask, when the wine is ordered, if a specific temperature is desired.

Ultimately the temperature at which a wine is served is a matter of individual taste. Different people appreciate different aspects of a wine's quality at different temperatures. However, the majority of people, amateurs and professionals alike, agree on some general guidelines. The way the wine reacts to various temperatures determines the basic rules.

Ideally wine is chilled (or warmed) slowly in a room or area of the proper temperature. It can also be chilled satisfactorily in a refrigerator. A freezer compartment may cause it to "break," or precipitate tartaric acid crystals, by chilling it too quickly. Ten minutes in a bucket filled with crushed ice and ice-cold water will chill a bottle, twenty minutes will make it quite cold, and forty-five minutes will make it ice cold. Salt may be added to the ice water to chill the bottle even faster.

If there is any doubt about the quality of the wine, the server or sommelier may taste the wine first. This should be only a tiny sip. A small amount of the wine is then poured into the host's glass to judge whether it is a suitable wine to serve with the food.

Aroma and flavor are the largest part of the pleasures to be had from wine. Therefore there must be space in the glass to hold the aromas, as well as the wine itself. The glass should never be filled more than two-thirds full.

The host should nod or indicate approval. When this occurs, all of the other guests are served before the host.

STEPS IN THE OPENING AND POURING OF WINE

White Wine

When the wine has been selected by the guest, transport the white wine in an ice bucket that is 90 percent filled with ice and water, and place it on the ice bucket stand. If there is no ice bucket stand, put the ice bucket on a large plate that contains a napkin, and place it on the guest's table or on a side table.

The following procedure should be followed for serving white wine:

1. Before drawing the cork, present the bottle of wine to the host to confirm that it is the wine ordered.
2. Replace the bottle in the ice bucket. Using the corkscrew knife, cut the foil covering the neck of the bottle just below the lip.
3. Strip the foil from around the lip of the bottle.
4. Wipe around the lip of the bottle with a service napkin after removing the foil.
5. Place the point of the waiter's corkscrew in the center of the cork.
6. Slowly turn the corkscrew so that it twists straight down into the cork. Continue turning until you reach the end of the cork, taking care not to pierce it so as to prevent chips from the cork falling into the wine.
7. Place the lever, which is at the end of the waiter's corkscrew, on the lip of the bottle.

8. Grip the neck of the bottle together with the lever and draw the cork up slowly.

9. When the cork is almost drawn, use the right hand to gently pull it out. Check the wine's quality by smelling the cork.

10. Wipe the top of the bottle again with the service napkin.

11. Take the bottle out of the ice bucket, and wipe it dry with the service napkin. Hold the bottle so that the label faces up. Pour the wine into the glass slowly, being careful not to touch the glass with the bottle. The glass should not be filled more than two-thirds full (for older reds many experts recommend that the large burgundy glass should not be filled more than one-third full to allow for the release of the bouquet). When finished pouring, twist the wrist slightly so that the top of the bottle is turned. By doing this, drips are avoided. If there are any drops left on the top of the bottle after pouring, wipe them off with the service napkin. After serving all the guests, place the bottle back in the ice bucket to keep it cool.

OPENING AND SERVING RED WINE

Red wine should be treated with care so as not to disturb the sediment in the bottle. A wine basket is usually used for serving red wine. If the wine basket is so shallow that wine might spill from the bottle when the cork is drawn, place a plate face down under the wine basket.

1. Place the wine bottle in the wine basket, which contains a service napkin to avoid dripping when pouring. Present the wine to the host, with the label facing up so the guest can confirm that it is the wine ordered.

2. Using the corkscrew knife, cut the underside of the foil covering the neck of the bottle just below the lip.

3. Continue carefully cutting the foil around the neck.

4. Remove the foil top.

5. Wipe around the lip of the bottle with a service napkin.

6. Center the corkscrew in the cork.

7. Keeping the corkscrew worm vertical, slowly turn the corkscrew clockwise so that the worm disappears into the cork.

8. Place the lever prongs on the bottle rim, holding it in place with the fingers.

9. Firmly holding the bottle and lever together, raise the opener handle until the cork comes out of the bottle.

10. When the cork is almost drawn, pull it out gently by hand. Check the wine's quality by smelling the cork.

11. Wipe the top of the bottle again with the service napkin.

12. Leave the bottle in the wine basket, label facing up, to pour the first taste for the host.

Note: History suggests that the ritual of having the host sample the wine first goes back to ancient times. A convenient way to eliminate one's enemy was to invite that person to your home to share a bottle of wine. It was easy to hide poison in wine. The guest was offered the wine first, drank it, and died. Logically, it was not long before guests demanded that their host drink the wine first. The obvious reason was that if the host drank first then the wine would be safe for the guest. The tradition continues to this day although happily for different reasons.

13. When the host has approved the wine, remove the bottle from the basket and hold it so that the label faces up.

14. Serve the other guests, moving counterclockwise around the table and serving from the right, completing the host's glass last. Pour the wine slowly, being careful not to touch the glass with the bottle. When finished pouring each glass, twist the wrist slightly with the neck of the bottle raised to avoid dripping. If there are drops left on the top of the bottle after pouring, wipe it dry with the service napkin.

If a guest refuses wine or turns the glass down, remove the glass so they will not have to refuse again. Replenish guests' glasses when most are empty. Continue to pour until bottle is empty.

When wine is ordered with dinner, do not serve coffee until dessert, unless the guest requests it.

OPENING CHAMPAGNE

Remove top of foil cap, then the wire hood. Hold your finger on the cork so it will not pop out too soon. Slant the bottle and be sure to point it away from your guest. Grasp the cork firmly. Twist the bottle, not the cork, slowly in one direction. Let internal pressure help push out the cork. Hold on to the cork as it leaves the bottle. A slanted bottle will not overflow as readily as an upright one, but have a glass handy just in case.

AERATING WINE

Uncork the bottle and pour its contents into a broad-basined vessel such as a carafe or a pitcher. This process essentially activates the aroma that carries the wine's signature. If you don't want to go through all this bother, simply pour the wine into a wineglass and allow several minutes for the surrounding oxygen to affect its unlocking. Old to very old red wines require little or no aeration to free their spirit.

White wines tend to be less complex in makeup than reds and seldom benefit from aeration. These should be served after an hour or two in the refrigerator but not icy. Wine that is too cold will be muted in aroma and flavor, and at the same time more astringent.

Contact with air over a prolonged period can absolutely ruin the flavor of most wines. If you do not finish a bottle of wine, transfer the contents to a smaller bottle (thereby minimizing airspace) and seal it tightly.

TEMPERATURE OF WINE FOR SERVING

The temperature of wine is a very important aspect of wine service; the sommelier must know the ideal or most suitable temperature for each wine.

Generally it is said that white wine is to be served chilled, and red wine is to be served at room temperature. However, "room temperature" originally meant the temperature of the dining room in a European palace in the eighteenth century. Today, with central heating and cooling, "room temperature" can be very vague.

Generally, the ideal serving temperatures of wines are as follows:

- 68 degrees F for full-bodied red wines that are rich in tannin (a high-quality Bordeaux, Burgundy, etc.).
- 64 degrees F for light red wines with less tannin.
- 55 degrees F for full-bodied dry white wines and very sweet white wines.
- 50 degrees F for light dry white wines, light sweet white wines, and rosé wines.
- 42–46 degrees F for sparkling wines and champagne.

Care should be taken not to spoil the flavor of the wine by chilling or warming it too rapidly to achieve the ideal serving temperature.

The sequence of wine service within the menu is as follows:

- Light wines should precede heavy or full-bodied wines.
- Dry wines should precede sweet wines.

- Dry white wines should precede dry red wines.

- Dry red wines should precede sweet white wines.

- Dry sparkling wines can be served either before or after dinner; sweet sparkling wines are best after dinner.

DECANTING WINE

Decanting requires little preparation and is extremely simple. Before starting, prepare the following pieces of equipment: a flashlight, a corkscrew, and a colorless glass decanter or carafe (thirty-three-ounce minimum). Be sure that it has been rinsed with a small amount of tepid water and is absolutely free of odor. Certain detergents, if incompletely rinsed away, can ruin a wine's bouquet. Do not store decanters closed with their own stoppers, but instead stuff the necks gently with a bit of tissue paper.

Red wines more than eight years old often have a natural, harmless sediment in the bottle. Hold the bottle up to a strong light to check it. If sediment is observed, decant the wine so no guest gets the gritty residue in his or her mouth.

Decanting is done either to separate the wine from any sediment deposited during the aging process, or to allow a wine to "breathe" in order to enhance its flavor.

1. Stand the bottle upright. Decanting should not be done more than one hour before the wine is to be served because the wine may lose its bouquet. Very old wines should be decanted immediately before serving, as the wine fades and oxidizes rapidly. Bottles of vintage Port might have to be stood upright for longer than twenty-four hours to allow the crusted sediment, known as the dregs, to settle to the bottom.

2. Gently uncork the bottle to avoid disturbing any sediment. If the bottle is lying horizontal, place it into a wine cradle and begin the uncorking process.

3. Stand a flashlight behind a clear carafe (between the wine bottle and carafe). Then carefully tilt the wine bottle toward the open mouth of the carafe and allow its contents to trickle in slowly, smoothly, and continuously. The flashlight should be directly underneath the neck of the wine bottle so as to follow the movement of sediment from the bottom of the bottle to the neck thus ensuring the decanted wine's clarity.

4. When the sediment reaches the point where the neck and shoulders of the bottle meet, you should be able to see some of the sediment, which is cloudy or hazy, starting to appear. You will find that only

one ounce or so of wine will remain in the bottle, and you will have a wine that is bright and clear in the decanter.

5. The remaining contents of the bottle should be discarded.

6. When first poured, the color of some older wines is often light orange red, and during a period of about five minutes, the color will deepen to a dark red.

WINEGLASSES

The proper glass should always be used. Using small glasses that are completely or nearly full is a mistake. Only a part of the wineglass should be filled, "to leave room for the nose."

A Burgundy wine requires a large, tulip-shaped glass; a claret needs a narrower one; a Rhine or Mosel should have a glass with a tall stem. The all-purpose wineglass is also proper.

Champagne is best served in a tall, narrow tulip glass. The so-called champagne saucer glass is improper for the serving and consumption of champagne. The bouquet for which the winegrower so painstakingly labored for is lost over the rim of the saucer.

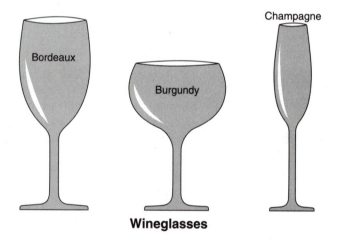

Wineglasses

The reason a wineglass is turned in slightly at the top is to concentrate the wine odor so that it is fuller as the wine is consumed. It is proper to hold the wine up to the light to check its clarity and color, or to look at it through the glass against the white tablecloth to note these visual qualities. A small amount of wine should be poured into the taster's glass so that plenty of space is left for sensing the bouquet.

The style and shape of wineglasses has evolved over time to ensure that the bouquet and full flavor of the wine may be savored and enjoyed.

THE FRENCH PARADOX

The research plans of a Boston epidemiologist and two recent biochemical research findings make intriguing current reading and give a tantalizing glimpse into the future of two areas of medical research involving grapes and wine.

According to Marian Baldy, Ph.D., writing in the University Wine Course, Dr. Curtis Ellison, an epidemiologist in the department of medicine at Boston University, is intrigued by the apparent paradox of the French, who eat a diet high in fat and cholesterol and yet enjoy a rate of heart disease lower than that of the U.S. population. Ellison wonders if the amounts and patterns of French wine consumption play a role in creating this "paradox." He plans to study the long-term health consequences of introducing wine into the diet early in life by comparing the dietary intakes, including alcohol, fat, cholesterol, and other nutrients, of children and adults in the United States and France.

Moving from Ellison's proposed macroscale study of wine and cardiovascular health (comparing populations of wine-drinking adults in different cultures) to a submicroscopic investigation of the same topic, Cornell pomologist Leroy Creasy has suggested that a substance called resveratrol may be the compound that explains how red wine can increase the level of high-density lipoproteins in the bloodstream. Resveratrol is the active ingredient in a traditional Japanese folk remedy for "cleansing the blood" using knotweed, and it is present in the skins of grapes—where it helps fight fungal disease—and in wines, especially lightly processed red wines.

The stage appears to be set for future studies to investigate the possible medical benefits of resveratrol and to discover whether it is indeed the solution to the French paradox that intrigues Dr. Ellison.

REVIEW QUESTIONS

1. Describe and indicate the steps in compiling a wine menu.
2. Outline the steps in wine service, along with the critical points associated with opening and pouring a bottle of red and white wine.
3. Describe the steps in opening a bottle of champagne.
4. Outline the service quality of serving wines at the correct temperatures.
5. Describe the steps and rationale for decanting wine and the use of the appropriate wineglasses.

Part Three

Bar Service and Mixology

An Overview of:

Liqueurs, Beers, Ales, Stout, Distilled Liquor, and Brandies—Their Varieties, Methods of Production, and Quality Points

Mixology, Bar Service, Training Intervention Procedures for Servers, Licensing, and Legal Issues Surrounding Alcohol

Bar Costing Procedures and the Effects of Alcohol on the Human Body

14
Liqueurs and Aperitifs

Outline

Liqueurs and cordials are the same thing. Europeans call them liqueurs, whereas in the United States, they are often referred to as cordials.

A liqueur is an alcoholic beverage made by combining a spirit with flavorings, then adding sugar syrup in excess of 2.5 percent of the volume. There are two major types of liqueurs, those that are fruit based and natural colored, and those that are plant or herb flavored. Liqueurs are simply whiskey, brandy, rum, or neutral grain spirits flavored with any herb, spice, seed, fruit, or syrup.

Italy is considered to be the "modern" home of liqueurs, that is, up to the fifteenth century. The Italians called this liquori, from which the word liqueur is derived. Catherine de Medici brought with her to France on the occasion of her marriage a number of culinary "secrets," as well as her Italian chefs. Among these "secrets" were recipes for liqueurs. The French were not slow to learn, and today perhaps more digestifs, as the French still call liqueurs, are now made in France.

The art of flavoring alcohol actually began in the Middle Ages when the "women of the house" found they could preserve fresh summer fruits for winter by bottling them in spirits. But flavored liqueurs, as we know them today, had their beginnings in the sixteenth century.

For many years, liqueurs were sold as medicine or love potions. Today, in most cases, they are served as after-dinner drinks or mixed with other ingredients to make cocktails.

The alcoholic spirit that the flavoring is combined with is usually grape brandy. Fruit-flavored liqueurs are the most popular.

Most commercial liqueurs are made with closely guarded secret formulas. Also called cordials and ratafias, liqueurs are usually high in alcohol and range from 49 proof for Cherry Heering to 110 proof for green Chartreuse. The crème liqueurs (such as crème de menthe) are distinguished by being sweeter and more syrupy. Liqueurs are also used in cooking, particularly for desserts.

METHODS OF PRODUCTION

There are basically two ways to extract flavors when making liqueurs, and these are referred to as the cold and hot methods, depending on the flavor to be made and its source. Fruit flavors are generally extracted by the cold method; other plant products, such as seeds, peels, and flowers, have their flavors extracted by the hot method. Each method encompasses several processes, and each fruit or plant product is handled differently.

INFUSION OR MACERATION

The cold method is used when the flavoring material is sensitive to heat. Cold extractions can take up to a year; attempts to make the process go faster by using heat would destroy the flavor.

1. If crushed fruits are steeped in water, it is called infusion.
2. If the fruit is steeped in alcohol, such as 120–130 proof brandy, it is called maceration.

There are three basic methods of flavoring the alcoholic spirits. These are:

1. Distillation.
2. Percolation.
3. Infusion.

Distillation

The flavoring agents—herbs and plants—are soaked in brandy overnight. The mildly flavored spirit and the herbs are then placed in a "pot still" and redistilled. The pot still resembles a large copper pot or kettle with a broad rounded base, topped by a long column. The flavored spirit is heated, the vapors rise to the neck of the pot still, which is kept above 173 degrees F but below 212 degrees F, where water vapor condenses and falls back into the liquid. The remaining vapor passes into the condenser, a coiled tube that is cooled from the outside with water, where it returns to the liquid state, and it is collected in another container.

The distillate derived from this process is a colorless, flavored spirit. Sugar is then added in the amount of not less than 2.5 percent by volume, to achieve the correct degree of sweetness. Vegetable coloring is sometimes added to produce color. Therefore, it is possible to have brown or white crème de curacao and even blue crème de menthe. Many of the plant liqueurs are aged in wooden casks to mature and achieve their fullness of flavor.

Percolation

The percolation method is also utilized in the production of plant liqueurs. It is similar to the process of brewing coffee. Brandy or neutral spirits are constantly pumped over the flavoring agent and allowed to percolate through it, soaking up the natural flavor of the plants. The resulting flavored spirit is then filtered, with sugar syrup and vegetable coloring added for sweetness and color. The liqueur can either be bottled immediately or aged in wooden casks.

Infusion

The third method of production (infusion) is used primarily in the making of fruit liqueurs. Brandy or neutral spirits are put in a vat with fresh or dried fruit and allowed to steep for up to a year. The liquid is drained off, the residue is distilled, and the resulting distillate added to the fruit brandy. Sugar syrup is added, and the product is aged from six months to a year.

Many different fruits are used, but the most popular are apricot, cherry, peach, and blackberry.

Liqueurs/Cordials are produced all over the world. The better varieties use brandy, not natural spirits, with true fruits, plants, and seeds, not essences. Each producer has his or her own secret and unique formula, some of which have never been duplicated by other producers.

ORIGINS AND FLAVORS OF WELL-KNOWN LIQUEURS

Amaretto

An Italian liqueur first created in 1525. It is almond-flavored, made from steeping apricot pits in alcohol. The original liqueur, Amaretto di Saronno, hails from Saronno, Italy. Many American distilleries now produce their own amaretto. The very best Amaretto is 40–56 percent proof.

Anisette

A clear, very sweet liqueur made with anise seeds and tasting of licorice. Anisette has a smooth, sweet taste. Marie Brizard is regarded as the best anisette because they use special green anise seed from Spain, rather than star anise seed. Anisette is 50–60 percent proof.

Advocaat

Reminiscent of eggnog, this Dutch liqueur is made with brandy, egg yolks, and sugar.

Bailey's Irish Cream

Fresh Irish cream blended with the finest Irish spirits and natural flavors to make this Irish cream liqueur. The alcohol in the whiskey serves as a preservative for the cream. Steeped in history and lore, it was named after one of Dublin's most famous "pubs," The Bailey. Soon to follow Bailey's into the marketplace were several other excellent "cream"-based liqueurs, which include Carolans and St. Brendans.

Benedictine

A sweet liqueur named after the Benedictine monks of the Abbey of Fecamp, France. Reputed to be the world's oldest liqueur, Benedictine has been produced since 1501. Though the recipe is a closely guarded secret, it is known that Benedictine is cognac-based and flavored with various aromatics such as fruit peels and herbs. Benedictine is aged for four years before being bottled, and is 36 percent proof.

Chambord

Chambord is a fine French liqueur made from wild black raspberries, honey, and other fruits and spices. It was the favorite of King Louis XIV, and the bottle is said to be shaped like the orb on his scepter. It is 33 percent proof.

Chartreuse

Chartreuse is made from a secret formula given to Les Peres Chartreux (the Carthusian Fathers) of the convent of the Grande Chartreuse at Grenoble, France. The original formula was slightly modified and perfected in 1737. There are two types of Chartreuse—yellow, which is 80–86 percent proof and green, which is 110 percent proof. Both yellow and green chartreuse are plant liqueurs with a spicy, aromatic flavor, made on a brandy base. The green is much drier and somewhat more aromatic than the yellow. Occasionally the monks age a small amount of the yellow and green chartreuse in oak casks for about twelve years. These are labeled "Chartreuse V.E.P." and state the year they were put into the casks. This extra aging makes the liqueurs softer and paler, with slightly lower proofs.

Cherry Heering

Cherry Heering is a Danish liqueur with a worldwide reputation, now known as Heering's Cherry Brandy. Peter Heering started selling this liqueur from a small shop a little more that 150 years ago and the company, now much enlarged, is still in the family. The only change has been in the shape of the bottle.

Cointreau

Cointreau is a brand name for one of the best "Triple Secs." Although the Cointreau family formerly made many flavors of liqueurs, the name Cointreau became synonymous with orange liqueur, and the other flavors are now produced under a different label. Made from bittersweet oranges, it is 80 percent proof.

Crème de Menthe (Clear)

Virtually identical to green crème de menthe. Because the green coloring has not been added, it can be used in cocktail recipes.

Crème de Menthe (Green)

Refreshing, tangy natural mint flavor, cool, clean, pleasant to taste, crème de menthe is made as a spirit and flavored with several types of mint and peppermint.

Crème de Cassis

This is a black currant-flavored liqueur and is an integral ingredient in Kir. It is rich, fruity, with the full flavor of black currents.

Crème de Cacao

Crème de cacao is a dark, chocolate-flavored liqueur with a hint of vanilla. White crème de cacao is a clear form of the same liqueur. The name Chouao, the district in Venezuela where the finest cocoa beans once grew, usually appears on crème de cacao labels.

Crème de Rose

This is an exotically scented liqueur flavored with rose petals, vanilla, and various spices.

Crème de Framboise

This is a rich, raspberry-flavored liqueur.

Curacao

Curacao has an orange character, from the peel of bittersweet "green" oranges grown on the Dutch island of Curacao in the West Indies. Clear amber in color, it is similar to "Triple Sec" but slightly sweeter and has more subtle orange flavor. It is a lower proof.

Danziger Goldwasser

This is a sweet kummel-type liqueur flavored with caraway and aniseed. It is colorless with flecks of real gold leaf. In ancient times alchemists presented gold as a cure-all.

Drambuie

The name drambuie was contracted from the Scottish Gaelic, Dram Buidheach, meaning "the drink that satisfies." It is made from old Highland Malt Scotch whiskey and heather honey, and is 80 percent proof.

Eau de Vie

French for "water of life," this term describes any colorless, potent brandy or other spirit distilled from fermented fruit juice. Kirsch (made from cherries) and Framboise (from raspberries) are the two most popular eaux de vie.

Frangelico

A liqueur made from wild hazelnuts, berries, and flowers. It is named after the Italian monk who first developed it, and is 56 percent proof.

Galliano

Galliano is an Italian liqueur flavored with vanilla and licorice. It is amber colored and sold in a tall slender bottle.

Grand Marnier

Grand Marnier is one of the finest orange Curacao liqueurs. It is made on a cognac base from small, green Curacao oranges that are hand-peeled. The peels are dried in the sun to concentrate the flavors and are then shipped to France for maceration and distillation.

Herbsaint

Developed and made primarily in New Orleans, Herbsaint is an anise-flavored liqueur that is used in such specialties as oysters Rockefeller.

Irish Mist

The recipe for this old Irish liqueur consists of four great Irish spirits, which are blended with honey, heather, and clover and a dozen hand-picked aromatic herbs. Originally from Tullamore in Ireland, the recipe was lost during the exodus of warriors in 1692. It was eventually located in Austria and returned to Ireland, and is 80 percent proof.

Jagermeister

From Germany, this distinctive flavor is a blend of 56 roots, herbs, and fruits.

Kahlua

Kahlua, the most famous coffee liqueur, is made in Mexico and is 53 percent proof.

Kummel

Kummel is a sweet, colorless liqueur flavored with caraway seed, cumin, and fennel.

Lochan Ora

This Scotch liqueur is made of 100 percent Chivas Regal Scotch whiskey blended with honey and native herbs. Lochan Ora means "golden loch." It is 70 percent proof.

Malibu

Malibu is a flavor blend of white rum and coconut from Canada.

Mandarin

Mandarin is a Curacao-type liqueur flavored from dried tangerine peel.

Maraschino

Maraschino is a sweet liqueur with a highly concentrated flavor distilled from fermented maraschino cherries and their kernels; it is used a great deal as a flavoring in certain sweet dishes. Maraschino was first produced over 200 years ago in Zara, Yugoslavia, and exported in distinctively shaped bottles. It is now also produced in Trieste, Italy.

Meade

Debate continues on which is the oldest—grape wine or a liqueur called meade. Meade is a fermentation of honey, water and herbs. History has recorded its use in Ireland before the fifth century, where it was made secretly by monks. This honey-wine was also believed to have the powers of virility and fertility, and it became the custom at weddings for the bride and groom to be toasted with special goblets full of meade which they would use for one full moon after the wedding. This tradition is the origin of the word "honeymoon."

Pear William

Pear William has the delicate flavor of fresh Anjou pears from France's Loire Valley.

Pernod

Pernod is a yellowish, licorice-flavored liqueur; it is a blend of select anise seeds, special flavorings, and natural herbs on a spirit base. Pernod is very popular in France and is usually mixed with water, which turns it whitish and cloudy.

Petite Liqueur

This champagne-based liqueur is made by the world's most well-known champagne producers, Moet and Chandon, the makers of Dom Perignon. It is fortified with cognac, therefore, Petit Liqueur has a higher alcohol and sugar content than champagne. Its slightly dry flavor develops chocolatey and nutty overtones when drunk, especially when consumed with dessert.

Sabra

This fine liqueur from Israel is made from the essence of the tangy Jaffa orange and fine Israeli chocolate (60 percent proof).

Sambuca Romana

This classic Italian liqueur is made from the elderberry, whose Latin name is *Sambucus*. It is traditional to serve Sambuca flaming, with three coffee beans. The beans are said to bring the guest good luck. Sambuca is 70–84 percent proof.

Sloe Gin

Sloe gin is a liqueur made by steeping pricked or crushed sloes in gin.

Southern Comfort

Southern Comfort was originally called "Cuff and Buttons" around 1875 when the phrase meant "white tie and tails." A moderate quantity of peach liqueur and fresh peaches is added to bourbon whiskey. The liqueur and fruit mellow the whiskey, even though it is 100 percent proof.

Strega

Strega is an Italian, orange-flavored liqueur made from distilled orange extract and seventy different herbs and spices. Directly translated, it means "Liqueur of the Witch," and is said to be made by the witches of Italy as a cure-all and love potion for the use of the townspeople. It is not marketed much in the United States, but in Italy it would be the top-shelf equivalent of Galliano, 80 percent proof.

Tia Maria

From Jamaica, Tia Maria is claimed to be the original coffee liqueur. It is made on a rum base with local Blue Mountain coffee and is 63 percent proof.

Triple Sec

A strong, clear orange-flavored liqueur very similar to Curacao. Triple Sec is used to make the mixed drink, Margarita.

Vandermint

Made since the seventeenth century, Vandermint is a blend of smooth, rich Dutch chocolate subtly flavored with a touch of fresh mint. It is 63 percent proof.

Wild Turkey Liqueur

One of the few American liqueurs, Wild Turkey is bottled exclusively in limited quantity in Lawerenceburg, Kentucky. It is made with Kentucky Straight Bourbon, from stock specially reserved for it. It is mellowed from its original 100 percent proof to 80 percent proof with the addition of honey, herbs, and spices.

APERITIFS

Aperitif is a French term referring to a light alcoholic beverage taken before a meal to stimulate the appetite. These beverages include spiced wines, such as vermouth, and various brand-name preparations and sherries along with champagne "cocktails."

Best-Known Aperitifs

Campari.   This is a bitter Italian aperitif. It is often mixed with soda. It is also featured as an ingredient in some cocktails. Regular Campari has an astringent, bittersweet taste. Sweet Campari is also available.

Dubonnet.   Dubonnet is a French bittersweet, fortified wine-based aperitif flavored with herbs and quinine. Dubonnet comes in both red and white versions—the white being the drier of the two.

Kir Royale.   Champagne mixed with crème de cassis—a black currant-flavored liqueur, which is rich, fruity, with a full flavor of black currant, from Dijon, France.

Lillet.   Lillet is made from a blend of wine, brandy, fruits, and herbs. It originated in the French village of Podensac and has been made there since the late 1800s. Lillet Blanc is made from white wine and is drier than Lillet Rouge (its red wine counterpart). Both are classically served over ice with an orange twist.

Ouzo.   From Greece, this clear, sweet anise-flavored drink is usually served as an aperitif. It's generally mixed with water, which turns it whitish and opaque. Ouzo is sweet, slightly drier, and a stronger proof than anisette.

Sherry.   Sherry is a fortified wine originally made in and around the town of Jerez, from where it derived its name. As with all wines, sherries range from the outstanding to the ordinary.

THE SOLERA SYSTEM

The solera system is used for all styles of sherry. It operates by a series of blendings. A proportion of the youngest wine in the bodega is blended into a butt of wine from the preceding year, where the younger wine begins to take on the character of the older.

To make room for this process, a third of the butt of second-year wine is transferred to the third-year wine, and a third of the third-year butt is moved into the fourth-year wine. After an average of five such movements, a third of the butt of oldest wine (called solera, because traditionally this was at the base of a tier of butts resting on the floor, or suelo) is drawn off for bottling.

Sherry is therefore a blended wine in many senses. The final bottle contains wines from a number of different soleras which are blended in a further series of butts before bottling.

There are no vintage sherries because of the "topping off" practice of the solera system.

Sherries range in color, flavor, and sweetness. Finos are dry and light, whereas Manzanillas are very dry, delicate finos with a hint of saltiness. Amontillados are considered a medium sherry. They are nutty-flavored, sweeter, softer, and are darker in color than finos. Olorosos are sweet, fuller-flavored, and darker than dry or medium sherries. They are usually aged longer than other sherries and tend to be more expensive. Olorosos are often labeled cream or golden sherries.

VERMOUTH

White wine that has been fortified and flavored with various herbs and spices. The name "vermouth" comes from the German *wermut* (wormwood) which, before it was declared poisonous, was once the principal flavoring ingredient. There are several types of this wine, the most popular being white dry vermouth, commonly thought of as French (although it's made in other countries including the United States).

It's drunk as an aperitif and used in nonsweet cocktails such as the martini. Sweet vermouth is reddish brown (colored with caramel) and is also used as an aperitif, as well as in slightly sweet cocktails such as the Manhattan. A third style—not as popular as the other two—is white and slightly sweet. It's called Bianco by the Italians.

REVIEW QUESTIONS

1. List and describe the methods of production and the principal flavor bases of liqueurs.

2. Explain the processes of distillation, percolation, and infusion.
3. Identify the origins and flavor bases of well-known liqueurs.
4. Explain aperitifs—their flavor bases and origins. Describe the solera system.
5. Define the essential elements of a "vermouth."

15

Beers, Ales, and Stout

Outline

WHAT IS BEER?

Beer is an infusion of malted barley boiled with hops and then fermented. The basic ingredients are malted barley, water, yeast, hops, and other cereals. Hops are added to give beer a special bitter flavor, as well as to act as a natural preservative. Yeast is added to cause fermentation.

The beers of early man were full of nutrition, primarily because they were almost fermented cereals. These beers were poorly strained, thus the drinker invariably ingested the nutritional value of the yeast and cereal sediment.

The earliest written reference to the brewing process appears on a Mesopotamian clay tablet circa 4000 B.C. A wooden model of a brewery dating back to 2000 B.C. was found at Meket-Re in Thebes. Shortly before this time, the Babylonians were brewing some eighteen different varieties of beer and even designated two goddesses, Ninkasi and Siris, to watch over its fortunes. In Western Europe, brewing was carried out in the family, usually by the women, and did not become commercially important until probably the sixteenth century. Most monasteries had their own brew house which became an important source of revenue.

HISTORY AND BEER IN THE UNITED STATES

Beer was quite a versatile product in colonial times. Beer stores better for longer periods than water; therefore, on long ocean voyages it was used by seafarers during their voyages of discovery. Beer was not only safer than water, but also provided the food nutrients necessary to prevent scurvy and beri-beri. Not surprisingly, therefore, on their voyages of discovery to the "new world" the Pilgrims on the Mayflower were dependent on beer for liquid sustenance.

In Colonial America, brewing was also carried out by the "women of the house," causing a brew house to become a common feature of most farms and plantations. George Washington was said to have had a brew house, and William Penn is reputed to have started the first commercial brewery in America.

It was during colonial times that beer drinking was advocated over hard liquor consumption, therefore, a duty lower than other harder liquors was applied. The purpose was to stimulate more beer drinking so as to reduce the excessive consumption of "King Devil," a name given to a particular type of rum being made in New England at that time.

Up to until 1840, most of the beer consumed in the United States were the traditional British-type ales—strong, heavy, and a bitter beverage with an alcohol content of about 8 percent. These beers, called stouts and porter, are what is known in brewing terms as top fermented beers (stout and porter remain popular to this day in Ireland and England). These types of beers have made a dramatic comeback in recent times in the United States due to the popularity of beer and the advent of "Microbreweries."

It was not until the influx of German immigrants in the late nineteenth century that brewing and beer styles changed in the United States. These new immigrants brought with them their ancient brewing skills. German brewing methods were brought to the United States, including the "bottom fermented" process, which produces a lighter, milder, lager-type beer. These beers became more attractive to American tastes. Their appeal was that they were lighter, less intoxicating, and highly favored, and their thirst-quenching properties were very desirable.

TYPES OF BEER FERMENTATION

The use of a type of yeast that will generally convert sugars to alcohol and CO_2 at lower temperatures is called "bottom fermentation." Bottom fermenting yeast is sometimes referred to as lager yeast, and a slower fermentation is characteristic.

The word lager is German and literally means to "store"; it is applied to bottom fermented beer because it has to be stored at low temperatures over prolonged periods of time. Traditionally almost all beers made in the United States (90 percent), unless otherwise described, are lagers.

Ales are usually "top fermented." This means they are fermented at higher temperatures than lager-type beers (between 60 to 70 degrees F), and are ready for consumption within a short period of time.

TYPES OF BEERS

Bock

This is a dark-brown German brew that is full bodied, slightly sweet, and almost twice as strong as lager.

Porter

Porter is a heavy, dark-brown, strongly flavored beer. The dark color and strong flavor come from the addition of roasted malt. Porters are usually higher in alcohol than regular lager beers. Porter has a slightly bittersweet flavor.

Stout

Dark-roasted barley gives this brew an intensely dark color, bitter flavor, and extremely dense body. Guinness began brewing their famous stout at St. James Gate in Dublin in 1759, where it is still brewed to this day. Guinness started by making traditional Irish ales. Later on Guinness changed to a new drink made from roasted barley. This new drink was called "Porter." Initially the drink was unpopular, so Guinness produced a "stronger extra stout." This was shortened over the years to stout.

In addition to the Guinness company, there are several other excellent Irish "stouts"—Murphys and Beamish & Crawfords. Both have brewed stout in Cork, Ireland, for over 150 years.

Malt

This is a robust, dark beer with a bitter flavor and relatively high alcohol content.

Wheat Beer

Made with malted wheat, this beer has a pale color and subtle, lagerlike flavor.

Fruit Beer

These are milk ales flavored with fruit concentrates.

Lager

From the German word "to store," lagers are brewed with a bottom fermenting yeast at cooler temperatures. Lagering or aging tends to give a smoother, more refined taste. It is America's most popular beer. Lager is pale-colored and light-bodied with a mellow flavor.

Light Beer

An American term indicating a watery, Pilsner-style, low-calorie lager. Generally it contains less than 5 percent alcohol. In the United States, this beer has reduced calories. In Europe, the term distinguishes between pale and dark lagers.

Ales

Ales are brewed using an ancient method with top fermenting yeast at warmer temperatures. It has a shorter brewing process than lagers, giving it a robust flavor. Blonde or golden ale is top fermented, made completely with barley, and seasoned with hops. Ales range from gold to amber in color. The golden ales are noted for their softness combined with rich complexity and distinctive strength.

Many consumers are moving toward the microbrewery/restaurants which have sprung up all across the United States. To some guests, American-produced beers from the giant breweries just do not satisfy them anymore. Microbreweries are small breweries of modest size and production. These breweries produce specialty hand-crafted small quantities of beer.

THE MICROBREWING PROCESS FOR ALES

1. Grist Case
   Malted barley is soaked and cured then roasted through kilning. The process is known as malting, and it is then sold to the brewer.

2. Milling
   In the mill, malt gets gently cracked, and the husk of malted barley creates grist.

3. Mashing
   After milling, the grist goes into the mash tun where it is mixed with warm filtered water, resulting in a sweet liquid known as wort. After about an hour, the wort is "run off" to a *lauter tun*.

4. Lauter Tun
   The mash is steamed and rinsed in the lauter tun to produce a liquid high in fermentable sugars.

5. Brew Kettle Boiling
   The wort is added to the brew kettle, and the liquid is brought to a boil. Hops are added to create bitterness, balance, and aroma.

6. Cooling
   After boiling, the hopped wort is pumped from the brew kettle through the heat exchanger. As it is cooled, the liquid is collected into a primary ferment.

7. Fermenting
   "Cultured yeast" is added to the wort to start the fermentation process. During several days of fermentation, the yeast consumes the sugars of the brew, creating carbon dioxide (carbonation) and alcohol.

8. Conditioning and Filtering
   The brew is conditioned at a cooler temperature and develops natural carbonation and full flavor. The beer is cold filtered to remove the yeast and bacteria so as to make it smoother and cleaner tasting.

9. Dispensing
   Once the brewing process is complete, the beer is held in cold dispensing tanks.

10. Storage
    a. Ales are ready for consumption within a short time (five to fourteen days) from start to finish, and should always be stored cool.
    b. Unlike wine, beer should not be aged. It is best when consumed as fresh as possible.
    c. Unpasteurized beer should be refrigerated and consumed within one or two weeks.
    d. Beer should always be stored standing upright. Laying it on its side exposes more of the liquid to the air in the bottle, which will diminish the beer's flavor.

FOOD AND BEER

Matching beers and food has increased in popularity in the United States. Generally beer is a great accompaniment to many dishes, including soups, sauces, stews, and breads.

Beer is also great for steaming clams and mussels or use as the cooking liquid when boiling shrimp.

A full-flavored brew such as ale or bock beer will contribute more flavor to a dish than a light lager.

Beer is a particularly compatible beverage with spicy cuisines such as Chinese, Indian, Mexican, and Thai. Spicy or smoked sausages are great paired with dark beer. As a general rule, the more highly seasoned the food, the more full-bodied the beer should be.

For maximum aroma and flavor, the ideal serving temperature for light (lager-style) beers is 45 to 50 degrees F; ales, porters, and stouts are best in the 50 to 60 degree range. Beer can begin to lose its flavor with temperature fluctuations, so do not move it in and out of the refrigerator excessively.

CIDER

Strictly speaking, cider is a stand-alone item. Sparkling cider is to cider what champagne is to sparkling wine. This light beverage is a perfect accompaniment to many foods and is delicious all by itself. Although most sparkling ciders are nonalcoholic, some ciders contain approximately 5 to 6 percent alcohol, with a few listed as 10 to 12 percent alcohol (the same as table wine). Sparkling cider contains no added sugar or preservatives.

BEER CLEAN GLASSES

Many bartenders conscientiously work and polish glasses until they sparkle, but a film of grease remains on the glass. This film quickly breaks down the creamy head of foam. Beer loses its delicate taste and zest when it is poured into glasses that have the slightest film of soap, grease, fat, or oil.

No single factor in retail beer operations is more frequently the cause of impaired quality, loss of eye and taste appeal, than improperly cleaned glasses.

As an exercise to check if glasses are "beer clean" or just look clean, wet the glass and shake salt into it as it is slowly turned in you hand, so that the salt will fall on the inner surface. In a "beer clean" glass, the salt should adhere smoothly to the entire surface.

Another way to check if the glass is "beer clean" is to dip the glass in fresh water and hold it, tilted downward, so that the water will drain out. A "beer clean" glass will have a completely smooth, wet surface. If there is any trace of grease, soap, or oil on the glass, the film of water on the glass will be in streaks and drops.

However, the most reliable way to check for "beer clean" glasses is by pouring or drawing beer into the glass, allowing a good head of foam to form. Then let it stand for a few minutes. In a "beer clean" glass, the head of foam should remain compact and firm. In a glass that is not "beer clean," the foam will break up rapidly and soon disappear, leaving a few large bubbles.

As beer is consumed from a "beer clean" glass, the foam will adhere to the inside of the glass in a ring design. A glass that has traces of greasy or oily film will have a spotty, irregular foam design; or, if the glass is covered with a soap film, no foam will adhere.

A "beer glass" should be washed each time it is used, unless the guest requests that the glass be refilled. It is recommended to stack cleaned glasses inverted, in a wire basket or on a deeply corrugated surface, where they can drain freely and air can circulate in them. Do not place them on a smooth surface, towel, or rubber drain pad, where they will pick up undesirable odors that will be offensive to the guest. Beer glasses should not be stored near the kitchen, where grease may be deposited on them by the air.

BEER SERVICE AND THE BEER LIST

As previously noted, beer is steadily growing in popularity in the United States. It is not uncommon now to find that restaurant guests drink it before, during, and after dinner. This type of guest might be one who simply refuses to pay high wine prices and drinks beer instead during dinner, or the guest may be a true beer lover, or simply seeking a beverage low in alcohol.

Obviously beer consumption also increases in hot weather. In any event it is wise to have a beer list on hand in those establishments that cater completely or even partially to beer-consuming guests.

Beer drinking nowadays has become trendy and sophisticated. Most restaurants now offer an extensive listing of domestic and imported beers.

The annual consumption of beer in the United States has increased enormously, particularly imported and speciality beers. However, overall the U.S. beer-consumption figure is low when compared with that of other countries.

Many restaurateurs now realize the potential for increased revenues to be gained from promoting beer in their establishments.

PROCEDURE FOR POURING AND SERVING BEER

1. Use beer clean glasses and, if possible, use chilled (frosted) pilsner glasses or mugs for beer. If there is not sufficient space to keep a freezer for "beerware," rinse the glass or mug in cold water before approaching the table.

Note: Some bars, particularly those serving fresh microbrewery products, will not chill a mug, but serve it at "cellar temperature" so the cold will not flatten the "head."

2. If the bartender does not open the bottle of beer, open the bottle either at an affixed bottle-cap remover at the bar area or with a "church key," bottle opener, or even corkscrew. If using a corkscrew, pry the cap off the bottle with the lifter that is part of a corkscrew. Don't flip the cap (where will it go?), but lift it off, then catch the cap in your hand. Remove the corkscrew from the bottle and dispose of the cap in a garbage container.

3. When you reach the guest, ask whether they would like the beer poured. If the guest says, "No," place the chilled glass to the guest's right, and the bottle of beer to the right of the glass.

4. If the guest says, "Yes," first place the chilled glass to the guest's right, if possible. If using a pilsner glass, hold the bottle directly over the center of the glass, with the rim of the bottle lip near one side of the glass. The glass should have sloping sides, with a small base and wide rim at the top to provide a sloped pouring surface.

5. If a large head is desired, pour directly into the center. Otherwise, the beer should be poured down the side of the glass to minimize the head. Those who are adept at pouring will be able to create a head that rises three-quarter-inch over the top of the glass and settles without spilling. The head should account for no more than 20 percent of the filled glass.

6. Place the bottle, with the remainder of the beer, on a coaster or beverage napkin.

7. Some guests will ask you to pour, "Just a bit." In this case, begin to pour the beer but stop after pouring two or three ounces, or when the glass is approximately one-third full. The guest can then refresh the glass as desired.

DRAFT BEERS

1. If stored in a walk-in cooler, beer in kegs should be kept at appropriately 36 to 38 degrees Fahrenheit. Beer is very sensitive to temperature and pressure, and foams as a result. If draft beer is allowed to warm, the liquid and gas will separate, and gas bubbles will form in the lines from the keg. When beer is drawn, it foams and gases. This wastes beer and profits go down the drain.

2. Draft beer is best when it is served in a "beer clean glass," with a good rich creamy head of foam. A thick rich creamy head should cling to the glass as each sip is taken. The bubbles that the foam

produce give a glass of beer the eye appeal essential to sales. The amount of foam also determines the number of glasses which can be drawn from a barrel. Foam is about 25 percent liquid beer.

Drawing the Perfect Glass of Beer

To produce the perfect beer head, the following steps should be observed:

1. Draft beer should be served at the correct temperature and in the proper glass shape and size.
2. Beer lines should be clean and well maintained, and never allowed to dry when not in use. Lines should be flushed at the end of each day.
3. The size of the head is controlled by the angle at which you hold the glass at the beginning of the "draw." If the glass is held straight, so that the beer drops down into the bottom of the glass, a deep head will result. If the glass is tilted sharply, so that the beer flows down the side, the head of foam will be minimized. The amount of foam beer produces also depends on its temperature. Ice-cold beer will produce light foam, whereas room-temperature beer promotes a thicker froth.
4. The beer head should be allowed to rise just above the top of the glass without spilling over, then settle down to a three-quarter-inch or one-inch head of frothy white foam.

REVIEW QUESTIONS

1. Describe and review the history of beer brewing in the United States.
2. Explain the basic method of fermentation of beer. Outline the major types of beers available in the United States.
3. Outline the major steps of the microbrewing process for ales.
4. Discuss the compatibility of beer and food.
5. State the process of pouring and serving beer. Outline the fundamentals associated with "beer clean" glasses.

16

Distilled Liquors

Outline

LIQUORS AND SPIRITS

In simple terms, distilled liquors or spirits are alcoholic beverages that are not wines, liqueurs, or beers. Distilled spirits include beverages such as rum, scotch whiskey, gin, and vodka. Spirits generally have a higher alcoholic content than wines, beers, and liqueurs.

Liquor/spirits, unlike wine, have no dependence on climate, regional, or cultural limits. They can be produced anywhere that a distiller decides to place the equipment.

DISTILLATION

The process of distillation is made possible by the fact that the boiling point of alcohol is about 173 degrees F or almost 40 degrees F lower than the boiling point of water. This means that if a mixture of water and alcohol is heated to the boil, more of the alcohol than the water will end up in the initial vapor. The vapor can then be cooled and condensed into a liquid (the word distill comes from the Latin *destillare,* which means to drip). The condensation of vapor on a cool surface will have a higher alcoholic content than the original liquid.

SO WHAT ARE STILLS?

Stills are the distiller's main piece of equipment for producing a distillate-concentrated distilled alcohol. This distillate is categorized by the method of introducing a fermented mixture.

THE POT STILL

The pot still resembles a large copper pot or kettle with a broad, rounded base, topped by a long column.

Using the pot still method, the flavored spirit is heated, and the vapors rise to the neck of the pot still, which is kept above 173 degrees F but below 212 degrees F, where water vapor condenses and falls back into the liquid. The remaining vapor passes into the condenser, a coiled tube that is cooled from the outside with water, where it returns to the liquid state. It is then collected in another container.

COFFEY STILL

A type of still named after the Irish inspector general of customs and excises. A patent for this was granted in 1832. Essentially it was to become known by its generic name of continuous still. Prior to this invention, all distilling took place in pot stills.

CONTINUOUS STILL

Along with the pot still are the two most widely used types of still in use. The continuous still is often referred to as a column, or Coffey, still. The continuous still, as its name implies, provides a continuous inflow of distilling liquid that greatly boosts volume while saving production time. However, it generally does not produce the same high level of quality as the pot still.

COLUMN STILL

This consists of two cylindrical columns fitted with a system of interconnecting steam-heated tubes. (Pot stills use a flame.) The steam, which is higher in temperature than fire, allows for different flavor profiles to be achieved. The alcoholic liquid is fed into the tubes, where it is distilled and redistilled, and taken off as highly concentrated alcohol. The vapor goes through a series of plates that holes with bubbler caps, after which it condenses.

SPIRITS

Whiskeys

Whiskey is the largest selling distilled spirit in the world. American whiskeys rank number one, with blended whiskeys being first, Scotch second, and Irish whiskey catching up fast. All whiskeys have their similarities, but they are all different.

American Whiskey (Bourbon)

In 1789, a baptist minister named Elijah Craig made a distilled spirit by combining spring water, corn, rye, and barley malt. Reverend Craig lived in Bourbon County, Kentucky. After the production of whiskey in Kentucky, the Reverend Craig became known as "The Father of Bourbon." By 1890, there were 1,576 registered distilleries throughout Kentucky.

Most whiskeys produced in the United States come from three areas: Kentucky, Western Pennsylvania, and the Midwest, specifically Indiana and Illinois. The properties of the limestone spring water found in these areas are conducive to the production of fine whiskeys.

Making whiskey is a simple process, and the quality of the product is dependent on the following factors:

1. The type and quality of the grains and malt used.
2. The properties of water used.
3. The type of still used (whether a "pot" or "twin column" still).
4. The amount of aging and degree of blending.

The process of making whiskey in the United States is strictly controlled by federal and state governments. The grains (corn, rye, barley, etc.) are ground into meal, combined with barley malt and water, and then cooked to convert the starches to sugar.

At this stage, the mixture is called "wort." The wort is cooled and transferred to fermenting tanks, and cultivated yeast is added. A sweet or sour mash process utilizes fresh cultivated yeast for fermentation and normally takes from thirty-six to fifty hours to ferment. The sour mash process uses two-thirds fresh cultivated yeast and one-third working yeast from a previous fermentation. This fermentation process takes between seventy-two and ninety-six hours. Sour mash produces a slightly sweeter whiskey.

The whiskey is then transferred to new, *charred white oak* casks and allowed to age. During the aging process, water evaporates, raising the proof, and the whiskey also mellows. The whiskey changes from white to amber in color. At the time of bottling, caramel may be added to change the color even further.

The use of charred oak barrels began in the United States in 1850. History suggests that while a barrel maker was steaming and bending barrels over an open fire, he accidentally charred the wood. Not wishing to throw the charred barrels away, he used them without telling the distiller. It was later discovered that the whiskey was considerably improved in the richness of its color and flavor as a result of the charring of the barrel. From then on the distiller insisted on having the oak in all his barrels charred.

Bourbon Whiskey

This whiskey is distilled from a fermented mash of grain that is no less than 51 percent corn grain. Both sweet and sour mash are produced. Normally sweet mash bourbon is bar bourbon, and sour mash is dispensed when specially requested. Bourbon, originally made in Bourbon County, Kentucky, is an American product now produced in all the whiskey-making areas of the United States.

Rye Whiskey

This is a whiskey distilled from a fermented mash of grain that contains not less than 51 percent rye grain. Rye whiskey has a distinct flavor all its own and normally is sold at 100 percent proof. It is particularly favored in the Midwest.

Malt Whiskey

Malt whiskey is distilled from the fermented mash of grain, of which not less than 51 percent of the grain is malted barley or malted rye grain. Very little malt whiskey is produced in the United States.

Corn Whiskey

This whiskey is distilled from a fermented mash of grain that contains not less than 80 percent corn grain. It is stored in uncharred oak casks and normally aged for only a limited period. Its color is white to pale yellow, and it has a very distinctive corn flavor. It is consumed mostly in the South.

Scotch Whiskey

Probably the best known of all whiskey, Scotch whiskey is only produced in Scotland. There are four major whiskey-making areas, and each one produces a whiskey with its own distinctive flavor and aroma.

The primary Scotch producing areas are the

1. Highlands
2. Lowlands
3. Islay
4. Campbeltown.

Scotch whiskey is made from malted barley grain. As with other whiskeys, there are five steps in making Scotch whiskey:

1. Malting
2. Mashing
3. Fermenting
4. Distilling
5. Aging and blending

The malting process is what makes Scotch distinctively different from other whiskeys. Barley is steeped in water until softened and then spread over the floors of the malting house to germinate and sprout for three weeks. The "green malt" is then transferred to a kiln where it is roasted over a peat fire.

During this process, the malt dries out and picks up the smoky flavor associated with Scotch whiskey. The degree of roasting is controlled, and the differences in Scotch is reflected in the darkness of the roasted barley malt. For example, Campbeltown is noted for its dark roast, whereas the Lowland Scotch is sought for its light, milk roast.

The barley malt is ground and mixed with warm water to convert the starch to sugar. The wort is transferred to a fermenting tank, and yeast is added. Beer is produced, then distilled in a pot still. It is then redistilled and proofed off at 140 percent to 142 percent proof. It is reduced to between 124 and 126.8 percent proof by the addition of distilled water. The whiskey is then aged in oak casks.

To create the perfect taste and aroma, the whiskey bottler blends whiskeys from all areas with grain whiskey (unmalted whiskey). This process takes place after the whiskeys are at least four years old. The fine art of making Scotch whiskey is in the hands of a blender who may use as many as fifty malt whiskeys, along with five or six grain whiskeys, to attain the desired taste. A small quantity of unblended malt whiskey is sold. These whiskeys must be labeled "Malt Whiskey." They are fuller bodied and sell at a premium price. In general Americans prefer light-bodied blended whiskeys. Scotch that has been aged over ten years tends to be softer and mellower.

Although Scotch whiskey can only be made in Scotland, it is bottled in the United States. Some bottlers import Scotch in bulk to reduce the amount of import duty, and bottle it at the port of entry.

Irish Whiskey

Most historians agree that the secret of distillation probably came from the Middle East and that it was brought to Ireland by missionary monks around the sixth century. These monks discovered that the alembic Arabs used for distilling perfume could be put to better use and adapted it into a pot still. They found that if a mash of barley and water was fermented with yeast, then heated in a pot still, the alcohol could be separated and retained into a spirit with wondrous powers. The monks called it "Uisce Beatha," Gaelic for water of life. Over the centuries the Irish words were corrupted into the anglicized sound of "Whiskey."

The oldest distillery in the world is located at Bushmills in County Antrim in Northern Ireland. Situated on the banks of the River Bush, it was granted its license by King James I in 1608, although distilling on this site goes back to 1276. The water from the River Bush tributary, St. Columbs Rill is still used to this day to make the whiskey. Other old and famous Irish whiskey distilleries include John Jameson, Paddy, and John Power.

Only in Ireland can Irish whiskey be produced. The process is similar to the production of Scotch whiskey. Irish whiskey is triple distilled in pot stills. Ireland produces both blended (malt whiskey blended with grain whiskey) and single malt. Irish whiskey is aged a minimum of seven years before bottling and has a less malty flavor than Scotch. In Ireland, whiskey is spelled with an "e" before the "y," whereas in Scotland it is spelled whisky.

The popularity of Irish whiskey is very much on the increase in the United States.

Canadian Whiskey

Canadian whiskey is a whiskey blend, and is light-bodied. It contains mostly Canadian corn, with a lesser amount of rye, wheat, and barley malt. For consumption in Canada, it is bottled at 70 percent proof. For export to the United States, it is bottled at 80–86.6 percent proof. It is usually six years old. If less than four years old, its age must be marked on the label, for example,

Seagram's VO 86.8 percent proof, Seagram's Crown Royal 80 percent proof, and Canadian Club 86.8 percent proof, 6 years old.

Gin

Gin is made by redistilling grain spirits with flavoring agents, especially juniper berries. Most brands of gin sold in the United States are distilled. Gin was first produced in Holland in the seventeenth century for medicinal purposes and was called "Genever" or "Holland." During the eighteenth century, England began producing gin, and since then its manufacture and use has spread throughout the world.

There are three basic types of gin; these are:

1. Dry gin, which is light bodied and aromatic in flavor and taste.
2. Genever, which is full flavored, with a malty aroma and taste.
3. Flavored gin, which has the additional flavoring of a fruit, such as orange, mint, or lemon.

Vodka

Vodka is made from potatoes and various grains, mostly corn, with some wheat added. Vodka, like whiskey, is an alcoholic distillate from a fermented mash, but vodka is distilled at a higher proof and then processed still further to remove all flavors. Unlike whiskey, vodka is not aged.

Vodka is integral to many cocktails, such as the screwdriver, Bloody Mary, and vodka martini. If served straight, it should always be icy-cold. Flavored vodkas—with anything from fruits to hot peppers—have become popular in the United States. Some flavored vodkas are even sweetened slightly.

Vodka was first produced in Russia in the fourteenth century. It was distilled by the famous Smirnoff distilleries in Moscow, from 1818, until it passed out of the family's control during the 1917 Russian revolution.

Rum

Rum is distilled from the fermented juice of sugarcane, sugarcane syrup, sugarcane molasses, or other sugarcane by-products. Although distilled at less than 190 percent proof, it must be less than 80 percent proof at the time of bottling. Rum is produced wherever sugarcane grows, but most rums are produced in the Caribbean Islands.

Tequila

Tequila is a colorless or pale straw-colored liquor which originated in Tequila, Mexico. Most tequilas imported to the United States range from 80 to 86 percent proof, although some versions are over 100 percent proof.

Tequila is obtained from the distillation of the fermented juice (sap) of the mescal plant, called pulque. The mescal plant is a species of the agava plant, which is a cactus plant that takes between ten and twelve years to mature. At harvest time, its long leaves, or spikes, are cut off, leaving only the bulbous central core called the pina (pineapple). The pinas weigh between eighty and 175 pounds each. They are taken to the distillery where they are cooked in pressure cookers for several hours. Then they are cooled and shredded, and the juice is pressed out. The juice, along with fibrous pulp, is mixed with sugar, and the mash is fermented for about four days. To make tequila, the spirit must be redistilled to obtain the pure colorless liquor. It is then aged in oak barrels for approximately thirty-five to fifty-six days. Gold tequila is left for nine months or more in fifty-gallon oak barrels that give it its color. Premium tequila is aged for over three years. Tequila is the base liquor in the popular Margarita cocktail.

Aquavit

Aquavit is made from a fermented mash of either barley, malt, and grain or potatoes. It is flavored with caraway seeds. It is first distilled as a neutral spirit at 190 percent proof, reduced with water to 120 percent proof, and then redistilled with the flavorings. Caraway is the principal flavoring, but others, such as lemon and orange peel, cardamom, or anise, are used. It is similar in production to gin, except that the main flavor in aquavit is caraway rather than juniper berries. It is generally not aged and has an alcoholic strength of from 86 to 90 percent proof. It is the principle beverage of Scandinavia.

SO WHAT IS PROOF?

The alcoholic content of spirits is measured in proof, expressed as a percentage of volume of water to alcohol. The term was originated by the British, who found that if gunpowder was mixed with alcohol and water, it would burn, but only if a *specific amount* of alcohol was mixed with the water. If even the slightest amount of water above the limit was added, the gunpowder would not burn. The British used this test as a means of checking the alcoholic content of spirits. If the spirit burned, they said it was "proof" that the spirit contained an adequate quantity of alcohol.

In the United States, proof of a spirit is two times the percent of alcohol by volume or weight. Thus, if a spirit contains 50 percent alcohol, the proof is 100. It is important to know whether alcohol content is based on alcohol by volume or alcohol by weight. This is because alcohol is lighter than water, so it takes more alcohol to equal water weight.

Wines have less alcohol (7 to 14 percent) than spirits, and beers generally have the lowest alcoholic content (from 2.5 to 8 percent). Spirits range widely, from 50 to 190 proof percent, depending on the type of spirit and the brand.

Angostura Bitters

Although not an alcoholic beverage, angostura bitters is worthy of mention here because it is a vital ingredient in many mixed spirit drinks. It is the most renowned brand of bitters. Compounded in the West Indian island of Trinidad from the bitter and aromatic bark of the Cusparia tree and a number of aromatic herbs and roots, it was originally prepared as a cure for malaria and other tropical diseases. It has been known medicinally for centuries to the people of the West Indies and South America.

It is chiefly used today, a few drops at a time, in gin cocktails and other similar drinks. It can also pep up soft drinks. Although not generally known, angostura bitters can also be used to flavor soups and sweet dishes. Vanilla ice cream faintly flavored with angostura bitters is very good, as is fresh grapefruit.

BRANDY

The word "brandy" means distilled wine. Brandies are made by taking a wine base, from grapes or other fruits, and putting it through the distillation process.

Although brandies are made in countries around the world, the best known are those of Cognac and Armagnac. Although all cognacs and Armagnacs are brandies, not all brandies are cognacs or Armagnacs. Only those brandies produced in the Cognac/Armagnac region of France are entitled to carry the word cognac or Armagnac on the label.

COGNAC

Cognac is a brandy distilled from wine, made of grapes grown within the legal limits of the Charente and Charente-Maritime departments of France. The city of Cognac, on the Charente River, is the heart of the district.

Cognac is distilled twice in pure copper pot stills soon after the wine has stopped fermenting. The wine is warmed in a tank and then boiled away by a steady coal fire. Two distillations are needed to get the fraction with exactly the right amount of alcohol. The first distillation produces a liquid of about 30 percent alcohol called "brouillis." This is redistilled to make the raw cognac, known as the "bonne chauffe," which runs from the still white and clear at about 70 percent alcohol.

It takes ten barrels of wine to make one barrel of cognac. The new cognac, which is colorless, is then aged in oak barrels. It is the interaction between oak and brandy, as well as the continual oxidation that takes place through the porous wood, that gives cognac its superb and distinctive flavor. Cognac, like all brandies, ages only as long as it remains in wood; it undergoes no further development once it is bottled. It is not the vintage that matters, as with wine, but the number of years spent in wood. Two years in a barrel is the legal minimum for any cognac. However, most good cognacs have three to four years in wood.

The Xs and Os of Cognac

By law, cognac is ranked in three categories: VS, VSOP, and XO. VS means "Very Special," and is the basic level. VS cognacs must be aged for at least two-and-a-half years in oak casks before being bottled. However, the majority of cognac at the VS level is aged longer—usually four to seven years. VSOP, or "Very Special Old Pale," must be aged for a minimum of four-and-a-half years to be labeled as such. As with the VS level, most producers mature VSOP for much longer than the required minimum, in some instances as long as twelve to fourteen years. The oldest cognacs are the XOs, or "Extra Old." This level can also be referred to as Extra, Napoleon, Vielle Reserve, or Hors d'Age. The minimum age at this unique level is six years, but usually falls within the broad range of forty years. Rarely does any cognac spend any more than four decades in wood.

When you see the words "Fine Champagne" on the label, it signifies that the cognac is a blend of brandies from the two best growing districts, Petite Champagne and Grand Champagne. The "Big Four" distillers in the cognac industry are: Hennessy, Remy Martin, Courvoisier, and Martell.

ARMAGNAC

Armagnac shares its refinement and very high standards with cognac; however, the two brandies are poles apart in style and in the techniques used to make them.

Armagnac is a remote country region located in the heart of southwest France, between Toulouse on the east, Bordeaux and Bayonne on the west, the Pyrenees on the south, and the Garonne Valley on the north.

WELL, CALL, AND TOP SHELF SPIRITS

Liquor can be divided into two broad categories: well liquor (or house liquor or bar liquor) and "call" brand liquor. Well liquor is that liquor served when a guest doesn't specify a particular brand. If a lounge has Schenley in the "well" for instance and a guest orders a martini, it will be made with the Schenley.

If, however, the guest orders a Beefeater martini, the bartender will use Beefeater gin to make it. Beefeater is a "call" brand.

Most bars carry a range of each spirit, beginning with the "well" package. The well package is the least expensive pouring brand that a bar uses when a guest simply asks for a "scotch and water." The call package is the group of spirits that the bar offers to guests who are likely to ask for a particular name brand, for example, Johnnie Walker Red Label.

Additionally another range of spirits is referred to as "top shelf" or "premium well." Examples of top shelf spirits are such premium and super premium spirits as Johnnie Walker Black Label or Chivas Regal.

POPULAR "CALL" SPIRITS

Rums

Myers (Dark)

Barcardi (Light, Dark, Gold Reserve)

Mt. Gay (Dark)

Tequila

Cuervo Gold

Gin

Beefeater's

Gordon's

Tanqueray

Bombay

Vodka

Stolychnaya (Stoly)

Finlandia

Absolut

Rye

Canadian Club (CC)

Seagram's 7

Seagram's V.O.

Bourbon

Wild Turkey

Old Grand Dad

Jack Daniels

Blended Scotch

Cutty Sark

Chivas Regal (top shelf)

Crown Royal

Pims

Johnnie Walker Red

Johnnie Walker Black (top shelf)

Unblended Scotch

Glenlivit (top shelf)

Glenfiddich (top shelf)

Irish Whiskey

Jameson's

Black Bushmill's

REVIEW QUESTIONS

1. Explain the process of distillation and the types of stills in use.
2. List and discuss the major types of whiskeys, their flavor bases, their origins, and their different flavor profiles.
3. Outline and review the flavor base and production methods of gin, vodka, rum, tequila, and aquavit.
4. Explain the concept of proof.
5. Define the variations of brandies. Explain the basics of cognac, Armagnac, and the Xs and Os of ranking.
6. Recall and discuss the elements of well, call, and top shelf spirits.

17

Mixology

Outline

MIXOLOGY

Mixology is the art of mixing cocktails. The skills of mixology do not define a mixologist's or a bartender's personality.

Bartenders can be compared with chefs who follow a recipe or formula to produce a dish to specifications. They are the representatives of the establishment's culture, and therefore must serve guests in a manner that reflects the hospitality and atmosphere of the establishments in which they work. To be a good mixologist, or bartender, one has to do a great deal more than mix drinks.

Essentially bartenders deal with people who desire to be entertained or to escape from the pressures of their normal lives. The bar is the bartender's normal surroundings because it is that person's place of work, but for guests it is a haven away from the constant turmoil of society.

In addition to being a skilled mixologist, a bartender must be a focused "people person" with the skills of a diplomat, and the patience of a saint. Bartenders are discrete, and most are required to be amateur psychologists. Bar guests expect the bartenders to be experts on almost every subject known to man. They need to know directions; provide advice, encouragement, guidance, solve problems, know the weather forecast, relate sports results, and take telephone messages for guests; be current on all political events; and have mind-reading abilities. They must also administer aspirin, as well as providing fast, friendly, and courteous beverage service.

My good friend and former colleague at C.E.R.T., Walter Flood (one of the great bartenders of the world) had the acronym DDA printed beside his professional title on his business cards. When queried as to what these letters stood for, his reply was "Diplomat, Doormat, and Acrobat!"

TOOLS OF THE TRADE

Every craftsperson learns to use some type of tools. Accordingly, the bartender (mixologist) needs to know what these tools are, and to learn how to use them in an efficient, safe, and entertaining manner (mixologists are always on stage).

The Jigger

This is used to measure the ingredients poured into a glass. It is generally a one-ounce glass. There is a bias by some bartenders (and guests) against a controlled measure. Some bartenders tend not to like it because it can slow down service, and guests don't like it because they feel they are not getting as much liquor as they would with a "free pour" method. The bartender's use of a jigger can be likened to a carpenter's use of a ruler. Given the current state of liquor liability, however, most bartenders should use a measured shot as part of a responsible beverage effort.

Lined Shot Glass

This is a short, thick-walled glass that holds two ounces. It has a white line across the one-ounce level. This glass is used for straight shots of liquor such as whiskey, bourbon, gin vodka, and so on.

Speed Pours

Speed pours are inserted into a bottle of liquor to regulate the flow of liquid. They come in different speeds: slow, medium, and fast. Speed pours that are assigned to pour exactly one ounce can be difficult to work with, primarily because they have a tendency to airlock. This can be a major source of aggravation during rush periods. As a result many bartenders prefer the measured shot to a speed pour.

The Mixing Glass

This is the tallest glass in the bar. Most have a 16-ounce capacity. It is used to mix a "stirred cocktail." Stirred drinks such as martinis, Manhattans, and Rob Roys are among the most popular of all cocktails. (There are basically only three methods of mixing drinks—stirring, shaking, and blending.)

Bar Spoon, Strainer, and Shaker

These three pieces of equipment are used with the mixing glass. The bar spoon is a stainless steel spoon with a handle about ten inches long, and it is obviously used for mixing drinks. The strainer is the device to hold the ice in the mixing glass while the drink is poured into the cocktail glass. The shaker is the metal container (stainless steel) approximately the same size as the mixing glass. It has a secure top to allow shaking. The shaker is used to make blended and shaken drinks.

Blender

The electric blender is used for the same purpose as the shaker: to make blended drinks.

Ice Scoop/Tongs

As a matter of safety, practicality, and sanitation, the ice scoop is necessary to prevent the bartender from digging up the ice by hand or with a glass. The ice tongs should always be used to place ice in guests' glasses.

Ice Pick

The ice pick is one of the most useful of tools in a bar. It is used to break up large chunks of ice cubes which tend to freeze together.

METHODS OF BUILDING COCKTAILS

Shaking

Ice is placed in the shaker, the alcoholic beverage is added, followed by the other ingredients (carbonated drinks are never shaken). The top is placed securely on the shaker, and the ingredients are shaken vigorously for about ten seconds. Remove the top of the shaker. For service the cocktail is strained into the appropriate cocktail glass, garnished, and presented to the guest.

Blending

Blended cocktails are made in the same way as shaken drinks, except that drinks containing frozen, partially frozen, or solid ingredients must be blended. The addition of shaved ice to the blender produces frozen drinks. As in the shaking process, carbonated beverages should never be used.

Stirring

The process for making and serving stirred cocktails is the same as that for shaken cocktails, except that they are stirred, not shaken. However, carbonated beverages can be added prior to stirring.

Cocktail Imperatives

Build. To pour the ingredients directly into the glass. Add ice only if required by the recipe.

Dash. A splash, a tiny amount.

Float. A tiny amount of liquor.

Mix. To pour the ingredients into the cone of an electric mixer and mix. The drink is then strained into an appropriate glass.

Muddle. Muddling involves mashing or grinding herbs such as mint to a smooth paste in the bottom of a glass. A wooden muddler is best as it does not scratch the glass.

On the Rocks. An alcoholic drink served over ice.

Neat.   Served with no ice and not mixed.

Spiral.   A peel of fruit cut in a spiral way, used either in the drink or as a garnish.

Twist.   A longish strip of peel twisted in the middle and then dropped into the drink.

COCKTAIL PREPARATION

Contrary to popular opinion, the purpose of cocktails is not to get drunk or high. They were invented to stimulate the appetite. Therefore a sweet cocktail is a bad predinner drink. A sweet cocktail amounts to having four or five candies before dinner (not a great stimulant for the appetite!). Many people have picked up the idea that cocktails filled with fruit juices, grenadine, and syrup are what all cocktails should be. These type of "fun" cocktails are fine when they are not intended for predinner consumption.

What Should a Cocktail Be?

A cocktail should be tart and dry. That's the reason vermouth has always been the most popular of all cocktail ingredients. And because cocktails are intended to stimulate the appetite, obviously too many of them should not be consumed. One or two is the proper number. The amount of predinner cocktails a guest consumes determines the amount of wine they can safely consume with dinner. *(See appendix 2 for cocktail recipes.)*

BAR AND LIQUEUR GLASSES

There are many varieties of glasses used for drinks. These include:
- *Stemmed Cocktail Glass*
  (Used for martini or Manhattans; ranges in capacity from 3 to 4 1/2 ounces.
- *Whiskey Sour*
  Has a capacity of 3 1/2 to 4 1/2 ounces.
- *Old-Fashioned*
  Capacity of 6 to 9 ounces, average size is 8 ounces. Used for "on the rocks."
- *Standard Highball or Tumbler*
  8- to 12-ounce capacity, straight-sided shell or sham.
- *Cooler*
  Tall slim glass for summer beverages (Zombie, Collins); varied capacity; 14 to 16 ounces are popular, often frosted.

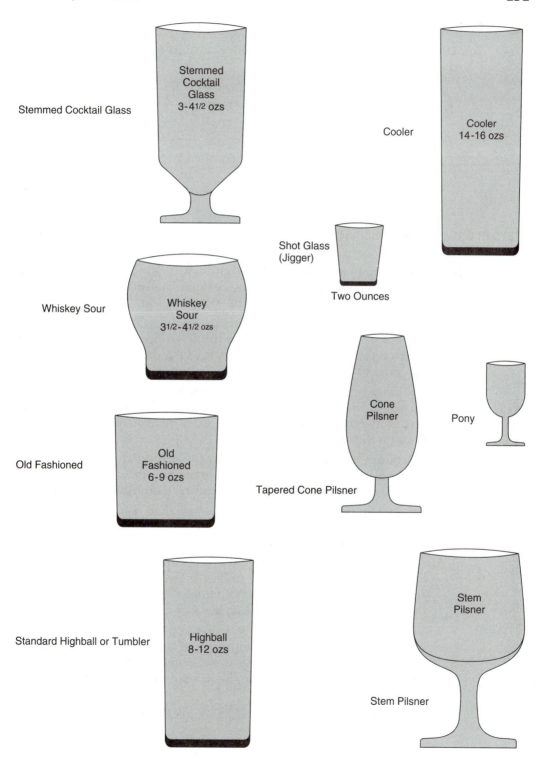

Stemmed Cocktail Glass

Stemmed
Cocktail
Glass
3-4½ ozs

Cooler

Cooler
14-16 ozs

Shot Glass
(Jigger)

Two Ounces

Whiskey Sour

Whiskey
Sour
3½-4½ ozs

Old Fashioned

Old
Fashioned
6-9 ozs

Cone
Pilsner

Tapered Cone Pilsner

Pony

Standard Highball or Tumbler

Highball
8-12 ozs

Stem
Pilsner

Stem Pilsner

Cordial, Liqueur

Sometimes referred to as a pony, one-ounce capacity is normal.

- *Shot Glass/Jigger*
  Lined or unlined, 1- to 2-ounce capacity.
- *Tapered Cone Pilsner*
  Beer glass with an 8- to 12-ounce capacity.
- *Stem Pilsner*
  As its name implies, it is a short-stemmed beer glass with an 8- to 12-ounce capacity.

STEPS IN BAR/BEVERAGE SERVICE

1. Place a napkin in front of the guest with the emblem facing the guest (if appropriate), smile and extend a greeting such as "Good morning" or "Good evening" and ask the guest, "May I serve you?" Suggest specific cocktails.

2. If there is more than one person in the group, take the order from left to right. If ladies are in the group, take their order first. Repeat the order to the guests when they have completed ordering.

3. Pay close attention to specific requests such as "with a twist," "no garnish," "on the rocks," or "very, very dry." This will help eliminate mistakes, guest dissatisfaction, and extra steps. Use shortened notations on the order form.

4. A whiskey service (jigger) glass must be used for measuring all drinks except for items which are served in a lined glass or a wineglass. Do not overpour or underpour. Try to pour without spillage.

5. Drinks should to be constructed as specified by the "House" and served in the proper glass, with proper garnish, unless the guest specifically requests a change.

6. Serve the ladies in the group first, and inform the guest as to the amount of the beverage sale. Collect money, ring up sales, present receipt, and thank the guest. Do not say "Do you need change?" as the guest may interpret this as an attempt for a bigger tip.

7. When collecting money in any denomination from a guest, always remind the guest of the denomination of the bill and the amount of the total check. This can help avoid potential problems, as many times a guest may think he or she has put out a bill of a higher denomination.

8. As soon as possible, the bar area should be cleared and wiped after guests depart.

9. Never use hands for handling ice. Use the ice scoop or tongs. Do not attempt to scoop ice up in a glass. This invariably results in chipped glass and can create the potential of litigation.

10. Return each bottle to its proper place after using it, so that you and other bartenders can reach for it without losing time looking for that bottle.

11. Be alert. Observe guests so that they do not have to strive to catch your eye for another drink.

12. Never fill a glass so full it spills over when the guest attempts to pick it up. Check for refills and needed extras before the guest is finished with his or her drink.

13. Present the check presentation folder. Pick it up and count the money before the guest leaves. Always thank guests and invite them back.

Bar Awareness

1. Bartenders are expected to monitor the barroom to ensure that guests are receiving the best possible service.

2. Acknowledge guests. Eye to eye contact is essential when acknowledging or dealing with a guest.

3. Be aware of boisterous, loud, or sloppy guests who already may be or are on their way to becoming intoxicated.

4. Observe the door and acknowledge guests when they enter. Be aware of potential problems with undesirable guests, and alert others if necessary.

5. Constantly survey the tables to see if any guests require attention. Alert other team members, or, when possible, take care of it yourself.

6. Be aware of intoxicated patrons and minors. You are responsible if you serve them alcohol.

REVIEW QUESTIONS

1. Describe a guest's expectations of a mixologist.

2. Identify the tools of the mixologist's trade.

3. Explain the cocktail building methods of shaking, blending, and stirring. State the cocktail imperatives of build, dash, float, mix, muddle, neat, spiral, and twist.

4. List the critical steps in effective and efficient bar service.

18

Intervention Procedures for Alcohol Service

Outline

The best known and most widely used alcohol service intervention program is TIPS (Training Intervention Procedures for Service of Alcohol). This is a certification program that informs participants about alcohol and the effects of alcohol on people, the common signs of intoxication, and how to help people to avoid drinking too much. It is available nationwide to provide training for servers of alcohol on ways to prevent alcohol abuse in restaurants and in other businesses where beverages containing alcohol are sold.

Through written materials, videotapes, and "role playing," bartenders, servers, and other team members learn important information on the effects of alcohol, how to identify potentially troublesome guests before they become a problem, and how they can deal with intoxicated guests or those who appear to be on the verge or overindulging without creating a scene.

COMMONSENSE APPROACH

TIPS is a practical, commonsense approach to helping prevent alcohol abuse. This training is an important asset for team members in dealing with this often difficult area of service. Research shows that laws in at least thirty-five states hold establishments liable for accidents caused by the intoxicated guests served at the establishment. And the number of lawsuits filed against hotels, bars, and restaurants is increasing each year.

Bartenders and other team members are legally responsible for serving either a minor or an intoxicated patron, and should never knowingly allow visibly intoxicated guests to enter the establishment or knowingly serve alcohol to intoxicated or underage guests.

An additional, potential problem of litigation may exist. Even if a drunk is not allowed to enter your establishment, you may still be liable. Technically, the police should be called and the intoxicated person detained until they arrive.

There should always be a certain amount of tact and professionalism used when it becomes necessary to end the service of alcohol to guests. If possible, explain to the guests in a diplomatic manner why they are being denied further service. The explanation should include the legal, moral, and safety issues for the guests, as well as for others. Be firm but polite. If the guests become abusive or outraged, tell them you will get a manager. Never second-guess yourself. Always "err" on the side of caution. Alert your other team members and the manager that you have denied service to someone and give as good of a description as possible of your rationale for this action.

MONITORING GUESTS' ALCOHOL CONSUMPTION

The simplest and most reliable way to monitor a person's degree of intoxication is by counting drinks. Only a carefully monitored breath analyzer is more accurate. A certain number of consumed drinks will signal when an intervention is necessary.

Also note how quickly a guest is drinking. Generally, a 150-pound person consuming four drinks (four ounces of alcohol) in an hour registers a 0.1 percent blood alcohol content (BAC) and is legally intoxicated (some states are have a lower BAC). Watch for these progressive symptoms of intoxication: lack of inhibition, followed by loss of muscular control, slurred speech, and impaired judgment.

If a guest seems to have reached his or her limit and asks for another cocktail, suggest a "mocktail" or something to eat instead. Encourage intoxicated guests to let a friend drive them home, or offer to call a cab. If you are serving a large group, suggest that someone become the "designated driver." Provide the driver with complimentary "mocktails." Call a manager and inform the manager of the situation. The intoxicated guest should be offered a cup of coffee or soda or other nonalcoholic beverage and allowed to remain on the premises, sobering up, if he or she is not unruly. If the guest is unruly, a taxi should be called and asked to take the guest to his or her hotel or home or place of residence. The establishment usually prepays the taxi for the cab ride.

If the guest has a friend, relative, or associate who is able and willing to take the guest home or to a place of his or her choice, management should request the person's phone number. The manager should call and ask the person to pick up the intoxicated guest. The intoxicated guest should be removed to a quiet area so as not to distract other guests and be provided with nonalcoholic beverages and perhaps a complimentary snack while awaiting the ride.

During an intervention, a person's behavior can be more easily managed if the person is provided with positive alternatives. Showing concern for the patron lessens the chance of confrontation.

Managing the intoxicated person requires skill, alertness, and patience; every situation is different. Role playing and reenactment of problem situations can become a regular part of team member meetings, developing greater confidence and perception among the team members. It can also be helpful to bring in a counselor or nurse from a community detoxification center or a local police officer to discuss the techniques they use when dealing with intoxicated persons.

MAKING AN INTERVENTION

As a server makes an intervention, it is important to remain calm: one must be quiet but firm, and not become defensive. The inebriated person will often not remember the encounter the next day. What someone who is inebriated says should not be taken personally, and a server should not get into a shouting match. Keep statements simple and direct; repeating statements can help reduce the chance of an aggressive escalation. Remember that the more complex behaviors, such as judgment, learning, and reasoning, are the first to be affected by alcohol. Trying to be rational and reasonable with an intoxicated guest can become quite frustrating.

Be assertive, and deal with issues at hand. Do not let the person sidetrack you. Making a statement such as "I am concerned about and want to be sure you get home safely" is much less threatening than "You have had too much, you are drunk and cannot drive."

A controlled drinking environment allows team members to pay more attention to guests, thereby increasing tips and creating a more enjoyable workplace.

Controlling intoxication is a challenge the hotel, restaurant, and retail alcohol beverage industry must meet if it is to continue to maintain the respect of the public. Training team members to recognize intoxication and to intervene in a nonconfrontative manner is one alternative, but preventing intoxication by creating a safe, responsible drinking environment is clearly the most sensible and cost-effective solution.

QUESTIONS REGARDING MINORS AND ALCOHOL SERVICE

In all states the legal drinking age is twenty-one years. Persons under the legal drinking age may not be served alcoholic beverages or be permitted to consume such beverages on the premises of the licensed operation.

If someone is suspected of being less than twenty-one years of age, proof of age should be requested. Proper identification consists of two pieces of identification, at least one with a recent photograph, preferably in color, and with signatures. It is proper to ask the person for a signature and compare it against the signature on one of the pieces of identification to see if they match. The person may also be requested to validate information on one of the pieces of the picture or photo identification. For instance, ask for the home street address, date of birth, color of eyes, and so on.

If adults order a drink for an underage person, it is important to know that this is illegal and cannot be permitted in a public establishment governed by the liquor laws of the state. Call a manager to the table. The underage person is not permitted to consume any alcoholic beverage on the restaurant premises regardless of who purchased the beverage or what may be done in the home.

The licensee is responsible for the "acts of their agents or employees," which means that the licensee is responsible, regardless or whether the license is on the premises, if an employee sells alcoholic beverages to a minor.

REVIEW QUESTIONS

1. Outline the fundamental concept and philosophy of "Training Intervention Procedures for Service of Alcohol" (TIPS).
2. Describe the methods of monitoring guests' alcohol consumption.
3. Explain the intervention steps a server may employ toward an inebriated guest.
4. Outline the major issues relative to minors and alcohol service.

19

Licensing and Legal Issues
Surrounding Alcohol

Outline

LEGAL ISSUES SURROUNDING ALCOHOL

The sale of spirituous liquors forms a very large segment of the foodservice industry. From the up-scale resort to the piano lounge bar, beer service in clubs, and minibars in guest rooms to the neighborhood tavern, the sale of alcoholic beverages represents a huge industry.

Each state has laws that regulate the sale of alcoholic beverages. Basically, according to these laws it is illegal to sell liquor without first obtaining a license from the state. States offer many different types of licenses; therefore, it is essential to obtain the type of license that permits the type of alcohol sales you intend to engage in, for example, an on-premise sale license is issued for a bar and for a liquor store, an off-premise license would be required. A restaurant license allows operators who derive most of their income from food to also sell liquor. Licenses may be granted to hotels, microbreweries, or even excursion boats.

A liquor license is one of the most valuable assets a restaurant can have. Loss of that license due to a violation of local liquor laws can be very costly. Typical violations include serving alcoholic beverages to minors or obviously intoxicated patrons, serving after legal hours, or employing individuals who are prohibited from working in licensed operations under the law.

ETHICS AND RESPONSIBILITIES ASSOCIATED WITH LIQUOR SALES

Selling alcohol has both its positive and negative sides. On the positive side, the alcoholic beverage industry is a great source of revenue for the government through taxes levied on alcoholic beverages. Moreover, alcohol is a profitable item for bars and restaurants. On the negative side, the abuse and misuse of alcohol cause many problems in our society.

Alcohol is an integral part of many of the celebrations and events of our culture. The New Year is customarily welcomed with a glass of champagne or sparkling wine, and weddings are frequently celebrated with festive alcoholic beverages.

Wine is part of many religious ceremonies. Sporting events, such as football or baseball, are often enjoyed with a cup of beer in hand, whether the fan watches from stadium seats or the living room sofa. It is common practice for many to enjoy a glass of wine with dinner and a cordial or liqueur afterward.

Because alcohol is consumed by such a broad cross-section of our society, it's not surprising that it has become our society's most abused drug. Unfortunately some people cannot control their consumption of alcohol, and as a result, become dependent and or dangerous after drinking it. The abuse of alcohol is a contributory factor to many of the problems of our society, including drunk driving. In fact the majority of automobile deaths among

American teenagers are alcohol-related. Because of its potential for abuse, alcohol is closely regulated.

LICENSES AND REGULATION OF LIQUOR SALES

Regulations governing the beverage industry fall into three categories: federal, state, and local communities, counties, or townships. The federal government controls the import of alcohol from foreign sources, and the production, labeling, packaging, and distribution of alcoholic beverages among states.

State governments regulate the distribution and taxation of alcohol within their borders. This may include such things as:

1. Location of the beverage operation.
2. Lawful times of operation.
3. Who may manage a bar.
4. To whom alcohol may be sold.
5. Whether alcohol may be consumed on the premises of an establishment or must be taken elsewhere.

LOCAL COMMUNITIES

To obtain a license, you must apply to the state liquor authority. If a license is granted, you may then engage in the activities that are permitted by that license. Each state has detailed rules and regulations with which you must comply.

Most states grant certain powers to communities and counties. These local option laws allow local governments to control the sale of alcohol within their jurisdictions. Towns, cities, and counties may pass regulations that are even stricter than state laws, or they may charge additional taxes. In fact local governments may choose to ban the sale of alcoholic beverages altogether. Therefore, communities in which the application for a license is being sought have a big say in whether they will agree to the granting of a liquor license.

A community usually restricts the number of licenses issued. Frequently the number of licenses issued is based on the population in that area; sometimes the ratio is computed to be one license for every one thousand persons. The community may also restrict the number of licenses by charging very high fees for the right to sell liquor.

Communities may also apply further restrictions. For example, they may specify: "No liquor establishment within three hundred feet of a school or church." Some communities modify this rule so that no bar entrance can be located "within three hundred feet of the main entrance of a church or school."

Communities are of course concerned about potential public nuisance caused by the licensed establishment. They generally monitor issues such as noise, drunkenness, fighting, crime, and other causes of public nuisances.

Those applying for a license must be of legal age, and not have been convicted of a felony.

Operations that sell alcoholic beverages are some of the most heavily regulated businesses in the country, for two different reasons: (1) to protect the revenue source for the government, and (2) to protect people from themselves.

THIRD-PARTY LIABILITY

A particular problem for hospitality and foodservice industry operations serving alcohol is third-party liability. This is the liability created by patrons served alcohol at an establishment who then cause damage. There are both specific statutes (Dram Shop Law) and common-law precedents governing this area. What is important is that the license holder, as well as the bartender (or servers of alcohol), may be held responsible for monetary damages caused by the person who was served at the restaurant.

Legal liability impacts operating expenses (the high cost of liability insurance) and the potential for lawsuits involving sales to minors and bar liability. To serve alcoholic beverages, an understanding of the legal framework of third-party liability is required. To understand what is meant by third-party liability, a simple but not an unusual set of circumstances demonstrates how dram shop liability has a trail.

The "Happy Hour" Drinker (A Case Study)

A college senior is coming home from football practice one evening. It is winter and it is dark outside, but the roads are dry and visibility is good. The young man is on a two-lane highway and sees a car approaching. For the most part it is staying on its side of the road, but it is beginning to swerve within its lane. As it gets closer, it strays across the double yellow line. He does what he can to avoid the oncoming vehicle. However, a head-on collision is unavoidable. Fortunately the young man is wearing his seat belt and is not ejected from the vehicle. However, he does sustain serious back, neck, and leg injuries. After a number of months of rehabilitation he recovers, but is told he will suffer some permanent leg problems that will cause him to walk with a slight limp.

The police send a copy of their accident report. Upon reading it, the young man discovers that on the night of the accident the driver of the other vehicle had been at a local bar. He would have been arrested for drunk driving except, unlike the young man, he did not wear a seat belt and was killed in the accident.

The issue becomes whether the deceased driver had too much to drink at the local bar. The bartender who was on duty at the bar the night of the accident was questioned. He stated that between the hours of 4:00 P.M. (the beginning of happy hour) and 6:00 P.M. when the other driver left the bar, he had consumed six double scotches. He left the bar after drink number six, and the accident occurred ten minutes later.

Dram Shop Law

The liability of the bar for those injuries is what is referred to as dram shop liability. Dram shop is another term derived from old English law. (A dram was a unit of liquid measurement equal to approximately one ounce or one shot, and a dram shop was a bar, a shop that served liquor by the dram—hence the term.)

Each state has its own laws regarding a bar's liability to an innocent victim of a person to whom they served liquor. A small number of states take the position that the bar should have no responsibility. Their reasoning is that it was not the bar that caused the injuries, it was the person that got in his or her car and drove while impaired. Other states take the position that the bar can be liable if it served the driver a drink when he or she was already drunk. Their reasoning is that it should be obvious to bartenders that if they serve a guest who is already intoxicated, he or she may operate a motor vehicle irresponsibly and cause an accident injuring another driver or pedestrian. Therefore, the bar must not serve such persons, they must be "cut off."

It is imperative that all hospitality operators be familiar with the dram shop liability imposed on them by the state in which they operate and that they strictly comply with the law. The service of alcoholic beverages is a very important part of the hospitality industry and can be very profitable. However, due to the nature of alcohol as a drug that can cause severe impairment, it must be dealt with properly.

REVIEW QUESTIONS

1. Outline and discuss the ethics and responsibilities associated with liquor sales.
2. Identify elements relative to the regulation of liquor sales. Describe the rules associated with the acquisition of a liquor license.
3. Describe third-party liability and Dram Shop Law.

20

Bar Theft and Special Problems

Outline

CONTROLLING LIQUOR COSTS

Alcohol beverage cost control is very different from food cost control, although there are similarities. The basic difference is that food cost control is primarily a problem of "product control," and liquor can be considered a problem of "personnel control."

On the other hand, liquor as a product is potentially much easier to control than food. It has few of the drawbacks of traditional food handling systems. Liquor is a homogeneous product. It is liquid, comes in glass bottles, generally all the same size, either quarts or fifths, and the packaging is consistent. Spirits are almost always packed twelve bottles to a case, and offer few storage difficulties. Liquor prices are far more stable than food prices. Variation of quality is not an area of concern—spirits are manufactured, and are totally controllable and generally standardized.

Liquor cost control appears to be easier to control than food cost, but in practice there is probably as much if not more mismanagement of beverage operations than food. This is why liquor control is primarily a "people control" challenge.

Liquor is not difficult to monitor, but the employees are; therefore, an effective set of controls must be put in place. The best control in a bar or lounge is simply supervision, and visibility. Supervisory visibility is an important factor in all operational areas, but most especially in the beverage cost control area. The vast majority of bartenders are honest and extremely diligent in their duties. However, sadly, some bartenders succumb to the temptation to steal or commit fraud. A common type of bar fraud encountered consistently is "short pouring."

Unfortunately no beverage control system is 100 percent perfect. However, beverage theft has to be kept to a minimum. With any system it is still possible for the dishonest or unscrupulous bartender to cheat both the guest and the establishment by pouring less than the desired amount. This becomes possible by pouring only one-fourth less per drink to sell so that the bartender may take home a bottle a day by cutting as small a volume of sales as 125 drinks daily.

Even with computers, sophisticated technology, and mechanical systems, a bartender may place a glass under the pourer and siphon off a portion of the measured amount. This is particularly easy to accomplish in service bars or when bottles are hidden or concealed so that the guest is unable to view the bartender's actions. The bartender might even place the merchandise that has accumulated into a nondeposit soda bottle and take it home when his or her shift is over. Should the bartender have access to cash, it becomes apparent that without ringing up a sale, he or she could collect money from a guest, sell the guest some of the stolen liquor, and still show the desired beverage cost percentage.

SIGNS OF BAR THEFT

The experienced dishonest bartender attempting this type of fraud may try to keep track of the amounts due by recording them somewhere. Signs of such things are broken matches or toothpicks which may mean that the bartender is counting how much he or she has stolen, so that they will know how much can be taken without affecting the beverage cost percentage.

There are several factors that increase risk of theft in a bar operation, as compared with a restaurant. The main factor is the intoxicating effect of alcohol on guests, the lack of tight inventory controls, and the different portion sizes served in most bars.

BAR THEFT OPPORTUNITIES

Servers in bars have more opportunities to steal from their employers and their guests than do servers in a restaurant. In a restaurant the server takes an order, delivers it to the kitchen where the cook prepares the food, which, once completed, is delivered to the guest by a server who may or may not be the same person who took the order. Once the guest is finished eating, he or she generally pays a cashier. The guest and employee transaction may be overseen by as many as four people, which greatly reduces the chance for theft.

This differs greatly in a bar operation. The bartender is in charge of all aspects of the transaction. He or she takes the order, prepares the drink, serves the drink, and collects the money. Because all the transaction elements center on only one person, the chance for theft increases. Even if the guest is sitting at a table, rather than at the bar, only one more person (the server) is added to the transaction, slightly reducing the opportunity for theft. The small number of people participating in the cycle increases the opportunity for theft, either from the bar or from the guest, or both.

People, as they drink, become less aware of what is going on or what they are drinking, opening the door for the possibility of being defrauded. After several drinks most people cannot tell the difference between the name-brand spirit they ordered and the nonname brand the bartender may have poured them. This allows the bartender to serve them a less expensive spirit and charge them for the more expensive spirit, pocketing the difference in price in the process.

CALCULATING BEVERAGE COST PERCENTAGE

There are two types of essential information required to understand and control alcoholic beverages, historical and analytical. Historical information outlines what has already happened, for example, the bar cost was 30 percent.

Analytical information, on the other hand, not only explains what has happened, but also why and how it happened.

An Example of Liquor Cost Differentiation

The overall bar cost was 30 percent versus a desired standard cost of 26 percent; the beer cost was 32 percent versus a standard cost of 31 percent, and the wine cost was 45 percent, the same as the standard cost.

The cost of distilled spirits was 25 percent, well over the standard of 20 percent. Banquet and catering costs were in line with the standard. Analytical information such as this makes decision-making easier. In this case it is obvious that there is no problem with beer, wine, or banquets. The entire cost coverage is evidently in spirits and on the main bar. There are still a lot of brands, hours of operation, and bartenders and servers to examine in order to see where the problem is, and even more detailed information would be helpful. If the variance to a particular bartender could be isolated, or to a specific shift, and if it could be determined that most of the excessive cost is in one type of spirit, such as Scotch, then troubleshooting and problem solving become even easier.

Beverage cost percentage is calculated in a similar way to food cost percentage. The method used most often is to determine first the unit cost and then mark up by the required percentage to arrive at the selling price. This number is generally rounded up or down to the nearest whole figure. The actual beverage cost percentage is then compared with the anticipated cost percentage, any discrepancy is investigated, and corrective action is taken.

However, cost, true cost, can only be obtained by the basic cost formula:

1. Beginning inventory (stock on hand, sometimes referred to as opening inventory).
2. Plus purchases (stock added).
3. Equals total stock or goods available.
4. Minus ending inventory (stock remaining).
5. Equals cost of goods sold or used.

INVENTORY SYSTEM

This inventory system is also called the ounce control system; it is an accurate but time-consuming and complicated method. The basic idea is that the standard usage of products is determined and then compared with the actual usage. It is similar to most food control systems in that it is product and cost oriented.

The system is set up as follows:

1. Obtain a daily count of every drink sold.
2. Calculate the liquor usage by multiplying the drinks sold by the amount of liquor in each drink.
3. Compare this calculated usage with the actual liquor used as determined by a physical inventory.

Although this will yield very useful information and can really help the operator zero in on problem areas, unless there is some type of electronic point-of-service (POS) equipment available so that the drink sales information can be readily, quickly, and accurately obtained, this system is not of practical use.

A point of departure from traditional control theory is the relative unimportance of percentages, but they are not a necessary part of this cost system. For example, if the gin-drink sales were all carefully tabulated and a calculation made that indicated that 15.4 bottles of gin should have been used for all purposes and physical inventories showed an actual usage of 15.5 bottles, there would be no problem. It is not necessary to make a percentage calculation. If the physical inventory showed a usage of 18.9 bottles, the percentage knowledge is still unnecessary. In the latter case, management would know that nearly 3.5 bottles of gin were used but not sold. The 3.5 bottles could have been stolen, wasted, spilled, given away, used for overportioning, sold but the money not collected, and so forth. Knowledge therefore of the percentage is of very limited use to management in so far as identifying and solving these problems.

PEOPLE CONTROL!

In many establishments beverage control revolves around "people control." Simple controls in response to liquor shortages often are the answer in many situations of liquor stock deficiencies. Some of the basic and elementary steps include checking what often are common items that can go unnoticed, such as the following:

1. Standardize cocktail recipes. If one bartender pours two ounces of gin and one ounce of vermouth into a martini and another bartender pours three and one-quarter ounces of gin and one-half ounce of vermouth, it becomes obvious that each bartender will have a different beverage cost percentage. Just as in food cost control, standardized recipes must be used by all bartenders to achieve the correct beverage cost percentage.

2. Standardized recipes in beverage operations are particularly important where large quantities of premixed drinks are made. This would normally be done (when legal) either for parties or for rush periods in which a large number of various cocktails (martinis, whiskey sours, daiquiris, and other cocktails) are sold.

3. Variations that may be undetectable when cocktails are made individually become quite noticeable when large numbers such as one hundred, or one thousand, are produced at a time. When these small deviations from the standard recipe are calculated over a period of time, they can cost the establishment considerable revenues.

4. Strange as it may seem, many bars use glasses of various sizes for the same drinks. Collins glasses and highball glasses normally have distinct differences in their capacities, and no bar should have two different-size collins glasses or two different-size highball glasses. Two glasses that look alike may actually hold different amounts.

5. If free pour is used, sometimes the same drink may be served in different glasses, such as drinks served on the rocks and straight up (stem glassware). Often the net capacities of the glasses are different. A martini straight up may be served in a four-ounce glass, but if it is served on the rocks, ice must be used and the total capacity of the glass may be more. If the glass is filled completely with ice, the amount of liquor that may be added may be more or less than for the stem glass.

6. Along with cocktail recipes and the use of standard glasses, the establishment must insist on the use of measuring devices such as jiggers. To allow a bartender to free pour is to give him or her the right to make portion decisions.

7. A great many hotels and restaurants have now moved to automatic beverage control systems. Modern, fast-developing computer technology has brought a level of sophistication and complexity to these systems. Most systems are integrated and produce instant access to sales, inventory levels, and cost of sales to revenue.

8. These systems measure out predetermined amounts of liquor when a button is pressed, and simultaneously display and record the correct sales price for the transaction.

ADVANTAGES OF USING COMPUTER OR AUTOMATED SYSTEMS

Automated beverage systems reduce many of the time-consuming tasks associated with controlling beverage operations. Although automated beverage systems vary, most systems can dispense drinks according to the operation's standard drink recipes and can count the number of drinks poured.

Automated beverage systems can be programmed to dispense both alcoholic and nonalcoholic drinks with different portion sizes. With many of the systems, the station at which drinks are prepared can be connected to a guest-check printer that records every sale as drinks are dispensed. Automated beverage control systems can enhance production and service capabilities.

Advantages include:

1. Less spillage of liquor, bottle handling is eliminated.
2. Overpouring is eliminated.
3. Accuracy—correct ratios of liquor are dispensed for cocktails.
4. Prevents tampering with the liquor supply.
5. Speed, as most bartenders can deliver an accurate ounce in approximately one second.
6. Accurate sales information, broken out into type of drinks sold.
7. Sanitation—less handling due to the closed nature of the system.
8. Uniformity of drinks—every drink is measured exactly the same.
9. Inventory control, instant access to available inventory.
10. Makes training of bartenders easier.
11. Eliminates pricing errors and tightens cash controls.
12. Much harder for bartenders to use their "own bottle."
13. Increased security.

Disadvantages include:

1. System failure, critical during busy periods.
2. Guests often don't like the system, primarily because of reduced brand identification.
3. The initial high costs of installing the system.
4. The possibility of lost sales due to the elimination of the personal touch.
5. Cost of maintenance.
6. Manual mixing is not totally eliminated. Not all brands can be accommodated by the systems.
7. Inability to handle special drinks.
8. Possibility of guest distrust.

The advantages may outweigh the disadvantages, but not in all cases.

No matter how well each system is designed, the experienced operator will find a way to bypass any control system. The possibility of stealing either merchandise or revenue always exists.

CHECKING FOR VARIANCES IN LIQUOR COST

To determine why liquor cost varies, the following set of guidelines may be used to find where discrepancies are:

1. *Inventories*
   a. Incorrect opening inventory figure.
   b. Incorrect ending inventory—miscount over or under.
   c. Incorrect inventory extensions, for example, whole bottles counted as tenths, or fifths counted as quarts.
   d. Incorrect inventory pricing—check invoices.

2. *Charges*
   a. Missing or incomplete requisitions.
   b. Requisitions to bar charged twice.
   c. Check transfer bills for proper charging.
   d. Incorrect assignment of beverage charges.
   e. Food department supplies being charged to beverage department food expense.
   f. Incorrect volume figures for period.
   g. Incorrect register/POS reading.
   h. Incorrect sales tax amount deducted (if appropriate).
   i. Recent state liquor tax increase?
   j. Recent liquor price increase by suppliers.
   k. Increase in sales tax.

3. *Sales Mix*
   a. Has there been a substantial change in sales mix?
   b. More name brands being sold.
   c. More beer being sold.
   d. More double liquor drinks being sold.
   e. More imported cordials being sold.
   f. More wine being sold.

4. *Drink Prices*
   a. Are correct prices being charged?
   b. Is pricing adequate?

5. *Par Stocks*
   a. Are they being maintained?
   b. Is merchandise missing?
   c. Are there constant par checks?

6. *Security*
   a. Is there a possibility of people gaining entrance after closing?
   b. Who has keys for gates or doors?
   c. Who locks up with bartenders?
   d. Are you sure there are no other keys available?

      e. Is it possible that spirits are being removed in other than original bottles?

      f. Do maintenance/cleaning crews have access to bar merchandise?

7. *Overpour/Spillage*

      a. Check whiskey service glasses every month for proper size.

      b. Check beer glasses for proper size.

      c. Do bartenders overpour when making highballs, rocks drinks or cocktails?

      d. Do bartenders spill abnormal amounts when building multi-drinks?

      e. Do bartenders free pour?

Basically overpour is a result of the bartender pouring a drink while holding the shot glass, and then dumping the drink into the highball or rocks glass. He or she commences dumping before the shot glass is full so as to avoid spillage, but then figures that to give the customer a full drink they should pour a little extra in the setup to compensate for this. Most often this results in excess of a one-ounce serving.

Spillage is usually a result of making two or three drinks (of the same brand) at one time. To expedite service the bartender snap pours one drink after another. This results in spillage between snaps.

8. *Cash Control*

      a. Was check recorded immediately after service?

      b. Was sale rung up on register/POS?

      c. Did sale rung on register correspond to number and type of drink served?

      d. Was check placed in front of customer immediately after sale?

      e. Did bartender charge customer one amount, then ring a lesser amount on register?

      f. A no-sale registered during a sale.

      g. Sale recorded with register drawer open.

      h. Were leftover stubs discarded (in trash) immediately after customer departed?

      i. Were there any leftover checks in evidence in service station area?

      j. Does bartender take abnormal time to count cash?

      k. Is bartender over or under in cash quite often?

9. *Liquor Control*

      a. Were all pourings (except liqueurs, brandies, wines, and beers) done with a shot glass?

      b. Was tall, unlined shot glass used for all drinks?

      c. Did bartender overpour or underpour?

      d. Did bartender free pour?

   e. Was proper glassware used for drinks?
   f. Were brand substitutions made?
10. *Basic Checklist—Cocktail Servers*
   a. Was check recorded for each round?
   b. Did the server take the check away after service?
   c. Was register/POS recording for proper amount?
   d. Did server have more checks on tray than parties on station?
   e. Did server discard leftover stubs in trash?

LIQUOR SHORTAGES!

The following are interesting instances of alcoholic beverage shortages discovered by Walter Flood (a colleague, friend, and wonderful bar professional) in the course of his training advisement on liquor control.

The "Bar" Fishing Pole

The liquor control system in a restaurant/bar frequently showed full bottles to be missing. This problem defied solution until a "spotter" was engaged to solve the case of the missing inventory. It wasn't long before the spotter discovered that an employee's prowess as a fisherman explained the situation.

At the close of business when all stock and bar areas were locked, the night cleaner would insert a fishing pole with a loop on one end through the mesh wire screen of the bar. Dropping it over the neck of a bottle and drawing it tight, he would lower the bottle to the floor, roll it with the aid of the pole to the opening between the screen and the floor, and make off with his catch.

Very soon there was a new cleaner, and no opening in the floor—and also no shortage.

The Refrigerator Compartment

In a small refrigerator were kept both wines and food for use after the main kitchen and storeroom were closed. The food was stored in the top compartment, which was not locked, and the wines in the bottom compartment, on which the steward had a special lock placed.

The control showed shortages of wines from this ice box and it was found that, as the shelf that divided the two compartments was removable, all a member of the night team had to do when a bottle of wine was wanted was to remove the shelf, reach down and help themselves. A lock on the food compartment solved this problem.

One Cash Register Too Many

The shortages encountered at a particular racetrack had all the control team members baffled. This occurred at an on-site casual catering operation in which permanent casual labor was used. The revenue continuously showed a shortage against closing liquor inventory. Careful observation was maintained on one bar where it was thought the shortages occurred. Despite the use of "spotters," nothing was ever discovered, that is, until an "unfortunate" bartender was involved in a minor fender-bender in the parking lot. The damage to his car caused the trunk to pop open. In the trunk a cash register was observed and reported to the authorities. The sham was up. The bartender had been operating his own cash till, bringing it in to the bar each time there was a race meeting.

Oversized Dispensers

Suddenly the beverage control report showed a daily shortage of over one hundred ounces of whiskey. For a week, in spite of a close watch, the cause could not be discovered.

It was then found that the new supply of whiskey dispensers from which individual "measures" of whiskey were served had a capacity of two ounces instead of one and one-half ounces. The difference in size was not noticeable, and the bartenders filled the glasses thinking they were serving only the prescribed amount. The larger dispensers were discontinued, and the shortage ceased.

The Cleaner with Expensive Tastes

The wine cellar of an up-market hotel maintained an inventory of expensive vintage Dom Perignon Champagne, on which a tight and careful watch was maintained, mostly because it was the most costly and valuable wine in the cellar.

It was soon noticed that the inventory and sales ratio for Dom Perignon was seriously out of line. Three bottles on average per week were missing over a period of three weeks. Intensive efforts were made to discover how this could happen. All the usual cash-to-inventory reconciliation methods were examined, and all failed to discover the shortfall.

The disappearance of the Dom Perignon was discovered by accident. Each day a cleaner was assigned to wash the cellar floor. This task was supervised by a manager. The cleaner used a large industrial-type mop and a large pail. His method was to wash the floor from the back of the cellar to the front, and when he finished cleaning, the cellar was relocked by the manager.

One particular day he was taking his mop pail full of dirty water from cleaning the floor to be emptied. He accidentally dropped the pail, and out rolled a vintage bottle of Dom Perignon, which was spotted by the manager. The mystery of the missing Dom Perignon was solved. The cleaner would place a bottle of the expensive champagne in the pail of dirty water at an opportune moment, and "mop" the Dom Perignon to freedom. Needless to say the cleaner was dismissed.

John's Short Pour

John, an excellent bartender, was much liked by his guests, colleagues, and supervisor. He was also a "short pourer." By short pouring all his drinks, he was able to pocket the additional cash from those guests who paid their bill and did not bother to get a receipt or to watch the register "rung up." The establishment was of course unaware and unable to observe any shortages, since by pouring short, John was able to keep his cost percentage right where it should be. For every $5 or $6 that the establishment takes in, John takes in $1 for himself, with no overhead or cost. John's shortages finally came to an end with the aid of a bar "spotter"—an experienced professional beverage controller versed in the habits of bartenders and short pours.

TWENTY-ONE WAYS TO ENSURE LOSSES IN A BAR

1. Permitting bartenders to mix all drinks according to their own individual recipes and ideas of portion sizes.
2. Not using a "jigger" to measure the ingredients of a mixed drink.
3. Not maintaining a "par stock" at each bar.
4. Not charging the bar for the olives, cherries, sugar, and other food items.
5. Placing wines and liquors within easy reach of those who might like to take a bottle home without taking the trouble of paying for it.
6. Failure of management to maintain positive control over sales and service from the bar, not reconciling inventory to sales, and assuming that there is no scamming going on in the bar.
7. Permitting an inexperienced employee to do the buying according to their own judgment of needs and quality.
8. Permitting wine and liquors to be issued from the cellar or storeroom to the bar without properly signed requisitions.
9. Not recording any requisitions.
10. Using inexperienced people as bartenders.
11. Not taking a physical inventory, and relying entirely on book or mechanical inventories.
12. Having inventories taken by persons who are also responsible for the storage and service of wine and liquor.
13. Permitting wines and liquors to be received, accepted, signed for, and stored without examination.
14. Selling mixed drinks for the same price as straight drinks. Allowing poor beer pouring and wastage.

15. Allowing bartenders to have a drink on the house occasionally which can become a big problem with regard to alcohol abuse.

16. Paying minimum wages to bartenders and allowing them to make up the difference between that and a living wage from the bar.

17. Permitting the bartender to serve drinks "on the house."

18. Not locking up the bar stock at night.

19. Not using the correct ingredients for certain cocktails.

20. Undercharging certain favorite guests of the house.

21. Saving the small cost of having a capable company install simple technology for wine and liquor control methods.

REVIEW QUESTIONS

1. Outline the essential difference between liquor control and food cost controls.

2. Explain the "opportunity" for theft and dishonesty within a bar operation.

3. Identify the methods of calculating beverage cost percentage and the different methods used to determine the cost.

4. Describe some of the methods employed to deal with liquor inventory discrepancies.

5. Describe the advantages and disadvantages of automated beverage control systems.

6. List and describe the steps for checking for discrepancies and variances in liquor cost.

21

Alcohol and Its Effect on the Body

Outline

ALCOHOL: HOW IS IT MADE?

Alcohol is a liquid whose chemical name is ethyl hydrate. It is derived from the reaction of double decomposition of glucose (sugar) by yeast. This process is termed fermentation. There are other forms of alcohol which can be chemically made. Ethyl alcohol is, however, the only alcohol produced in any quantity that is reasonably safe to drink.

Alcohol is made by fermenting naturally sweet fruit juices (musts), such as grapes, apples, pears, plums, or grains such as corn, rye, and barley, in which the natural process of converting starch to sugar has begun. The distillation of these musts into a purer or more concentrated form produces a high-proof beverage.

The strength of alcohol produced by natural fermentation normally cannot exceed 14 percent. Above this strength the alcohol renders the yeast impotent. Wine, or any other beverage requiring greater strength than this, must have alcohol added. This is called fortifying. Wines of less than approximately 14 percent alcohol content tend to have shorter storage life than those of higher proof. Fortified wines such as port or Madeira, with proofs ranging upward of 23 percent, have a life of over one hundred years.

ALCOHOL: STIMULANT OR DEPRESSIVE?

Alcohol is a food substance that passes direct and unchanged from the stomach and intestines into the bloodstream.

Alcohol is not a stimulant as most people believe; it is in fact a depressant. Figures indicate that 70 percent of the adult population in the United States drink an alcoholic beverage.

Alcohol is a food product that is classified as an intoxicating drug that depresses the brain and central nervous system. Alcohol contains what is described as "empty calories." One ounce of pure alcohol (100 percent) contains 210 calories. One ounce of whiskey (43 percent alcohol = 86 percent proof), has 75 calories, and a 12-ounce bottle of beer has 150 calories. These "empty calories" contain no vitamins, minerals, or other essential substances. Alcohol does interfere with the body's ability to use other sources or energy.

ALCOHOL AND DIGESTION

Alcohol requires no digestion and is absorbed through the bloodstream and transported to all parts of the body in a very short period of time. A small amount is immediately taken into the bloodstream by way of the capillaries in the mouth. The remaining portions travel to the stomach, where 20 percent is absorbed through the stomach lining. If food is already present in the stomach, the alcohol mixes with it and prevents the remaining amount of alcohol from moving into the small intestines where the remaining 80 percent is absorbed into the bloodstream. The amount of food in the stomach is an important factor when drinking because it slows down the absorption of the remaining 80 percent of alcohol as the stomach completes its digestion of the food.

The door between the stomach wall and small intestine will remain closed as long as there is food to be digested, and it is sensitive to the presence of alcohol. When a person overindulges, the large concentration of alcohol tends to get "stuck" in the closed position. When this pylorospasm happens, the alcohol trapped in the stomach may cause sufficient irritation and distress. (It's a self-protective mechanism to prevent overconsumption of alcohol.)

Once in the small intestines, alcohol is absorbed by the bloodstream and becomes the body's transportation system. Alcohol is soluble in water and is able to pass through the cell walls.

The percentage of alcohol as well as the presence of carbonation are important factors in the rate of absorption. The higher the percentage of alcohol the quicker it is absorbed into the bloodstream. Beer has some food substances that will slow down the absorption rate. The rate of absorption into the bloodstream determines the level of intoxication. The faster the alcohol is absorbed the more rapidly the blood alcohol level rises and the greater the impairment.

SPEED OF ALCOHOL ABSORPTION

This is dependent on the following factors:

1. The rate of consumption.
2. A person's height and weight.
3. The amount of food in the stomach.
4. Gender, because females have less water in their system to dilute alcohol, where men have more water. The amount of water in the body determines the blood alcohol concentration. Also there is a certain enzyme in the stomach that helps our system to speed metabolism of alcohol. Greater quantities of this enzyme exist in a man's stomach.
5. A person's mental disposition, for example, moods swings, from high to low, or a state of general depression.
6. If the person is taking some form of medication, this speeds up the effects of alcohol.
7. The greater the strength of the alcoholic beverage, the higher the percentage of alcohol, the faster it enters the bloodstream.

8. The type of alcoholic beverage, that is, carbonated drinks enter the bloodstream faster, straight distilled spirits are second, followed by cream and juice based drinks, wine then beer (which contain carbohydrates that will slowdown absorption in the stomach).

BLOOD ALCOHOL CONCENTRATION

Blood alcohol concentration (BAC) represents the alcohol content of any body tissues composed of water. The tissues' alcohol content varies in proportion to the amount of water. It takes very little time for the tissues to absorb the alcohol circulating in the blood. For example, within two minutes the brain tissues reflect accurately the blood alcohol level. The higher the concentration of alcohol (up to 43 percent or 86 percent proof) the faster it is absorbed. Impairment is based on both the amount absorbed and the rate of absorption.

Alcohol will affect the brain and central nervous system more rapidly than any other organs in the body. The concentration of alcohol causes the effect of intoxication and or impairment.

Behavioral changes are related to the concentration of alcohol in the blood, and usually follow a recognizable pattern, beginning with a loss of inhibition, progressing to slurred speech, loss of concentration, and aggressiveness, and culminating in loss of consciousness.

DIFFERENCES IN BAC AND WOMEN

A 120-pound female would get intoxicated faster due to a higher proportion of fat and correspondingly lower amounts of water. Alcohol is not fat soluble. A female and a male at the same body weight, both drinking the same amounts of alcohol, will have different blood alcohol levels. Hers will be higher due to less water in her body to dilute the alcohol. The difference in weight and body fat will speed up the absorption rate so that with:

1. One drink in one hour = BAC .03.
2. Two and a half drinks = BAC .07.
3. Five drinks = BAC .14.
4. Fifteen drinks = BAC .45 (in a coma at this stage).

Most states define 0.10 BAC as legal intoxication. (Some states define intoxication as 0.08 BAC, and some suggesting this should be lower.)

BREAKDOWN AND REMOVAL

The removal of alcohol from the body begins as soon as the alcohol is absorbed by the bloodstream. Ten percent of the alcohol consumed is excreted through the breath, sweat, and urine. The rest has to be changed chemically. The alcohol has to metabolize and change to acetaldehyde. The acetaldehyde breaks down very rapidly to form acetic acid. It then leaves the liver and is dispersed through the body, where it is oxidized to form carbon dioxide and water, so that 90 percent is metabolized and excreted by the liver. The liver is the key organ in the breakdown process. The rate alcohol is metabolized by the liver may vary a little between individuals.

EFFECTS ON A PERSON'S HEALTH

Although moderate drinking causes no direct harm, continued heavy drinking can result in permanent damage in the following areas:

1. Digestive system.
2. Circulatory system.
3. Central nervous system.
4. Brain.
5. Liver.
6. Kidneys.

ALCOHOL AND DRUG ABUSE

Drug-Free Workplace Act (1988)

The Drug-Free Workplace Act requires each employer-holder of government contracts to certify to the federal contracting agency that it will provide a drug-free workplace by publishing a company policy statement describing unlawful behaviors, required employee employment conditions, and violation penalties; by publicizing the program within the company; and by taking appropriate disciplinary or rehabilitation step for violators. This act does not mandate drug testing. It applies to employers with employees that hold or seek federal contracts of $25,000 or more and on federal grants.

Penalties may be suspension or termination of grants and/or debarment from the federal procurement process for up to five years.

The regulatory agency for the Drug-Free Workplace Act is the Federal Contracting Agency.

Consequences of Abuse

It is estimated that drugs and alcohol abuse costs U.S. businesses over $150 billion annually in lost productivity, and that one in four U.S. workers has personal knowledge of coworkers using illegal drugs on the job. Additional industry statistics reveal a strong correlation between substance abuse and decreased productivity, increased employee absenteeism, requests for early shift releases, and workers' compensation claims.

Employees working under the influence of drugs or alcohol function at approximately two-thirds of their potential.

It is estimated that one out of every sixteen workers in the United States is affected by alcohol. This results in lost work time, declining productivity, and increased absenteeism. Alcohol abuse has been a problem for the hospitality industry in general. Many theories for its prevalence have been put forward, from the notion that its accessibility contributes to the problem, to the idea that employees watching and observing others enjoy themselves while they work unsocial hours. It has been suggested that the unsocial hours that foodservice team members work encourages the use and, sadly, the abuse of alcohol.

APPROACHES TO ALCOHOLISM

The approach to handling alcoholism is to monitor all team members regularly and systematically. Mention of alcoholism should be avoided. The team member should be allowed to seek aid the same as they would for any other health problem.

Drug abuse among workers is one of the wider societal issues confronting industry in general. Although alcohol is the most abused substance, marijuana, cocaine, heroin, crack, and varieties of abused prescription drugs are found to be in use in the foodservice industry.

THE MOST COMMONLY ABUSED DRUGS

The most common illegal drugs that plague the hospitality industry include the following stimulants or (uppers): amphetamines (benzedrine, dexedrine, methamphetamine, "speed"), cocaine, crack (smokable cocaine), and crystal methamphetamine or "ice." Sedatives (downers) complete the drug inventory. These include alcohol (alcohol is a drug and is regarded as such by foodservice and hospitality organizations), Barbiturates (tranquilizers or sleeping pills), codeine, Demerol, heroin/opiates, loads (codeine and Doriden, which produce a semicomatose condition), marijuana/cannabis, Valium, and Xanax.

MEDICAL CONSEQUENCES

Some of the medical consequences and toxic effects from the abuse of stimulant drugs (uppers) and sedatives (downers) include the following: sweating, foul body odor, poor dental traits, rapid pulse, dilated pupils, euphoria, agitation, progressive weight loss, and insomnia followed by hypersomnia.

As the substance abuse continues, the medical consequences become more severe: premature aging, lethargy, slurred speech, depression, mood swings, sinusitis, bronchitis, dry mouth, heart palpitations, heart infections, heart attacks, strokes, blood infections, tuberculosis, impairment of the immune system, and AIDS through sharing needles with other infected users.

THE TELLTALE SIGNS

Indicators of chemical dependency in the workplace include:

1. Frequent absences.
2. Longer absences.
3. Multiple instances of unauthorized leaving of the workplace.
4. Excessive morning or noontime tardiness.
5. Increased number of "cuts" during workday.
6. Difficulty in concentrating.
7. Difficulty in recalling simple instructions.
8. Increased inability to learn from or recall previous mistakes.
9. Alternating periods of high- and low-work performances.
10. Marked inattention to detail.
11. Increased overt boredom, tiredness, or disruptive behavior.
12. Marked decline in productivity.
13. Missed deadlines.
14. Increased excuses for incomplete, missing, or unacceptable work.
15. Increased signs of disorientation, frequent instances of loss of train of thought.
16. Sleeping on the job.
17. Lowering of ability to assume responsibility.

Within emotional and personal crises, alcoholism and drug abuse are considered to be personal matters. They also become the supervisor's problem when they affect a team member's ability to perform satisfactorily in the workplace.

EMPLOYEE ASSISTANCE PROGRAMS

More and more employers are making a more humane response to employee wellness through adopting EAPs (Employee Assistance Programs). These programs are in place to help team members overcome problems, and they provide guidance and referrals to outside professional help.

In addition, Alcoholics Anonymous, church support groups, and various hospital therapy programs are excellent and inexpensive routes to rehabilitation.

The wellness model implies a continuum rather than a sick or well choice. It includes psychological wellness as well as physical wellness. Wellness programs are designed to help team members with substance addictions while aiding them with other personal problems. Help may be offered in the form of outside counseling by referrals to agencies specializing in problem resolutions. Many employers agree to pay for the initial visits and/or cover the entire treatment cost through their insurance plans. Organizations who invest in wellness programs report that these programs make a significant contribution to employee retention, and the investment in these programs has financial and practical impact with decreased absenteeism and improved productivity.

REVIEW QUESTIONS

1. Identify the makeup of alcohol and describe its effect on the human body.

2. Explain alcohol—its digestion and its absorption into the human body.

3. Describe and discuss what Blood Alcohol Concentration (BAC) is. Outline its breakdown and removal and its effect on male and females.

4. Describe the effects of alcohol and drug abuse relative to personal health.

5. Outline the principles of Employee Assistance Programs. Explain the benefits and philosophies of such programs.

Part Four

Toward Teamwork

An Overview of:

The Critical Elements and Issues Related to Sanitation and Safety

Approaches to Diversity, Respect, Leadership, Quality Management, and Training

Issues of Teamwork Relative to a Holistic Approach to Guest Satisfaction

22

Issues of Sanitation

Outline

SANITATION AND HEALTH

Guests rate and judge the cleanliness of a foodservice operation in all phases of their dining experience. Both consciously and unconsciously, they use their sense of smell to determine whether an operation is acceptable. They scan the appearance of the exterior and the interior of the establishment to determine the general level of maintenance and sanitation. They judge team members by their personal hygiene, the cleanliness of their uniform, and their general grooming.

However, a lack of sanitation in a foodservice establishment has more serious consequences than the negative impressions given to the public by unclean conditions. Unsanitary conditions and careless handling of food, equipment, and utensils can result in the spread of disease, food poisoning, and even death.

The U.S. Public Health Service has identified sixty-two diseases that are communicable to humans through human to human or animal to human channels.

Over 10,000 people annually in the United States have diagnosed incidents of food poisoning of various types. Many other incidents apparently take place, but go unreported. Food poisoning is, in the main, a direct result of a lack of sanitation.

The key to having a sanitary foodservice operation is education and training. All team members must become knowledgeable about sanitation. Persons who prepare and serve food for guest consumption should know the purpose of and how to use the Hazard Analysis Critical Control Point (HACCP) system. The HACCP system enables an operation to identify the foods and procedures most likely to cause illness. It also establishes procedures to reduce the risk of foodborne illness outbreaks and allows management to monitor and ensure food safety. To be successful, an HACCP system needs an involvement and commitment from all team members. Effective day-by-implementation involves all employees who receive, store, cook, and serve food.

THE SEVEN PRINCIPLES OF THE HACCP SYSTEM

1. Assess the hazards at each point in the flow of food through the operation Hazards include any biological, chemical, or physical factors that may cause an unacceptable risk to the health of the guest and team members.

2. Identify the critical control points. A critical control point is any step in the preparation of an item in which a preventative control can be implemented to eliminate or prevent potential hazards. It is important to observe the preparation, holding, and service processes, as well as team member care in handwashing and food handling. Flowcharts can be used to map the steps in the processing of food items in order to monitor areas of concern.

3. Set up procedures for critical control points. This step involves the establishment of key activities at each control point. These activities should be well defined, observable, and measurable. For the procedures to be effective, team members must be trained properly and provided with the proper tools and equipment.

4. Monitor critical control points. Using a flowchart (step 2) as a guide, examine each point through which the potentially hazardous food passes, and make sure that the recommendations at each point are being followed.

5. Take corrective action. If problems are discovered in the monitoring of control points, quick and corrective action must be taken to remedy the problems. Management must ensure that control procedures are followed. Repeated problems or infractions may indicate a need for retraining.

6. Set up record-keeping procedures. Documentation should be maintained in order to monitor the success of the system and to provide information to aid in its periodic updating.

7. Verify that the system is working. Spot-checks must be made to ensure that critical control points are under control. A common misconception is that if a system is in place it is being used correctly. Therefore, frequent checks are essential.

SANITATION: A WAY OF LIFE

The word sanitation is derived from the Latin word *sanus*, meaning sound and healthy, or clean and whole. The modern interpretation of the term is broad, including knowledge of health and of sanitary conditions, as well as the full application of sanitary measures.

Only since the work of Louis Pasteur was the way made possible to the understanding of infection as the cause of communicable diseases. The route of infection was found to be from person to person, from person to spoon, cup or plate to person, or from person to food to person. In most, if not all, cases, the human element is found in the pattern.

Sanitation must be a way of life in the hotel and foodservice industry. It is a quality of living that is expressed in cleanliness. Being a way of life, it must come from within each team member. It is nourished by education and training and grows as an ideal in first-class foodservice operations.

BACTERIA

The presence and growth of bacteria in food depends on the opportunities for their introduction at some stage of the food handling and service process. Some bacteria grow best on low-acid foods, others in acid foods, and still others (the majority come in this category) prefer food that is neither acid nor base. Some grow best if sugar is present in the food; others, if gelatin is a component part of it; and still others, if proteins are present. Some need air for growth, and others thrive in its absence.

TEMPERATURE DANGER ZONE (TDZ)

Most organisms, including bacteria, function most effectively within a certain range of conditions. The temperature most favorable to bacterial growth is between 60 to 110 degrees F. Temperatures below 45 degrees F inhibit their growth, and temperatures above 160 degrees F tend to be lethal to many varieties.

Once in this temperature range, the bacteria must have enough time to multiply to significant numbers to cause a problem (bacteria multiply by their own number every twenty minutes).

Some bacteria can and will grow in a freezer at 0 degree F, and some will survive and grow in a holding box at 155 degrees F. However, most bacterial action occurs within the range called the *Temperature Danger Zone (TDZ)*, which is 40 degrees F to 140 degrees F. Room temperature and body temperature are within the TDZ, which is why these bacteria cause so many problems in food. Food spends time at room temperature while being prepared. Once it enters the human body the temperature is conducive to growth.

COMMUNICABLE DISEASES: WHAT ARE THEY?

As previously discussed there are at least sixty two different communicable diseases. A common route of travel is from person to person through direct contact. This direct contact is made through carriers or infected persons. A "carrier" is defined as a person who, without symptoms of a communicable disease, harbors and gives off the specific bacteria from his or her body. An "infected person" is one in whose body the specific bacteria are lodged. An infectious disorder of the respiratory system, such as the common cold, may be spread by a droplet of infected discharges from coughing and sneezing without safeguards. An indirect route of infections spread through respiratory discharges is by the used handkerchief, the contaminated hand, and the subsequent handling of plates and cups in serving.

The realization by team members of the meaning of good health, the importance of good health habits, and how to maintain them is of major concern in any sanitation training program.

PERSONAL HYGIENE AND HEALTH

Personal hygiene and good health include clear skin, lustrous hair, good appetite, the ability to work without undue fatigue, and freedom from colds, headaches, or other physical disturbances. Team members possessing these attributes have enthusiasm, buoyancy, optimism, and zest for their jobs. The desirable habits of personal hygiene are obtaining adequate sleep and rest, bathing daily, caring for the skin and hair, following an adequate diet, wearing clean clothes, and taking an interest in personal grooming and appearance.

PERSONAL SANITATION CHECKLIST

A checklist for use in inspecting team members usually covers the following points:

1. Good posture; clean, well-fitted uniform; clean, well-kept hair; clean hands; clean, well-kept nails; clean skin; lack of any body odors; and freedom from colds or other respiratory difficulties.
2. Protective measures taken by wearing hairnets, hats, and caps should be observed by all food production team members.
3. Clean aprons, clean uniforms, and comfortable, well-fitted shoes are essential.
4. Elimination of jewelry and avoidance of excessive makeup and nail polish are common requirements.

Correct sanitary work habits of team members must be stressed at all times.

CORRECT SANITARY WORK HABITS

1. Hand Washing
   Washing hands with soap and water upon reporting for work, whenever hands are soiled, after use of a handkerchief, and, above all, after each visit to the rest room.
2. Work Areas
   Keeping work surfaces clean and the work area well organized and orderly so that each part of the work may be carried through to completion without hazard.
3. Food Service—Serving Food
   Using only clean utensils in preparing, cooking, and serving food.
4. Utensils
   Keeping fingers and hands out of food as much as possible. Using spoons, forks, tongs, or other appropriate utensils.
5. Proper Utensil Use
   Grasping utensils such as spoons, spatulas, tongs, and forks by handles.
6. Glassware and Cups
   Picking up and conveying glasses by the bases, cups by their handles, and plates by the rims, being careful to avoid possible contamination of the serving surface.

7. Tasting Food
   Using a clean spoon each time for tasting food.

8. Smoking
   Observing the "no smoking" rule in the preparation and serving areas.

9. Cleaning Up
   Refrigerating unused foods and the clean up of any spillage promptly.

10. Sanitation Courtesy
    Extending the same sanitation courtesy to guests and other team members that you would like to receive from them.

AIDS (ACQUIRED IMMUNE DEFICIENCY SYNDROME)

In recent years few workplace issues have received as much attention as AIDS (Acquired Immune Deficiency Syndrome). This is particularly important for the foodservice industry from the standpoint of transmission of the virus.

There is no evidence that AIDS can be transmitted through casual contact or through food preparation. One of the major problems that employers face is the fear that fellow team members and customers have of contracting the illness. Because no cure or vaccine for AIDS presently exists, many foodservice organizations are turning to education as the most viable means of combating both the medical and social dilemmas posed by AIDS.

The potential benefits of an AIDS education program for team members are:

1. Prevention of new infections among individuals by helping everyone understand how HIV is and is not transmitted. (HIV is the first stage in full-blown AIDS.)

2. Alerting managers and supervisors to the legal issues raised by HIV infection in the workplace.

3. Education programs help prevent discrimination by fearful or misinformed employees. Through education, the same team members are equally capable of creating a humane and supportive (and therefore healthy) working environment.

Individuals who test HIV positive are protected under the Americans with Disabilities Act (ADA). This act provides comprehensive civil rights protection to individuals with AIDS. It bans discrimination against people on the basis of their disability.

Employers are prohibited from dismissing or transferring infected team members out of food handling duties simply because they have AIDS or have tested HIV positive. The majority of AIDS-related lawsuits in the past have been related to the workplace, and usually have involved discrimination and confidentiality.

REVIEW QUESTIONS

1. Discuss the importance of sanitation relative to customer perceptions.

2. Describe the imperatives of correct sanitation in regard to health.

3. Outline and restate the seven principles of HACCP.

4. Explain the critical elements inherent in the Temperature Danger Zone (TDZ).

5. Identify what communicable diseases are, and discuss the elements of correct personal sanitation.

6. Indicate the critical issues associated with AIDS and the foodservice industry.

23

Safety

Outline

We care about each other and we don't want people to get hurt. We monitor our environment continually, and immediately address areas of concern which threaten the life or injury of our colleagues or guests.

—Fairmont Hotel Core Values

Safety is closely related to sanitation and is also of great importance to the well-being of both team members and guests. Sadly for many years the food-service industry has had a poor safety record. The nature of the work requires the use of many pieces of equipment and tools that can cause cuts and abrasions. The steam, electricity, and gas used in foodservice facilities are potentially dangerous sources of explosions, burns, and accidental shocks to employees. Foods served at very high temperature present a danger to both guests and team members.

The term accident implies a random act or occurrence, or something that is unavoidable. Most such occurrences in foodservice operations are preventable.

An accidental injury to a guest may result in litigation against the food-service organization and a monetary judgment against it. At the very least, it can create bad publicity for the facility and discomfort for the guest.

Additionally an accident to a team member causes the loss of their services for a period of time. The establishment may be required to pay a higher workers' compensation insurance premium because of an increase in accidents.

Federal law requires that a safe working environment be provided for all team members and guests. Common sense demands that a safe establishment be maintained for everyone who enters.

Moreover, foodservice employers are required by law to provide working conditions that do not impair the safety or health of employees or, indeed, any other unit or department team members. Therefore, an environment must be provided that protects employees from physical hazards, unhealthy conditions, and unsafe or dangerous practices by other team members.

OCCUPATIONAL SAFETY AND HEALTH ACT (OSHA)

In the late 1960s, Congress became increasingly concerned about workplace injuries and worker deaths. Eventually, these concerns led to the passage of the Occupational Safety and Health Act (OSHA) in 1970.

The Occupational Safety and Health Act of 1970 was passed "to assure so far as possible every working man or woman in the Nation safe and healthful working conditions and to preserve our human resources." Every employer engaged in commerce who has one or more employees is covered by the act. Federal, state, and local government employees are covered by separate provisions or statutes.

The act established the Occupational Safety and Health Administration, known as OSHA, to administer its provisions. The act requires that in areas in which no standards have been adopted, the employer has a general duty to provide safe and healthy working conditions. Employers who know of, or who should reasonably know of, unsafe or unhealthy conditions can be cited under OSHA.

Employers are responsible for knowing about and informing their employees of safety and health standards established by OSHA and for displaying OSHA posters in prominent places. In addition they are required to enforce the use of personal protective equipment and to provide communications to make employees aware of safety considerations. The act also states that employees who report safety violations to OSHA cannot be punished or discharged by their employers.

Both union and nonunion workers have refused to work when they considered the work unsafe. Current legal conditions for refusing work because of safety concerns are:

1. The employee's fear is objectively reasonable.
2. The employee has tried to get the dangerous condition corrected.
3. Using normal procedures to solve the problem has not worked.
4. To implement OSHA, specific standards were established regulating equipment and working environments.

Inspection Requirements

The act provides for on-the-spot inspection by OSHA representatives called compliance officers or inspectors. Under the original act, an employer could not refuse entry to an OSHA inspector. Further the original act prohibited a compliance officer from notifying an organization before an inspection. In 1978, the U.S. Supreme Court ruled on this no-knock provision, holding that safety inspectors must produce a search warrant if an employer refuses to allow an inspector into the plant voluntarily. However, the Court ruled that an inspector does not have to prove probable cause to obtain a search warrant.

In conjunction with state and local governments, OSHA has established a safety consultation service. An employer can contact the state agency and have an authorized safety consultant conduct an advisory inspection.

Citations and Violations

As noted, OSHA inspectors can issue citations for violations of the provisions of the act. Whether a citation is issued depends on the severity and extent of the problems and on the employer's knowledge of them. In addition, depending on the nature and number of violations, penalties can be assessed against employers. The nature and extent of the penalties depends on the type and severity of the violations as determined by OSHA officials. There are basically five types of violations, ranging from severe to minimal and including a special category for repeated violations:

- Imminent danger.
- Serious.
- Other than serious.
- De minimis.
- Willful and repeated.

Imminent Danger. When there is reasonable certainty that the condition will cause death or serious physical harm if it is not corrected immediately, an imminent danger citation is issued and a notice posted by an inspector. Imminent danger situations are handled on the highest-priority basis.

Serious. When a condition could probably cause death or serious physical harm, and the employer should know of the condition, a serious-violation citation is issued.

Other than Serious. Other-than-serious violations could have an impact on employees' health or safety but probably would not cause death or serious harm.

De Minimis. A de minimis condition is one that is not directly and immediately related to employees' safety or health. No citation is issued, but the condition is mentioned to the employer.

Willful and Repeated. Citations for willful and repeated violations are issued to employers who have been previously cited for violations. If an employer knows about a safety violation or has been warned of a violation and does not correct the problem, a second citation is issued. The penalty for a willful and repeated violation can be very high. If death results from an accident that involves a safety violation, a jail term of six months can be imposed on responsible executives or managers.

OSHA has established a standard national system for recording occupational injuries, accidents, and fatalities. Employers are generally required to maintain a detailed annual record of the various types of accidents for inspection by OSHA representatives and for submission to the agency. Employers that have had good safety records in previous years and that have fewer than ten employees are not required to keep detailed records.

As a further measure of safety awareness, in 1998 OSHA issued the "Hazard Communication Standard" (HCS) which requires employers to inform employees what chemicals they are working with, to detail what the risks or hazards are, and what can be done to limit these risks. HCS is achieved through training programs and detailed labeling on or near chemical containers. Material Safety Data Sheets (MSDS) are part of this standard.

A system of priorities for workplace inspections has been established by OSHA.

These are as follows:

1. Inspection of imminent danger situations.

2. Investigation of catastrophes, fatalities, and accidents resulting in the hospitalization of five or more employees.

3. Investigation of valid employee complaints of alleged violation of standards or of unsafe or unhealthful working conditions.

4. Follow-up inspections to determine if previously cited violations have been corrected.

OSHA provides a free on-site consultation service which helps employers identify hazardous conditions and identify corrective measures. The penalties for violations were raised in 1990. According to the new law, a minimum fine of $5,000 is mandatory for intentional violations with a maximum fine of $70,000 for intentional or repeat violations. A maximum fine of $7,000 applies for all other violations, including failure by an employer to post the required OSHA notice.

IDENTIFYING HAZARDS

The nature and scope of foodservice operations requires that many items of equipment be sharp or hot. Therefore, one of the best methods for identifying potential hazards is to simply consult team members. Have them develop a list of accident prevention measures. They see hazards in and around the foodservice facility every day.

Through mandatory and proper supervision, unsafe work practices can be corrected.

Safety committees should be established. The safety committee provides a means of getting team members directly involved in the operation of the safety program. The committee should meet regularly, at least once a month, and attendance should be mandatory.

Other helpful items which promote safety include:

1. Publishing safety statistics. Monthly accident reports should be posted. Ideas and suggestions should be solicited as to how these accidents can be avoided.

2. Using bulletin boards to display posters, pictures, sketches, and cartoons depicting safety situations.

3. Set high expectations for safety. Encourage the team to recognize positive safety actions and acknowledge those who contribute to safety improvements.

ACCIDENTS IN THE FOODSERVICE INDUSTRY

Most accidents in the foodservice industry involve falls, burns, lacerations, and strains caused by improper lifting.

The most common type of injuries that team members encounter most frequently revolve around, in most cases, carelessness. These include *lacerations, cuts,* and *bruises* which are caused by improper use or handling of knives, slicers, choppers, and broken ware or glass. Glasses, bowls, cups, and plates are also sources of injury. Broken glass in dishwashers or sinks cause accidents.

Cuts and bruises are a common problem in the food service industry. They are usually related to equipment or utilities and may be prevented or reduced if proper precautions are taken.

Steps to Reduce Accidents

- Posting the operation regulations for all equipment and requiring strict observance of them.
- Keeping all knives sharp, and using the proper knife for the job. Dull knives require more pressure than sharp ones and cause more cuts.
- Using cutting boards for slicing items. If a knife or implement falls, step back and allow it to hit floor. Attempts to catch a falling knife usually result in grabbing the sharp blade.
- Holding materials to be cut in ways that avoid finger injury.
- Keeping side towels available so that team members can keep their hands and utensils free from grease.
- Not placing knives or cutting blades from equipment in pot sinks filled with water. Knives should be washed at once.

Strains

The lifting of heavy or cumbersome objects can cause injury to team members.

The following are good lifting practices: Lift with the heavy muscles of the legs so that strains are not taken on the back. Bend the knees, and push while lifting. Arrange equipment properly so that extremely heavy loads do not have to be lifted.

Burns

Burns and scalds of varying degrees of severity can result from contact with the hot surfaces of grills, ovens, stove burners, steam tables, fryers, and any other heating equipment that might be in use.

One simple step that should be ingrained into all team members is the need to announce their presence when passing others with loaded trays. Phrases such as "passing please," "behind you," or "hot coffee" should be used.

By the very nature of the work being done in a foodservice establishment, burns present a serious hazard. The following suggestions are made to prevent them:

- Require food preparation team members to wear well-fitting uniforms with long sleeves.
- Keep handles of pots and pans turned in from the edge of the range so that they are not hit, causing spillage. In case of a minor burn or scald, put the injured part under cold water or apply ice immediately to prevent blistering and pain.

Slips and Falls

Falls are typically caused by wet or greasy floors which have been left unattended. The danger from greasy or wet floors is compounded by team members rushing about during busy periods.

Simple safety steps include:

- Watching for possible problem areas, such as the floor around the ice machine, where water may cause slipping. Team members should be made aware of the necessity to keep these floor surfaces safe.
- It is also recommended that team members wear sensible shoes, such as those with rubber soles, or ones made from neoprene to prevent slipping.

Gas Explosions and Electric Shocks

The following suggestions are made to prevent these problems:

- Be sure that all electrical equipment is grounded.
- Protect all gas equipment against explosion with gas cut-off devices that are activated at pilot light failure.
- Vent all gas equipment before lighting.
- Never work near electrical equipment with wet hands or while standing on wet floor surfaces.
- Unplug all electric equipment before attempting to clean or adjust it.
- Keep covers near deep fat fryers.

WORKPLACE STRESS

Stress comes from two basic sources: physical activity and mental or emotional activity. The physical reaction of the body to both sources is the same. Diningroom work can produce a stressful environment, particularly at busy service periods.

Not all stress is harmful. Positive stress is a feeling of exhilaration and achievement: This can be associated with a successful busy service period, during which everything went well. The team performed well as a group, record numbers were served, and 100 percent guest satisfaction was achieved.

Negative stress may cause people to become ill. Work induced stress can be caused by:

1. Conflicting expectations between supervisors and team members.
2. Uncertainty over team members' expected contributions to the team effort.
3. Poor preparation for the job, an environment that is physically unpleasant, and a climate of threats and hostility.
4. Noise levels, excessive temperature levels, long and irregular hours, and working during public holidays.
5. Poor supervision and organization.

Other strains include lack of communication on the job and lack of recognition for a job well done. Stress has been linked to many ailments. It manifests itself in several ways: increased absenteeism, job turnover, lower productivity, and mistakes on the job.

FIRE SAFETY AND EMERGENCIES

Fire safety ordinances have come a long way since the disastrous 1942 Coconut Grove fire in Boston which claimed 491 lives, yet in June 1970, 160 people died and more than one hundred were injured in a Kentucky supper club. More recently the tragic fire in Las Vegas in 1980 took 85 lives, and in Puerto Rico in 1986, 96 people lost their lives in a hotel casino fire.

Major Sources of Fires

Because most kitchens usually have open flames of some type, potential fire hazards are obvious. More fires occur in foodservice establishments than in any other type of business operation. These potential fire hazards should be checked regularly.

Special fire protection equipment should be provided in all areas where fires are likely to occur such as hoods, grills, deep fryers, ovens, and stove tops.

Directions in the use of fire extinguisher and evacuation procedures for guests and team members should be part of every new team member's induction and orientation training. When unsafe actions are observed, immediate corrective action should be taken.

The following is the Occupational Safety and Health Administration's, fire prevention checklist for restaurants, hotels, and motels:

1. Emergency plans developed and discussed with team members?
2. Emergency drills conducted (at least annually)?
3. Employee emergency alarms distinctive, operating properly?
4. Alarms, smoke detectors in good working order?
5. Water sprinkler systems in good condition?
6. All exits clearly marked and unobstructed?
7. All exits and exit signs appropriately illuminated?
8. Sufficient exit capacity available for occupancy?
9. Stairways in good condition with appropriate railings?
10. Fire doors installed as required and in proper operating condition?
11. Fire walls located as required?
12. Flammable materials stored in improper containers?
13. "No smoking" areas clearly marked?
14. Portable fire extinguisher readily accessible, inspected monthly, recharged regularly?
15. Team members trained in the use of fire extinguishers?
16. Local fire department aware of hotel facilities and fire protection systems?

In addition, a major guest expectation is a need for visible evidence of fire safety and security for themselves and their property.

WHAT TO DO IN EMERGENCY SITUATIONS

Accidents

1. Inform an other team member, preferably a manager.
2. Locate a team member with CPR and first aid training who is willing to assist.

3. Do not move the person. Often the injury is not visible and movement can cause further injury. (Call 911, or the local police.)

4. Obtain the facts pertaining to the accident such as names and addresses, and what happened, when, where, and why if appropriate.

5. Complete an "Accident Report Form" with the ascertained information.

There are generally two report forms:

    a. Public Accident Report Form, for accidents involving guests.

    b. Employee Accident Report Form, for accidents involving team members.

6. Ask the persons involved (the guest and other team members, as well as witnesses, if any) to sign and date the Accident Report Form.

Emergencies

1. Sadly, in common with other parts of the world, public places in the United States, such as restaurants and hotels, have become terrorist targets.

2. Policies and procedures should be in place in the event of such an emergency (e.g., bomb threat or armed person on the premises). Team members should be provided with the following instructions:

    a. Don't panic. Remain calm and notify a supervisor or manager immediately if possible. Let the manager handle the situation.

    b. Do not alarm guests.

    c. If directed to do so by management, evacuate guests in a calm, orderly manner.

    d. Do not play hero. Unless trained, do not touch a suspected bomb, try to talk to or disarm an armed person, or do anything to endanger anyone's life, including your own.

3. Call the local police department number. Post the number to be called conspicuously and in as many places as possible, such as the front desk or by the cashier station.

4. Generally it is advisable to call the police and ask for "police and medical personnel," including an ambulance, to be sent to the establishment as soon as possible.

5. If there is a fire, call the local fire department.

6. Each team member must practice safety awareness by thinking defensively, anticipating unsafe situations, and reporting unsafe conditions immediately. Team members should have a thorough understanding of all the safety and emergencies procedures.

Public facilities with the numbers and types of guests restaurants have are bound to experience some aspects of emergencies such as choking, fainting, and heart attacks. The Heimlich maneuver and CPR procedures (cardiopulmonary resuscitation) are very effective in controlling these serious episodes. In certain cities and states, one person in every licensed establishment must be trained in these procedures. A professional should be used to train employees and/ supervisors.

The Heimlich Maneuver

Named for the doctor who first used this maneuver, the Heimlich maneuver has become a most effective technique to aid those who are choking. This maneuver squeezes out the air trapped in the person's lungs. This burst of air forces the obstruction out.

1. Stand behind the victim and wrap your arms around his or her waist, allowing the head and arms to hang forward.

2. Make a fist with one hand and clasp it with the other hand. Place the fist against the victim's abdomen just above the navel and below the rib cage.

3. Press in forcefully with a quick upward thrust. Repeat several times. This pushes the diaphragm up, compressing the lungs, and may force the object out of the windpipe. (This maneuver may be used on children and adults. Infants and small children should be held upside down, over the arm of the rescuer, and then struck between the shoulder blades.)

4. After the obstruction is removed, restore breathing by artificial respiration. Keep the victim warm and quiet. Seek medical attention immediately.

Artificial Respiration

Artificial respiration is used when a person's heart or lungs have stopped because of choking, a heart attack, or some other serious health threat. In most cases, a fatality can be avoided if prompt action is taken.

Cardiopulmonary resuscitation (CPR) is a technique used to provide artificial circulation and breathing to the victim. The American Red Cross regularly conducts CPR courses consisting of lectures, demonstrations, and student practice. This valuable training usually takes approximately eight hours, and it could save a guest's or a team member's life. It is a sensible idea to have someone who has received a certificate of completion in a CPR course on duty in the establishment during the hours of operation (many states now mandate this).

REVIEW QUESTIONS

1. Outline and discuss the Occupational Safety and Health Act (OSHA). Discuss the importance of safety as it relates to the workplace.
2. State the common cause of accidents in the foodservice industry.
3. Define workplace stress. Outline the causes of stress.
4. Describe the steps for the prevention of fires.
5. Identify the steps involved in dealing with emergency situations in the foodservice industry.
6. Describe the Heimlich maneuver and the critical elements of cardiopulmonary resuscitation (CPR).

24

Quality Management, Diversity, and Respect

Outline

PRINCIPLES OF QUALITY MANAGEMENT

> Quality...we are always challenged by improvement. We strive to "make things better" everyday. We honor the elegance of our tradition and make sure our improvements are aligned with how we want to do business. Because we value the quality of our environment we work in, we protect and care for all the assets entrusted to us.
>
> —Fairmont Hotel Core Values

Quality can be defined as anything that enhances the product from the viewpoint of the guest. Some aspects of quality are easily identified, other aspects of quality are not, but the absence of it in restaurants stands out like a sore thumb.

Over the past decade, hundreds of articles and books have been written on quality, and thousands more have been written on service. Quality service is not unique or particular to upscale restaurants and hotels. Fast-food operations, casual restaurants, and institutional and industrial foodservice establishments have the same opportunity to achieve quality service as do fine dining and luxurious establishments. Why? Because each area of the foodservice and hospitality industry has guests with their unique set of expectations. Every area has the same opportunity to exceed, meet, or fall short of the expectations of its guests.

More and more high quality has become essential to the success of the hospitality and foodservice industry. Nothing attracts guests like quality. The goal of quality is very simple and straightforward: to consistently meet or exceed guest expectations by providing products and service at prices that create value for guests and profit to grow the organization. Quality not only must exist, it must also be perceived by the guest because *perception is reality.*

In addition, the application of total quality management (TQM) will reduce waste, build teamwork, increase the motivational environment, and improve team member retention. It will develop institutional pride and increase and expand technical knowledge and understanding.

CHEFS AND QUALITY MANAGEMENT

The concepts of quality management along with the role the chef has to play in it is the glue that holds together all the elements vital to success in the foodservice field. Future culinarians will need to understand and embrace the tenets of quality management if they are going to play an important and valuable role in the overall development of themselves and the industry.

Quality management will help gain that competitive edge over other establishments. Quality management principles change the kitchen team's relationship with dining room colleagues, guests, and suppliers through greater focus on meeting and exceeding customer expectations.

When quality service is absent, it is obvious. Quality is a moving target. Perceptions of quality and value fluctuate with changing guest expectations.

According to Lilian Vernon, CEO of Lilian Vernon Corporation, "Quality is the essential element in gaining a customer's trust. To forfeit it once is to lose it forever."

There's always room for improvement—and there always will be. In a quality oriented organization, "good enough" is never good enough. Every aspect of the foodservice or hospitality organization must be used to ensure guest satisfaction, or quality will not be achieved. Even if your guests are satisfied with how they are served, keep looking for a better way. In a fast changing industry, it is only a matter of time before guests' needs change. When they do, the foodservice organization will want to be ready to maintain the competitive advantage built over the competition.

> Quality is never an accident; it is always the result of high intention, sincere effort, intelligent direction and skilful execution; it represents the wise choice of many alternatives.
>
> —Willa A. Foster

TOTAL QUALITY MANAGEMENT, SO WHAT IS IT?

In recent years we have witnessed the rise and fall of many approaches to quality. However, one of the most important lessons learned from the past is that *quality is not a destination, it is a journey.*

Quality management is essential for survival in today's competitive foodservice business arena. The ability to create a quality consciousness in an organization is the foundation on which quality improvements must be built.

As we proceed into the next century and beyond, TQM will influence everything we do. The goal is excellence. Committed to quality management, it is possible to maintain and improve our operations. Quality management builds teamwork, increases the motivational environment, develops institutional pride, and increases and expands the technical knowledge of culinarians.

FUNDAMENTALS OF TOTAL QUALITY MANAGEMENT

1. **A guest orientation:** The guest defines quality and is the focus of improvement processes.

2. **Empowering leadership:** Management is committed to leading change toward a shared objective and gives authority and resources to team members so that they may bring about improvement.

3. Across-the-board employee involvement: All team members, at every level, are involved in strategic planning and continuous quality improvement training. Quality products and services evolve from a quality work environment.

4. Education and training: Team members are given opportunities to better understand their jobs and roles. They are given a bigger picture of their part in the organization's processes and encouraged to focus their energies on producing a superior product.

5. A team approach: This is the heartbeat of TQM. Here the focus is on collaboration. The team approach solicits multiple perspectives (on product, processes, guest satisfaction, and so on) and builds on each individual's strengths.

   Many chefs recognize that it is necessary in today's foodservice industry to be more than an excellent cook with first-class culinary skills, they also recognize that it is necessary to be a first-class leader with great team building skills.

6. Procedures and process controls: The team must gain full knowledge of processes and systems, including knowing whether a given procedure, method, or process is in control or out of control. Decisions made are based on facts.

7. Continuous quality improvement (CQI): The organization should no longer be satisfied with meeting an established threshold or endpoint but will strive constantly to provide a higher quality of hospitality and services. Continuous improvement must become the norm. The status quo is no longer an option in an increasingly competitive and uncertain foodservice industry.

One hotel chain set the following criteria for implementing and measuring quality. Although the main thrust here is to define quality service in more of a customer satisfaction program than a total quality management program, it never the less captures the essence of what TQM means in terms of guest service.

1. Assess the situation regarding quality levels.

2. If required search for causes of variation.

3. As a team agree on and target solutions.

4. Take action.

5. Measure the results.

6. Provide an environment that empowers everybody from chefs to servers.

7. Provide appropriate training at all levels of the organization.

To facilitate these steps, the company identified six principles (key characteristics) of excellent service:

1. Warmly greet and acknowledge every guest encountered.
2. Take care of every guest's request quickly and in a friendly manner.
3. Project a professional image through appearance and conduct.
4. Be committed to guests comfort, safety, and security.
5. Provide reliable information about the services available in the establishment and the local area.
6. Work to make everything right for the guest.

TQM challenges every employee to collaborate so as to create the environment and culture which will provide service that meets or exceeds customer expectations every time. Quality is not a procedure, it is a process, and as such is never finished. If you are not in the total quality business, be assured your competitors are.

DIVERSITY

There are a number of characteristics of diversity. The most widely recognized deal with age, gender, ethnicity, sexual preference, and education. We too often approach others from our own cultural perspective and expect them to think like us. We react when people respond or behave in a way that is "different." These behaviors may lead to stereotyping, which happens when we always consider certain groups behave in a certain way. A bad experience with one person does not mean that all experiences with others from that culture will be bad. Preconceived negative attitudes about certain groups is prejudice.

DIVERSITY AND FUTURE CHALLENGES

One of the major reasons for the emergence of diversity as a future challenge for the foodservice industry is that of changing demographics. Older workers, women, minorities, and those with more education are now entering the foodservice industry in record numbers.

The foodservice industry has always had higher numbers of minorities and women than most other industries in the United States. However, it has not always enjoyed the best of reputations in its handling of women and minorities. All analyses and indicators show that 65 percent of the new jobs created during the 1990s were filled by women. By the year 2050, one-half of the U.S. population will be composed of African Americans, Hispanic Americans,

Native Americans, and Asian Americans and these minorities will make-up a high percentage of the foodserver workforce. There's probably more diversity in the foodservice industry—more women, more minorities—than in any other industry.

As we look forward to the next century, the foodservice industry not only is faced with issues of leading greater numbers of people, but also a more diverse work force. This diversity will require a greater awareness of total quality respect for the values and cultures of all team members.

An establishment that values diversity is one in which team members learn to appreciate individuality and to avoid prejudging people. An encouraged awareness of diversity will facilitate the discussion of assumptions each team member may hold regarding certain groups of people. Understanding and accepting diversity enables us to see that each of us is needed. "Recognizing diversity helps us to understand the need we have for opportunity, equity, and identity in the workplace.

Generally, until human beings have the opportunity to learn otherwise, they assume that other people look at the world just as they do, that is, everyone has similar values, and everyone is motivated for the same reason.

Acceptance of diversity can mean getting used to speech in a different accent or people who dress differently. It means feeling comfortable with team members whose skin is a different color. Diversity in a team refers to physical and cultural dimensions that separate and distinguish us as individuals and groups. Failure to understand and to respect the diversity of employees can result in misunderstandings, tension, poor performance, poor employee morale, and higher rates of absenteeism and turnover. When diversity is respected, the working environment is richer.

THE CULTURE OF RESPECT

When there is a culture of respect in the workplace, whether in the kitchen, diningroom, or in the rooms division, productivity increases. A "total quality" respect toward all team members builds total quality service.

Total quality respect (TQR) is linked closely to valuing the differences among individuals. It is about driving fear out of the establishment and adopting a sense of tolerance toward all ethnic, gender, and other differences among team members.

Understanding and valuing diversity within the team enables each person to see they have a special contribution to make. The self-esteem of diverse team members will stay intact if they believe their backgrounds are accepted and respected.

A team filled with ethnic diversity always has the potential for conflict based on differences. This conflict may be based on misconceptions or stereotypes, and each side can misinterpret or dismiss the viewpoint of the other by failing to understand the framework in which the other person operates.

INTEGRATING A CULTURE OF RESPECT FOR DIVERSITY

The first step in improving respect for diversity is communication. Establish a climate that encourages a free exchange of ideas. Explore how all team members come to the establishment with a unique combination of backgrounds and influences.

Get to know other team members. Don't make ethnic or gender oriented jokes; good-natured jokes in this area should not be tolerated.

If individuals are having difficulty with English, be patient and encouraging. Ask them for their input—because even though some people don't say anything, it does not mean they have nothing to say. Persons changing from one culture to another may experience culture shock which may manifest itself in fear. Encourage the rest of the team to understand and respect differences in people

The self-esteem of diverse team members remains intact if they believe their backgrounds are accepted and respected. You get people to do what you want not by bullying or tricking them, but by understanding them.

THE CIVIL RIGHTS ACT, EEOC, AND SEXUAL HARASSMENT

The Civil Rights Act of 1964, particularly Title VII, the new Civil Rights Act of 1991, and the various regulations of states, counties, and cities over the past thirty years have given rise to some of the most important aspects of legal liability that have confronted the hospitality industry. These laws prohibit discrimination because of race, color, religion, sex, national origin, or age.

Title VII of the 1964 Civil Rights Act concerns the Equal Employment Opportunity Commission (EEOC). In 1980, they issued guidelines on sexual harassment, indicating that it is a form of discrimination. Employers are also guilty of sexual harassment when they allow nonemployees (guests or salespersons) to sexually harass employees. In recent times harassment in the workplace has become mostly synonymous with sexual harassment. Unfortunately many other forms of harassment may be encountered in the foodservice industry, that is, harassment of gay people, minorities, and physically or mentally impaired people. In addition to the Civil Rights Act, federal laws, executive orders, court cases, and state and local statutes provide a broad legal framework to protect employees.

According to EEOC guidelines, sexual harassment is a form of discrimination prohibited by Title VII of the Civil Rights Act. It can occur in any of several forms, including unwelcome sexual favors and other verbal or physical conduct of a sexual nature when:

1. Submission to such conduct is made either explicitly or implicitly a term of an individual's employment

2. Submission to or rejection of such conduct by an individual is used as either the basis for or a factor in an employment decision affecting such individual; or

3. Such conduct has the purpose or effect of unreasonably interfering with an individual's work performance or creating an intimidating, hostile, or offensive working environment.

CONDUCT AND BEHAVIOR THAT MAY CONSTITUTE SEXUAL HARASSMENT

Personal behavior and language that are "acceptable" to one individual may be "offensive" to another. Therefore, each individual must use sound personal judgment concerning the possible effects on others of his or her actions.

Examples of conduct that may constitute harassment are off-color jokes; repeated unsolicited sexual flirtations, advances, or propositions; continued or repeated verbal comments of physical actions of a sexual nature, sexually degrading words to describe an individual; touching, patting, or pinching; or display in the workplace of sexually suggestive objects or pictures.

Isolated comments of a sexual nature, while possibly objectionable, are not necessarily sexual harassment. Furthermore, as a general rule, conduct between consenting parties, or actions arising out of a current personal or social relationship where there is no coercion involved, may not be viewed as harassment.

Harassment of one employee by another employee or supervisor on any basis including, but not limited to, age, race, color, handicap, national origin, religion and/or sex is strictly forbidden. The purpose is to assure no employee harasses another on any of these bases. Any employee who feels that he or she is a victim of such harassment should immediately report the matter to the appropriate member of management. Zero tolerance of these issues is the expected response to these complaints.

The best cure for workplace sexual harassment is a policy and an educational program designed to prevent it. Policy statements should be in writing and stress that harassment will not be tolerated.

The following are the fundamental elements of an effective sexual harassment policy:

1. A systemwide comprehensive policy on sexual harassment should be developed. Experts in the area of sexual harassment, including a lawyer, should be involved in its preparation. This policy should be part of all new employee orientation training programs.

2. Procedures for dealing with complaints in this area should be established.

3. Action should be taken immediately to investigate complaints of harassment.

4. Offenders should be disciplined and dismissed instantly in serious cases. The policy should be equally and fairly applied to all team members.

When people are sexually harassed, they have legal recourse, but many times they hesitate to speak out. Some of the most common reasons include fears regarding losing their jobs, being rejected by other team members, or being accused of being overly sensitive, and feeling embarrassed.

REVIEW QUESTIONS

1. Define the concept of Total Quality Management (TQM). Outline the role chefs play in TQM.
2. Outline the fundamentals of Total Quality Management.
3. Describe the characteristics of diversity. Discuss the challenges of respect for diversity.
4. Outline the benefits of the creation of a culture of respect in the foodservice industry.
5. Discuss the Civil Rights Act and sexual harassment in the workplace.
6. Outline conduct that may be construed as sexual harassment.

25

The Dynamics of Leadership

Outline

LEADERSHIP: CAN I BECOME A LEADER?

Anybody can become a leader. Excellent personal qualities and characteristics help in becoming a good leader. However, leadership skill sets are learned and are not something a person is born with. Real leaders are ordinary people with extraordinary determination.

Leadership transforms problems into challenges, excites the imagination, calls on pride, develops a sense of accomplishment and achievement, and provides opportunities to overcome obstacles.

One well-known phrase often used in describing a leader is: "A leader is a person you will follow to a place you wouldn't go by yourself."

Leadership is demonstrated by a person who:

1. Can sacrifice personal glory for the good of the foodservice establishment team, who has strength of purpose to achieve the goals, who cannot be easily discouraged, who does not compromise, but adapts.

2. Does not allow a team members' weaknesses to prevail over their strengths, one who will always set realistic goals for a fellow team member, based on individual ability. (Foodservice establishment team leadership impacts performance.)

3. Has an open and approachable style and believes in a "win win" relationship with the team. Uses diplomacy based on respect, trust, and courtesy toward the foodservice establishment team.

4. Has a clear vision of the possibilities of the foodservice establishment team's potential and inspires them through motivation, aims high and goes after things that will make a difference, rather than seeking the safe path of mediocrity.

5. Has stamina, high-energy levels, tenacity and a positive attitude. Once committed to the foodservice organization's goals and objectives, sees them through. Communicates openly with the foodservice establishment team, shares risktaking, and leads by example.

6. Shuns publicity at the expense of the foodservice establishment team and the organization. Accepts failure in some things in order to excel in more important ones.

7. Focuses on problems as opportunities, is tolerant and never confuses power with leadership.

8. Invests of himself or herself in adequate training, adopts a coaching and correcting style, and understands that training is the vital ingredient for quality service.

9. Shows concern for the welfare of their team, and is sympathetic and caring.

10. Celebrates the foodservice establishment team and their success, as well as their promotions, awards, birthdays, marriages, reunions, anniversaries, and holidays.

11. Builds individual self-esteem, so that each team member feels important and empowered.

ON BECOMING A LEADER

1. Become a leader by seeking out situations and volunteering to be a leader whenever you can.

2. Be an unselfish teacher and helper to others. Others will come to you for leadership. Treat those you lead with respect—always.

3. Develop your expertise. Expertise is a source of leadership power.

4. Develop self-confidence, become an uncrowned leader, do things without being first directed to do so.

There are many opportunities for individuals to become leaders. Within the dining room and kitchen, there are team members who need help. Seizing the opportunity to lead can help these people build confidence in you as a leader.

According to Mary Parker Follet, "The most successful leader of all is the one who sees another picture not yet actualized."

LEADERSHIP MYTHS

A leader is a dealer in hope.

—Napoleon Bonaparte

Myth associates leadership with superior position. It assumes that when you are on top you are automatically a leader. But leadership is not a place, it is a process. It involves skills and abilities that are useful whether one is in the executive suite or on the front line. The one who influences others to lead is a leader without limitation.

Bennus and Nanus observed the following myths in their book *Leaders: Their Strategies for Taking Charge:*

Myth 1: "Leadership is a rare skill." Nothing could be further from the truth. Although great leaders may be as rare as great runners, great actors, or great painters, everyone has leadership potential. The truth is that leadership opportunities are plentiful and within the reach of most people.

Myth 2: "Leaders are born, not made." Biographies of great leaders sometimes read as if they entered the world with an extraordinary genetic endowment, that somehow their future leadership role was preordained. Don't believe it. Whatever natural endowments we bring to the role of leadership can be enhanced.

Myth 3: "Leaders are charismatic." Some are, most aren't. Charisma is the result of effective leadership, not the other way around.

Myth 4: "Leadership exists only at the top of an organization." In fact, the larger the organization, the more leadership roles it is likely to have.

Myth 5: "The leader controls, directs, prods, and manipulates." This is perhaps the most damning myth of all. Leadership is not so much the exercise of power itself as the empowerment of others. Leaders are able to translate intentions into reality by aligning the energies of the organization behind an attractive goal. Once these myths are cleared away, the question becomes not one of how to become a leader but rather how to improve one's effectiveness at leadership.

The traits that are the basic elements of leadership can be taught. When the desire is present in the foodservice establishment team leader to be a good leader, nothing can stop the process. Ninety percent of leadership can be taught through development. The 10 percent who are gifted will succeed only if the development and growth of leadership are pursued.

The terms management and leadership are often used simultaneously. They can be synonymous, but both mean different things. In the past terms such as "people management" were used to indicate authoritarian controls. This "people management" philosophy has been shown to be folly.

CONCEPT OF AUTHORITY

Leadership success is dependent on more than the source of authority. It is dependent on many skills. The greater the foodservice establishment team leader's skill in developing a foodservice establishment team, the greater the productivity and satisfaction of all the foodservice establishment team. When team building skills are applied to people rather than solely authoritarian leadership, foodservice and hospitality team members have been found to cooperate more with each other and other departments, as well as developing better interpersonal relationships and a great team spirit.

You can't declare yourself a leader. You become the foodservice establishment team leader the moment the team decides to follow you. There's no other way to do it. And they only follow when they believe the team leader has their best interests in mind.

Authority must strike a balance for individuals to follow:

1. The goal is to lead individuals toward growth.
2. Practical judgment skills are required.
3. Authority acts as a uniting element of a team's common goals.
4. Authority enhances cooperative efforts.

Traditional authority is the right and power to make decisions assigned to bosses and supervisors.

For authority to be real and genuine, leaders exercising that authority must know what they are requesting of team members and why they are making those requests. Authority for the sake of power is useless, it must seek to inspire desired outcomes from each person. Requests or demands made on a team member without good reasons often lead to anger and frustration on the part of both the member and leader. Remember members will respond more freely to a request than they will to an order.

As H. Ross Perot states: "People cannot be managed. Inventories can be managed, but people must be led." The following article appeared in the *Wall Street Journal*. It subtly attempts to demonstrate the differences between management and leadership:

> *"Let's get rid of management"*
> People don't want to be managed.
> They want to be led.
> Whoever heard of a world manager?
> World leader, yes.
> Educational leader.
> Political leader.
> Scout leader.
> Community leader.
> Labor leader.
> Business leader.
> They lead.
> They don't manage.
> If you want to manage somebody, manage yourself.
> Do that well and you'll be ready to stop managing
> and start leading.

Developing leadership skills requires a great deal of persistence.

> Nothing in the world can take the place of persistence
> Talent will not; nothing is more common than unsuccessful men with great talent.
> Genius will not; unrewarded genius is almost a proverb.
> Education will not; the world is full of educated derelicts.
> Persistence, determination alone are omnipotent.
>
> —Calvin Coolidge

BEHAVIORAL THEORIES

Behavioral theories were directed toward the study of leaders, supervisors, and foodservice establishment teams, rather than just focusing on the characteristics of successful leaders. In the past emphasis was placed on studying the behaviors that provided effective interaction among work-team members. Studies have shown that two characteristics which were arrived at independent of one another were important elements of leadership behavior. These were grouped as *consideration* and *structure*. Elements of consideration include behaviors indicating mutual trust, respect, and a certain warmth and rapport between the team leader and the team. Structure includes behavior in which foodservice establishment team leaders organize and define team activities and their relations to the group.

In their book *The Leadership Challenge*, Kouzes and Posner similarly reported that the behaviors followers expect from their leaders include honesty, competence, vision, and inspiration. Another study conducted by Cichy, Sciarini, and Patton, reported in the Cornell Quarterly, discussed fourteen desirable leadership behaviors and qualities.

These leadership behaviors and qualities were those that:

1. Provide a compelling message or vision.
2. Have a strong personal value or belief system.
3. Recognize that the ability to adjust is a necessity.
4. Make desired outcomes tangible.
5. Encourage and reward risk taking.
6. Listen as well as, if not better than, they speak.
7. Provide appropriate information, resources, and support to empower team members.
8. Are inquisitive, ask questions.
9. Emphasize quality continuously.
10. Know personal strengths and nurture them.
11. Place a high value on learning.
12. Maintain precise desired outcomes.
13. Change their minds seldom.
14. Have strong family values.

In *Coaching for Commitment*, Denis Kinlaw also uncovered similar behaviors of superior leaders, which he summarizes under six sets of common practices. These are:

1. Establishing a vision: Superior leaders create expectations for significant and lasting achievement. They give meaning to work by associating even menial tasks with valued goals.
2. Stimulating people to gain new competencies: Superior leaders stimulate people to stretch their minds and their wills. They freely share their own expertise and keep people in touch with new resources.
3. Helping people to overcome obstacles: Superior leaders help others to overcome obstacles. They help others to find the courage and strength to persevere in the face of even the greatest difficulties.
4. Helping people to overcome failure: Superior leaders help people to cope with failure and disappointment. They are quick to offer people who fail new opportunities.
5. Leading by example: Superior leaders are models of integrity and hard work. They set the highest expectations for themselves and others.
6. Including others in their success: Superior leaders are quick to share the limelight with others. People associated with superior leaders feel as successful as the leaders.

SITUATIONAL LEADERSHIP

The emphasis of leadership study has shifted from the trait and behavioral approach to the situational approach. This modern situational approach to leadership is based on the assumption that all instances of successful leadership are different and require a unique combination of leaders, followers, and leadership situations.

According to Kenneth Blanchard and others writing in the *One Minute Manager,* the four basic styles of situational leadership are:

- Style 1 Directing
  The leader provides specific instructions and closely supervises task accomplishment.

- Style 2 Coaching
  The leader continues to direct and closely supervise task accomplishment, but also explains decisions, solicits suggestions, and supports progress.

- Style 3 Supporting
  The leader facilitates and supports subordinates' efforts toward task accomplishment and shares responsibility for decision making with them.

- Style 4 Delegating
  The leader turns over responsibility for decision making and problem solving to subordinates.

This has also been summarized as "different strokes for different folks." There is no one best or appropriate style suited to all situations. Leadership style, often described as the three Fs—"Firm, Fair, and Friendly"—is the combination of many elements, but there are times when the firm, fair, friendly style does not work. The three Fs presupposes there is a homogenous team who will readily react and perform favorably to this leadership style.

As a situational leader, the team leader needs to analyze the team. Within the foodservice establishment team, there will be team members who have high commitment to the team and its goals, but without the necessary array of skills. In this situation the team leader uses a detailed set of instructions to lead the foodservice establishment team member—a directing style. A team member who is sometimes committed and has a lot of skills will require a supporting leadership style. These team members are capable of working alone with little direction. Team members with well-developed skills and a great deal of team commitment require tasks delegated to them in order to feel fulfilled.

Leadership ability is inextricably linked to motivation. What motivates one person may not motivate another. Motivation comes from within the individual team member. Leadership and leadership style provide the basis for a motivational environment.

Extremes in leadership styles include the strict authoritarian, aloof person who rules with a rod of iron. The advantage of this style is good control and discipline over the foodservice team. The disadvantages are resentment, no cooperation, and poor communication with subordinates. These are certainly not the ingredients of a coaching leadership style in a quality management environment.

The other extreme is the "Democrat" who needs to be accepted by other team members as a complete equal. The "Democrat" style promotes a good atmosphere, good communication, and cooperation. However, the disadvantages can outweigh the advantages because the "Democrat" is taken for granted, has no authority, and will eventually lose control of the foodservice team. Somewhere between these two extremes is the ideal leadership style.

The old-fashioned authoritarian, dictator style has no place in the complex diversified modern world of hospitality and foodservice. Team members need to be led, not controlled or managed. The best leadership style is one that works for the individual team leader; it is based on the makeup of the team, the personal characteristics of the team leader, and the ever changing daily situations facing the foodservice team leader. Situational leadership provides the team leader with a flexible approach to each situation as it arises.

There are three types of leaders:
Those who make things happen;
those who watch things happen;
and those who wondered what happened!

—Old American military saying

LEADERSHIP AND QUALITY

> Lead, follow or get out of the way.
>
> —Col. Harold P. Knutty

As part of a quality management process, leadership confers on the team leader the privilege and responsibility to direct the actions of the team in carrying out the pursuits of the organization and quality management.

Quality thrives on inspirational leadership, and the culture of total quality will generate leadership. The distinction between a supervisor and a leader is that the supervisor is an assigned organizational role, whereas the leader is a role that can be assumed by anyone. Therefore, not all supervisors are leaders, and not all leaders are supervisors.

Leaders play a crucial role in quality. Leaders are primary agents for improvement. They work to create an environment where the team can experience pride. Their efforts are directed at allowing each team member to perform their job to the utmost.

Leaders take risks based on the self-knowledge that mistakes are opportunities, not failures. They have the ability to let go of concepts that block new ideas of learning. Leaders balance action against inaction and praise against correction. Competent leaders have sufficient expertise to make good judgments and get things done.

LEADING THE FOODSERVICE TEAM

> A sense of humor is part of the art of leadership, of getting along with people, of getting things done.
>
> —Dwight D. Eisenhower

Leading is not the same as supervising, although some supervisors are leaders. There is no model or system of leadership behaviors which can be applied to all situations or circumstances in which team leaders can influence the actions of others.

The terms management and leadership are often used simultaneously. They can be synonymous, but both mean different things. In the past terms such as "people management" were used indicating authoritarian controls.

Just about anyone can become a competent leader. The only thing which needs to be known is what to do and then do it. President Eisenhower summarized leadership as follows: "The one quality that can be developed by studious reflection and practice is leadership."

Leadership does not depend on team member incentives or pleasant working conditions. The foodservice establishment team leader's ability to motivate people to perform is independent of these factors. Leaders are made, not born. Leadership can be learned. Myth associates leadership with superior position.

It assumes that when you are on top you are automatically a leader. But leadership is not a place, it is a process. It involves skills and abilities that are useful whether one is in the executive suite or on the front line.

The traits that are the basic elements of leadership can be taught. When the desire is present in the supervisor to be a good leader, nothing can stop the process. Ninety percent of leadership can be taught through development. The 10 percent who are gifted will succeed only if the development and growth of leadership are pursued.

In order to skillfully lead the team, the supervisor must master the skills of leadership and have a passion to succeed: They must show the way, and lead by example. They must have a clear idea of what they want to do and the strength of purpose to persist in the face of setbacks, even failures, to do it. They know where they are going and why.

LEADERSHIP STYLES

Durable and solid leadership can be established through a combination of methods. A true leader is a person who people want to follow because they trust and respect that individual. Leadership style is something that each team leader will develop individually. Essentially style is based on two behaviors known as directive behavior and supportive behavior.

Directive behavior is the authoritarian behavior which concentrates on control, structure, and strict supervision. Supportive leadership behavior style is about enabling, coaching, facilitating, and praising.

Leadership development is a process of self-development. It is facilitated by education, training, mentoring, and experience.

The greater the leadership skills of the team leader, the greater the satisfaction and productivity of the team.

Parts of these leadership skill sets include:

1. Creativity.
2. Confidence in your abilities.
3. Good communication skills.
4. The ability to make decisions.
5. Trust in the foodservice establishment team to do the job.
6. A desire to develop skills in others.
7. Comfortable in giving directions.
8. Ability to motivate the team.
9. Ability to take risks.

Trusting the team leader is also vital to leadership in order to have a productive foodservice establishment team environment. It is essential to practice open and honest communication so as to promote loyalty and commitment within the team.

USE A LITTLE HUMOR

Humor can be a powerful tool for enhancing self-confidence and building empathy. Humor promotes positive attitudes within the team, thus making it easier to hear feedback and new information. Humor is also a great lubricant for team work.

Humor also distracts from worry; it lightens stress, anxiety, depression, and pain. It increases creativity and offers perspective and balance. It can help express the truth when the truth is feared and repressed. The use of humor decreases discipline problems and pressures on team members. It also improves listening, and creates a comfort level within the group.

Humor can be used to illustrate points and create retention of ideas and scenarios. Team members can view themselves more objectively. It increases spontaneity, allowing flexibility of thinking; it facilitates change and helps build rapport and trust among the team.

Remember, laugh with your team not at them.

MOTIVATION AND TEAM LEADERSHIP

Could you motivate the team?

To motivate we need to understand why people act as they do, and what sort of behavior they are likely to exhibit in different situations. This involves being able to see through problems and situations from the team members' points of view. These basic talents enable team motivation.

Team members like and expect competent leadership; they like to do things that are worthwhile and like to have the feeling that they are contributing something new. They naturally turn to a person who can lead, but they want to be led in a way which allows them to keep their self-respect and sense of personal worth. The best type of leader, motivator, or coach is one who deliberately sets out to earn and keep the respect, confidence, and cooperation of each team member by helping them demonstrate their capabilities and by boosting their morale. This puts them in the best possible position for imparting skills, knowledge, and quality guest service techniques effectively.

REVIEW QUESTIONS

1. Name the qualities demonstrated by leaders.
2. Describe the "myths" of leadership.

3. Describe the concept of authority.

4. Explain what behavioral theory outlines.

5. Define and discuss the elements of situational leadership.

6. Explain the connection between leadership and quality.

7. Identify the different styles of leadership, the benefits of humor and leadership, and the issue of motivation and leadership.

26

Teamwork: Putting It All Together

Outline

> I've learned one important thing about living. I can do anything I think I can—but I can't do anything alone. No one can go it alone. Create your team.
>
> —Dr. Robert Shuller

Working together to accomplish success creates a synergy that everyone can count on. Within the foodservice establishment, department teams must constantly interact, because guests think and react holistically to their experiences. They don't separate segments of their interactions, they react and evaluate the entire food product and service. A restaurant or foodservice establishment can be likened to a living organism. The whole organism or system consists of a series of parts. Each part plays an important and vital role in the provision of a complete and high-quality guest experience.

If any part of the system is defective, it will damage the entire foodservice organization. If teams within the restaurant or foodservice establishment are not "sympatic" to one another and do not work together in a complementary fashion, the overall "service" may break up.

A key function in maintaining a healthy foodservice product is for the boundaries that exist among its parts (front-of-house and back-of-house) to remain open, allowing for the exchange of ideas and information. If boundaries are closed, the organization itself will be seriously damaged.

The process of improving interteam dependence requires a conscious effort at cross-team communications. Teams that work well together strengthen the entire organization. Each team has both internal suppliers and internal customers (the server is the chef's internal customer). As internal teams learn to collaborate, they overcome insularity and narrow thinking.

GUEST SERVICE FACTS

1. If 20 guests are dissatisfied with the foodservice product, 19 won't tell, and 14 of the 20 will take their "business" elsewhere.
2. Dissatisfied guests tell an average of 10 other people about their bad experience.
3. Satisfied guests will tell an average of 5 people about their positive experience.
4. It costs 5 times more money to attract a new guest.
5. Up to 90 percent of dissatisfied guests will not call again.
6. Quality of service is one of the few variables that can distinguish any foodservice organization from its competition.

WHAT IS A TEAM?

A team is a group of individuals working together to achieve a common goal. Plain and simple! A group of individuals performing their jobs to the best of their ability while supporting each other is successful teamwork. Members recognize their interdependence and understand both personal and team goals. According to Ken Blanchard, writing in the *One Minute Manager,* "None of us is as smart as all of us."

When one person is unable to perform at 100 percent, the difference must be made up by the other team members. This places additional stress on those teammates because they have to work harder to meet the same goals. When this happens it is clearly noticeable.

It is extremely gratifying at the end of a successful day to know all team members have pulled together and reached the goals. Most of all the guests you've served will tell others of the excellent service.

Team members like to feel a sense of belonging and ownership in what they are doing as a group.

For all of us to make a team effort, here are some ideas to think about:

1. Don't be critical of fellow team members, help them with constructive comments.
2. Take pride in the excellence of your duties.
3. Give that "extra effort." Up-sell whenever possible as this will increase sales, as well as guest satisfaction.
4. Do everything to avoid waste.
5. Never take the attitude, "Let someone else worry about it; that's not my job."
6. Take instructions willingly and constructively.
7. Continue to strive for self-improvement and to be the best at what you are doing.
8. Input and constructive criticism is welcome. Voice opinions in a positive and constructive manner.
9. Be hospitable and polite with all guests at all times.
10. Be attentive and anticipate guests needs.
11. Possess excellent communication skills with guests, fellow staff members, and management.
12. Continually promote teamwork. People support what they create.
13. Pay attention to detail.
14. Have confidence, a positive attitude, and an outgoing personality.
15. Have a complete knowledge of food and beverage products, their description and prices.
16. Have a strong understanding of the organization's goals and values and be supportive of them.
17. Have a complete knowledge of your specific job and its requirements.
18. Maintain high standards of grooming and sanitation.

19. Cooperation is spelled WE. Individuals say I—teams say WE. Each person and each department contribute to teamwork, which equals guest satisfaction.

20. You become successful by helping others become successful.

There is no exercise better for the heart than reaching down and lifting people up.
—John A. Holmes

SUCCESSFUL TEAMS

What is it that most of us want from teamwork? We want to find the most effective, most rewarding, and most productive way of working together.

Team building involves getting employees to feel a sense of belonging and ownership in what they are doing as a group. To be successful in the hospitality industry, teamwork within and between all departments is essential.

The diningroom and kitchen are often pressure-filled places during busy meal periods. A team spirit with good morale can reduce this pressure; increase the confidence, ability, and harmony of the team; and help them to deal with these busy service periods.

When the concept of team building is adopted, it becomes easier to apply quality service philosophies. It also provides encouragement for each team member to work together to develop a team spirit. It helps people to get to know each other so that they in turn can learn to trust, respect, and appreciate each individual's talent and abilities.

COMMUNICATION

Good and effective communication is important to team building. Effective, clear, and accurate understanding of information is critical in the foodservice industry.

Within the team, individuals come from many different backgrounds. Each team member will interpret a message differently based on their backgrounds.

Often, jargon, or the use of French terms, or complicated culinary technical terms are used to describe skills and various techniques. Assuming that each individual has a clear understanding of these terms and jargon may frequently cause communication gaps.

Within a group or team it should never be assumed information has been transferred and interpreted in the way it was intended.

Assuming that each team member has understood can cause confusion and frustration for both parties. Check for understanding. The aim is to ensure that the "sender" and "receiver" both have the same picture of the message in their minds. Simply put, communication should mean the same thing to both the "sender" and the "receiver." For example, the server places a guest order in the kitchen—did both parties understand and interpret the guest's desires correctly?

GUIDELINES FOR TEAM COMMUNICATION

As a rule of thumb, involve everyone in everything.

—Tom Peters

1. Communicate ideas at the proper time and place. Try to catch a team member at a time when their frame of mind is receptive to information. Use nonverbal signals. This shows you are interested in what is being said.

2. Include the team member's name whenever possible. This demonstrates respect and acknowledgment.

3. Take care in the use of tone of voice, facial expressions, words, body language, and appearance. All these factors affect the reception of the message.

4. Summarize the information by paraphrasing or restating the core of the message.

5. Ask questions when unsure. A lot of confusion may be avoided by asking the team member to repeat or rephrase the message.

6. Sincerity and insincerity in communicating will become apparent if careful thought is not part of the reception of ideas and opinions. The receiver should be made to feel free to respond fully.

7. Not only seek to be understood but also to understand and be a good listener.

8. When you talk, you can only say something that you already know. When you listen, you may learn what someone else knows.

DEVELOPING A POSITIVE TEAM AND WORK CLIMATE

Essentials of building a great team include the following:

1. Clarifying each team member's role and clarifying and sorting through any interpersonal conflict.

2. Setting time aside to learn and apply quality improvement methods and reviewing work methods which affect team member performance and quality.

3. Listening, receiving, and reacting to team input. It is impossible to affect quality service without the direct participation and involvement of the dining room or service element of food. Failure to do this usually results in a poor team climate, which in turn transfers into dissatisfied guests. If the kitchen team produces the best possible meals and these meals are served by indifferent, grumpy wait-staff, then obviously the overall team has lost.

Any barriers to team-building success that are present in the establishment must be removed. Each person must be valued and treated with dignity and respect.

MAKING TEAMS WORK

A team of foodservice and hospitality individuals—chefs, servers, stewards, storeroom, supervisors, guest relations agents, front desk employees, management, and so on—requires a great deal more coordination and integration of its efforts than a "group."

Working together, ordinary people can perform extraordinary feats; they can push things a little higher up, a little further on toward the heights of excellence.

Just because it is called a team doesn't mean it will automatically function as a team. Teams may appear to be easy to form and operate, but it takes hard work by everyone involved for a team to be successful.

Team activities such as discussions, role plays, or case studies provide an opportunity for team members to explore topics, interact with each other, and share information by expressing views and responding to ideas and opinions.

TEAM FACILITATORS

The role of a team facilitator or leader consists of leading team discussions and group processes so that individuals learn, and team members feel that the experience is positive and worthwhile.

Typical activities for a team leader are group activities in which quality improvements are assessed. In group discussions where all team members feel committed to the quality improvement actions, an enhanced awareness of team efforts usually exists. Participation by all team members is facilitated; they are invited to present their viewpoints, levels of expertise, and attitudes regarding topics of quality.

Team activities stimulate thinking, create enthusiasm, and assist in analyzing different approaches to quality service. Aspects and characteristics of a great team environment are:

1. An informal relaxed atmosphere.

2. Understanding of the total quality philosophy.

3. Willingness to act as a group, communicate, and listen to each other.

4. Willingness to share new ideas.

5. A focus on differences about concepts—not about team members.

6. A readiness for action once a course of action has been arrived at through consensus.

Leaders must come forward from within a team. This is especially important in the beginning when the group needs guidance, coaching, and feedback.

If the group does not have a formal leader, then it should draft a person from among its members to serve this function.

PITFALLS IN TEAM BUILDING

1. Allowing a team to work alone without support from upper management.

2. Allowing the team to become isolated in its goals causes the team to lose track of its end goals.

3. Not providing a sense of direction to the team or allowing it to develop its own goals and visions in isolation to the organization's culture.

4. Another pitfall is overenthusiasm without "pulse taking" or any measurement of accomplished goals. (Organizations initiate empowerment programs and then forget to monitor how the group is doing, or to check whether the team has the resources, expertise, and authority to carry through its actions. They forget that the idea is for the group, not for one "empowered" person to take over. If this happens, it will not provide any improvement over the old process.)

5. Teamwork does not happen automatically. Training is needed. The training must take into account that some of the people involved have been operating in one way for years, so it will be hard to change their mode of behavior. It is hard to train people to handle empowerment, especially if they have been complying with directives for years in the workplace.

6. Getting teamwork started and keeping it going can present a challenge. At first, there is usually resistance to a new way of doing things. Then comes a period of information sharing and

development of expectations, followed by commitment to particular roles and expectations.

TEAM BUILDING SUGGESTIONS

1. The corporate culture of the organization must support the team effort.
2. Teams should compete with themselves to do more and to do better.
3. Provide retraining or bring in an outsider to observe and report the findings to the team.
4. Allow the team to work on problem solving, not just operational issues but also sorting through interpersonal, and technical skills issues.
5. Provide career paths and opportunities for some team members to transfer out of the team if necessary, so that unresolved personality clashes between key people do not persist and drag everyone else down with them.
6. Expand teams to other parts of the hospitality organization, or work on removing external barriers that may be hampering team operations.
7. Provide team members with the full picture by providing information to give them more context.
8. Make sure personal and team growth is an objective.
9. Team development is a process that requires constant refining and improving. Recognize team successes, and make sure that the team receives a great deal of acclaim, approval, and visibility.
10. Most people in positions of authority want to use this authority wisely and they're always looking for someone with common sense to help them.

TRAINING INDIVIDUALS IN TEAMWORK

For teamwork of any sort to be successful, the members of the team must be trained for the task. Training is the key to successful teams.

There are a number of ways to train team members, one of which is role playing or simulations. Simulations provide imaginary or real-life situations that a team member figures out how to solve. The advantage of this method over the traditional ways of learning is that the members have an opportunity to try out the actual behaviors as they are learning. They learn about the power of a group working together, as opposed to one person working alone.

They learn to trust others, to work together with them, and to give feedback. They learn also to deal with conflict resolution. In using simulations, feedback is very important from the facilitator to the team member. Teams need an objective observer to tell them what they are doing right or wrong.

By focusing on past case studies of problem hospitality operations and by placing high importance on guest satisfaction, quality or operational gaps can be identified. Discussions, comparisons, and observations on shortcomings can be noted.

To achieve total quality, each team member can draw comparisons between what was in a case study and what should be. People can relate to problems associated with quality issues when they are presented in a carefully prepared case.

GETTING THE BEST FROM TEAM MEETINGS

Effective quality guest service requires team meetings on an ongoing basis. These meetings should proceed on the basis of what is already known by the team to the unknown. However, meetings can be time-consuming. The following guidelines facilitate the team leader in developing a more productive meeting:

1. Keep the meeting to under twelve people.
2. Start the meetings on time.
3. Be informal. This is key to putting the team at ease.
4. Respect the contribution of each team member. Every individual has the desire to be recognized. In their minds, whatever they say is worthwhile.
5. Always avoid arguments.
6. Avoid personality disputes. Quickly involve other team members and seek their opinions.
7. Exercise tactfulness when correcting a team member's statement or opinion.
8. Help each team member in the group to share in the discussion. Ask people in the team to speak up. It can be most annoying to the team when an answer is given to a question that most of the group has not heard.
9. The team leader should be alert to guide and encourage nervous or timid members of the team. They should be brought into the discussion by seeking their opinions.
10. Control the meeting if it gets out of control. Interrupt and then summarize key points under discussion. Conclude with correct information and begin discussion on another topic.

11. Stimulate discussion if the team appears disinterested or is slow to offer opinions.

12. Ask debatable questions such as, "Which is a better method?" or "Which is more practical?"

13. Compliment the team before closing the meeting.

14. Develop interest in the next meeting by giving a brief overview of the highlights of the next session.

TEAM TRAINING

The hiring and training of people that have the skill sets to deliver quality service is the first step to guest satisfaction. Training is the basis for total quality management success in the foodservice organization. Without a strong and committed investment in training, neither the organization nor the team will be successful. The principles of total quality are rooted in a trained team approach.

Total quality management does not happen within the organization unless the team and the leader do certain things, which require money and time. Time costs money, therefore, quality has a cost. This cost should be viewed as an investment in the future growth of the foodservice organization. Quality and training can be viewed as an investment, rather than an expenditure.

In his book *Quality Is Free*, Philip Crosby argues that achieving quality costs nothing. He also points out that the real cost of quality is doing things wrong—the cost of waste.

QUALITY MANAGEMENT AND TRAINING

As previously stated TQM requires that each and every function required to produce quality food, ambience, and service within the restaurant be identified, and then ongoing continuous development and improvements can be applied at every stage. Proficiency in total quality management skills cannot be achieved through study—study must be accomplished by a well-organized sequence of applications to actual processes.

The key to this success is training each team member to contribute to total quality management. Commitment to total quality must emanate from the top levels of the organization. It involves the challenge of developing appropriate attitudes and values within the team and throughout the entire foodservice organization.

The aim of adopting a quality approach to training is to provide a service that meets and hopefully exceeds customer needs every time, and to deliver what we promised we would deliver.

TYPES OF TRAINING

There are many types of training: each has relative strengths and weaknesses. The following training methods are considered appropriate to total quality enhancement training in a foodservice environment. They are listed so that each may be evaluated relative to the appropriateness of the training mission.

1. **Job Talk:** This is commonly a speech by the team leader with limited opportunities for open discussion.

2. **Team Meetings (group discussions):** A speech by the team leader with a lot of participation and interaction with the team. Always requires leadership. Particularly useful for teams with mixed experience levels.

3. **Role Playing:** Creating a realistic situation and having team members assume parts of specific personalities in the situation. Their actions are based on the roles assigned to them.

4. **Demonstrations:** In a demonstration, actual equipment is used to demonstrate the action. Demonstration is the most effective method for instructing manipulative skills. Its use of the learner's visual sense.

5. **Case Study:** This is a written narrative description of a real situation. Team members are required to propose one or more suitable solutions and make appropriate decisions.

6. **Apprenticeship Training:** Trainee's work under guidance; The trainee rotates through all the organization's departments in a planned sequential way.

7. **On the Job Training (OJT):** No two people learn at the same rate. Some team members pick up new skills very quickly; others require repeated instruction and supervised practice.

The most important training sense is seeing. When giving instruction, demonstrate visually as often as possible. For example, if demonstrating sauce preparation, show the ingredients. Explain the method (learning), demonstrate skills (seeing), what the texture should be (touching), and finally taste.

Adults learn by doing. They want to get involved. Adults relate their learning to what they already know. This presents a challenge for the supervisor to incorporate participative activities into training. A variety of training topics and methods tends to stimulate and open all of the team members' senses.

The need for positive feedback is also a characteristic of adult learners. Adults prefer to know how their efforts measure up when compared with the objective of the training program. Additionally adult learners may have personal doubts when it comes to training. Among these doubts are their ability to learn, fear, embarrassment, and failure. Each training session should be opened with a good introductory activity which will put everyone at ease.

Facilitators of the adult learning process can be described as change agents.

TRAINING DELIVERY

Be conscious of body language. Good posture is important. Use body language that expresses confidence and enhances the training presentation. Maintaining eye contact is essential. Put enthusiasm in your voice, speak clearly, and don't start with an apology for being there. Create a comfortable atmosphere. There is no reason why a warm friendly atmosphere cannot be created and maintained throughout the training session. Try to establish this at the beginning.

The following are some helpful training suggestions:

1. Use effective facial expressions.
2. Use and maintain eye contact.
3. Move around the room and gesture.
4. Use gestures that are not distracting.
5. Communicate with the team members in the training session on a personal level.
6. Vary tone and pitch of voice.
7. Emphasize key points and use relevant examples.
8. Be certain to talk to, not at, the organization team.
9. Select and use appropriate media technology.
10. Plan to make logical smooth transitions between topics.
11. Give clear directions for all subsequent activities.
12. Greet each team member as they arrive for the training session.
13. Be available during breaks to visit with each member to answer individual questions.
14. Be available after the training session to answer any additional questions or to discuss concerns.
15. Provide clear oral and written instructions for all assignments and activities.
16. Maintain alertness.

UNDERSTANDING TEAM BEHAVIORS

Within groups people often act out roles which are closely related to their individual personalities. Each person plays out a particular role or assume a certain mental posture during training. Team leaders should be aware of these various roles. There are three categories into which these role dynamics fall. These are a building and supportive role, a self-centered role, and a task role.

Within the building and supportive role are team members who may be categorized as:

- Supporter. Praises, agrees, goes along with the team.
- Harmonizer. Mediates differences between team members.
- Tension reliever. Jokes or brings out humor.
- Facilitator. Opens channels for communication.

The self-centered roles include:

- Blocker. Constantly raises objections, revisits topics when the rest of the team have moved on.
- Aggressor. Expresses ill-will and makes sarcastic remarks.
- Recognition seeker. Calls attention to him- or herself during the training session.
- Dominator. Tries to run the session by giving orders, interrupting, and attempting to get his or her own way.
- Apathetic member. Nonparticipant in team activities.

In the task role, team members demonstrate problemsolving and task performance. Within and among groups, many other roles are played out, including the following:

- Initiator—proposes new ideas, goals, and procedures.
- Information seeker—seeks facts and additional information before making decisions.
- Information giver—offers facts and information.
- Opinion seeker—seeks clarification of the values involved.
- Opinion giver—states own opinions.
- Clarifier—elaborates on ideas offered by other team members.
- Coordinator—brings together ideas offered by the team.
- Energizer—prods the team to a greater level of activity.

By listening carefully and watching the various verbal and nonverbal clues, each of the described roles may be observed. Recognizing these behaviors is the first step in developing a method of coping with them.

DIFFICULT PEOPLE AND TEAMWORK

When team members disagree, the major outcome in doubt is how individuals will feel about working together in the future, and how individuals will deal with each other as people.

Be unconditionally constructive. Many people deal with difficult people in the same way those people treat them, by reciprocating what they receive. This may be called an "eye for an eye"policy. If the other person yells at them, they yell back. If the other person insults them, they insult that person right back. If the other person cheats them, they cheat the other person.

Unfortunately in a modern foodservice organization, it is largely ineffectual and even dangerous, because the "victim" often is harmed as much as the perpetrator. Reciprocation sets off a negative spiral and does not resolve anything.

Each of us sees the events in our own lives and other people's behavior from our own vantage point. Thus we see only "part" of the whole. We tend to think, nevertheless, that our perspective is accurate and representative of what is occurring.

Unfortunately there are at least two sides to every story and many ways to view every incident. At the end of a hard week, for example, a leader and a team member may reflect on life in their organization, but each sees things a little differently.

Balance reason with emotion. We all know that in some instances too much emotion can diminish performance. The person who is very agitated is less likely to be rational. On the other hand, a foodservice organization with little or no emotion is dull and lifeless. Responding impulsively and emotionally to a difficult person usually only worsens the relationship, especially if the person is making you angry. A good working relationship with a difficult person requires a reasonable approach. What can you do to balance emotional and rational reactions to behavior that upsets you?

1. Take a break.
2. Count to ten if an official break is not possible.
3. Consult a third party.
4. Acknowledge and talk about your emotions.
5. Accept responsibility and apologize if an argument erupts.
6. Prepare yourself when you know an emotional situation is likely.

We cannot deal effectively with difficult people unless we understand them. However, people usually overestimate their understanding of others. When you feel that someone is being difficult, it is always best to assume that there is a good reason for their behavior which you do not as yet understand. Unfortunately most people assume that what other people say is absurd or untrue and try to imagine what could be wrong with them to make them say something so ridiculous.

Be trustworthy. Working relationships are better among trusting people. People who can be counted on to keep their word are trustworthy. Trustworthiness is not an objective measure of honesty and reliability. It is a qualitative measure. If I believe you will do what you say, then I perceive you as trustworthy. If I suspect you will not, your credibility with me is low.

Faith in people is fragile. Once broken, it is difficult to restore. You may think, "I have good intentions; I usually come through with most things I promise; I'm not trying to hurt anyone; I should be trusted." However, being trustworthy in three out of five instances does not earn you trust. Every breach of trust diminishes people's confidence in you. Even if you keep your word nine out of ten times, others will remember the one time you did not and wonder when you will disappoint them next.

Use persuasion, not coercion. When people are being difficult and you have more authority than they do, it is tempting to force or coerce them to do as you wish. However, compliance through coercion (such as threatening harm) provides only short-term gains and long-term losses. People resent being coerced and eventually express that resentment in angry outbursts or acts of revenge. Coercion creates competition to see who will win, as methods to create win/win solutions are overlooked. Rather than solve difficulties, coercion usually just perpetuates or escalates them.

A difficulty should be seen as a problem that both parties wish to solve through cooperation. Both should be on the same side of the line, attacking the problem instead of each other. Managing difficult behavior is not a contest. It is a challenge to invent a solution both people support and feel committed to implementing.

Accept and deal seriously with difficult people. It is tempting to scorn and reject people who do not fulfill our expectations. When disappointed, we become critical and disdainful. We slam the door on communication and give up on problem solving. The "types" described are part of the normal human mix within a team. Some team members have a number of these characteristics, and they can take on these descriptions at different periods. They are:

- *Hostile-aggressives.* These are the people who bully and overwhelm by bombarding others, making cutting remarks, or throwing tantrums when situations don't go the way such people are certain they should.

- *Complainers.* These people gripe incessantly but never do anything to resolve what they complain about.

- *Silent and unresponsives.* They are the types who respond to every question and every plea for help with a yes, a no, or a grunt.

- *Superagreeables.* These are the type who are very reasonable, sincere, and supportive in the presence of others but do not produce what they say they will or act contrary to the way they have led others to expect.

- *Negativists.* These are the people who always claim or proclaim to the rest of us, "It won't work" or "It's impossible" every time something new is proposed. All too often they deflate any optimism others might have.

- *Know-it-all experts.* These are the types who are "superior." They believe and want others to recognize that they know everything there is to know about anything worth knowing. Such people are condescending, imposing (if they really do know what they are talking about), or pompous (if they don't); and they often make others feel like idiots.

- *Indecisives.* These are the types who stall major decisions until the decisions are made for them. They can't let go of anything until it is perfect, which means never.

RESOLVING CONFLICT WITHIN THE TEAM

Conflict is inevitable within all foodservice teams. It is not bad or harmful if handled correctly. In fact, it can lead to far greater creativity and innovation by challenging assumptions, values, and proposals.

Possible causes of conflict in teams include the following:

- *Confusion.* The overall team goal or objectives are unclear or unacceptable to the team.

- *Perception.* Some aspects of the task are interpreted based on past experiences. These experiences influence the way in which the members of the team see themselves or the task.

- *Emotions and egos.* Emotions can cloud judgment, confuse facts and feelings, and get things out of proportion. (They are also a tremendous source of energy and morale, so should not be ignored!)

- *Communication.* The complexity of human communication, both verbal and nonverbal, always provides an opportunity for misinterpretation of meaning or intention.

To overcome and resolve, the following are helpful:

- Present the issue unemotionally—use an "I" message and ask the other team members for help. "Can we agree to work together on this? I really need your help."

- Clarify and define the issue. "Here's how I see the problem. What do you think is the issue?"

- Understand the other person's position, listen without judgment or rebuttal, and ask for clarification (probe as needed), "Can you tell me more about that?"

- Give your point of view. Use "I"statements—express it assertively and take ownership for it. Test for understanding.
- Within the team develop objectives or conditions on which both parties agree: "What are we all after?" "The problem will be solved when."
- Brainstorm alternatives, put judgment on hold, check egos and emotions.
- Jointly choose one alternative as a tentative solution.
- Finally, decide how each member of the foodservice team will know if the solution is working.

RECOGNIZING TEAM MEMBERS

Ways to champion the entire front-of-house and the back-of-house teams include the following:

1. Send letters to team members, thanking them for their involvement; send another one at the end of their project of key action, thanking them for their contribution.
2. Develop a "behind the scenes" award specifically for those whose actions are not usually in the limelight.
3. Create a "best ideas of the year" booklet and include everyone's picture, name, and description of their best ideas.
4. Feature a quality idea of the month.
5. Honor peers who have helped the organization by recognizing them at meetings.
6. Create a visibility wall to display information, posters, and pictures, thanking individuals and describing their team contributions.
7. Mention a member's outstanding work or their ideas during meetings and at other meetings with peers and management.
8. Take an interest in a team member's development and set up appropriate training and experience to build on initiatives.
9. Get your teams' pictures in the company newspaper.
10. Ask people to help you with a project you consider to be especially difficult which provides real challenges.
11. Send team members to special seminars, workshops, or meetings outside that covers topics they are especially interested in.
12. Have a stock of small gifts to give to people on the spot whom you "catch doing things right."

REVIEW QUESTIONS

1. Describe the benefits of a team approach in the foodservice industry.
2. Outline the attributes of successful teams.
3. Describe why effective communication is vital in the foodservice industry.
4. Outline the essentials of developing a positive team and work climate.
5. Explain the steps in conducting effective meetings.
6. Outline the benefits and elements associated with teamwork and training.
7. Describe the methods of training used in the foodservice industry.
8. Explain the complexities involved with understanding team member behaviors, and discuss how to deal with difficult people and resolve conflict.

About Wines

Acetic   Vinegary taste or smell resulting from overexposure to air.

Aging   It's a common misconception that all wines improve with age. Over 90 percent of all wines made in the world are meant to be consumed within one year.

Alcoholic   Term used to describe a wine that has too much alcohol for its body and weight, making it unbalanced.

Anjou Rose   A rose wine from the Loire Valley in France made from the Gamay grape.

Antioxidants   Phenolic compounds present in grape color and tannin which provide protection to the human body, inhibiting low-density lipoprotein cholesterol and stimulating high-density lipoprotein cholesterol.

A.O.C.   An abbreviation for Appellation d'Origine Controlée—the government agency that controls wine production in France. Only 24 percent of all French wines are worthy of A.O.C. designation.

Aperitif Wines   Specifically created to be drunk before a meal or as a "cocktail." These beverages include spiced wines, such as vermouth, and various brand-name preparations, such as Dubonnet, Campari, Punt e Mes, and Lillet. Sherries and similar wines, which may be drunk during a meal but are not likely to be, are also included in this category.

Appellation   In the wine world, this term refers to a designated growing area governed by the rules and regulations established by a country's federal government or local governing body. Such rules vary from country to country but are somewhat similar in their attempt to stimulate the production of quality wines. These regulations are established by the Appellation d'Origine Controlle (A.O.C.) in France, the Denominazione di Origine Controllata (D.O.C.) in Italy, the Denominaìao de Origem Controlada (D.O.C.) in Portugal, the Denominaciùn de Origen (D.O.) in Spain, and the American Viticultural Area (A.V.A.) in the United States.

A.P. Number   The official testing number displayed on a German wine label that shows the wine was tasted and passed government quality-control standards.

Aroma   The smell or bouquet of a wine. Used only in a favorable context.

Aromatized Wines   Flavorings in the form of herbs and spices, as well as barks, roots, and flowers, are added to certain wines. Many of these wines fit into the group known as vermouths, and many of these wines come from southern France or southern Italy. Aromatized wines come in both sweet and dry versions.

Asti   Capital city of the Piedmont region of northern Italy. Asti Spumante is a white sparkling wine that is sweet and very fruity.

Astringent   The term used to describe a wine with a drying or puckering of the mouth quality due to a high content of tannin. Found in young red wines. Tannins come from the grapes skins and from oak barrels in which the wine is aged.

Auslese   German ("selected harvest") wines are made from the ripest bunches of grapes and are individually selected and pressed. Some of them have noble rot (edelfaule or Botrytis cinerea), which concentrates their juice and sweetness.

Bacchus   Roman god of wine.

Balance   Describes the haronony among the various components of the wine. In a well-balanced wine, the flavors of fruit, acid, tannin, and alcohol are experienced in proper proportion to one another.

Beaujolais   A light, fruity red wine from the Beaujolais district of France. "Beaujolais-style" refers to a wine with similar sensory qualities.

Beaujolais Nouveau   This is a light fruity-style wine that is best to drink young. "New" Beaujolais is picked, fermented, bottled, and available in a matter of weeks. The exact date of release of Beaujolais nouveau each year is November 15.

Beerenauslese   Any of several fine, sweet German wines made from superior, slightly overripe grapes which have been individually picked or cut from their bunches. Some Beerenausleses are made from grapes that have been infected with Borttis Cinerea (noble rot). Because of their special selection and picking, these wines are very choice and expensive.

Big   An intensely flavored, full bodied, and textured wine. Having a weighty quality that can be sensed in the mouth.

Blanc de Blancs   A white wine made from white grapes.

Blending   Legitimate method of improving the quality of different wines. Nearly every wine involves some blending, whether between grapes, vintages, different vats, or other ingredients.

Blush Wines   These are generally made with red grapes (some producers mix red and white grapes), but the juice has had a very brief contact with the grape skins. This produces wines that can range in color from shell pink to pale orange to barely red. Blush wines can range from dry to sweet and may be light to medium bodied. The term blush wine has all but replaced the more dated term "rosé."

Body   This describes the texture, weight, and flavor intensity of the wine.

Bordeaux   Large wine region along the Gironde and Dordogne Rivers in southwestern France best known for dry red and dry to sweet white table wines of high quality.

Botrytis Cinerea   Noble rot. A mold that forms on the grapes that is necessary to make Sauternes, and the rich German wines (Beerenauslese and Trockenbeerenauslese). The German name for noble rot is *Edulfaule*.

Bouquet   Smell or aroma. An especially intense, flowery bouquet may be called a nose.

Breathe   To breathe a wine means to allow air to come into contact with it to improve the bouquet and taste.

Breed   The most seductive and rarest quality of wine; also the most difficult to describe. It is the privilege of the finest wines that is endowed with an outstanding personality, a discreet yet fragrant bouquet, perfect poise of flavor and strength.

Brut   The driest style of champagne and, by extension, other sparkling wines.

Burgundy   A wine district in France centered around Beaune and the wines from that district.

Buttery   Used to describe a wine having the flavor of butter. Evident in some new world Chardonnays and white Burgundies. The word creamy is also used in the same context.

Carafe   The open container usually used for serving wine at the table, often the container for house wine.

Chablis   Wine from grapes (Chardonnay mostly) grown in the Chablis district of France.

Chablis Grand Cru   The highest classification of Chablis in terms of quality.

Chambrer   French wine term meaning "to bring to room temperature."

Chaptalisation   The French term for the addition of sugar to fermenting must to build up the alcoholic content of the wine being made. A declared percentage is permitted but the practice is controlled by the authorities. The process is named after the Comte de Chaptel, a chemist and minister of Napoleon who first experimented in sugar addition.

Charmat Method   French tank method of producing sparkling wines. Least-expensive method for producing reasonable-quality wines.

Chateau   The "legal" definition is a house attached to a vineyard having a specific number of acres with winegrowing and storage facilities on the property.

Chateau Bottled   A wine that has been *Mis en Bouteilles au Chateau*, or bottled where it was made and by the people who made it. It is a guarantee of authenticity, and it used to be also a guarantee of quality when the owners of the chateau refused to give the "chateau bottling" to any of their wines that they did not consider up to standard. Now there are chateaux where every vintage is bottled at the chateau, good or not so good. The owners claim never to make bad wine.

Chateauneuf-du-Pape   Rhône village that lends its name to the sturdy, full-bodied red wines from nearby vineyards of Grenache and Syrah.

Literally, "new castle of the pope," for its fourteenth-century summer home of the Avignon popes.

Chianti   Wine from the Tuscany region of Italy.

Claret   A dry red wine from the Bordeaux region of France and a semi-generic wine type in the United States. The English name for red wines of Bordeaux since the twelfth century. There has never been any other red beverage wine to possess so great a variety of styles and types, or a better balance of the qualities wine should have, that is, color, bouquet, flavor, breed, and charm.

Complex   Challenging and interesting, with several dimensions.

Corkage   A fee charged by some restaurants to open and serve a bottle of wine brought in by the patron. A quick call to the restaurant will confirm the amount of the corkage fee. Some restaurants charge a lower fee if the patron's wine is not on the restaurant's wine list, such as might be the case with an older wine or a particularly distinctive vintage.

Corked   Used to describe a wine that is not fit to drink because it has acquired an objectionable smell like a dirty, mildewed basement due to a bacterial infection of its cork. This is an increasingly common problem.

Corkscrew   The modern version of the corkscrew was invented about 1700. It was different in shape and greatly improved over the early medieval corkscrew. Nowadays every possible variety of corkscrew is found on the market, from the simple spiral variety to elaborate models employing air pressure. However, the great secret of getting a cork properly out of a bottle is to screw the worm well into the cork.

Côte d'Or   French region that includes the most important Burgundy vineyards: the southerly Côte de Beaune—famous for Pinot Noir. Literally, "golden slopes."

Cru   Growth or vineyard.

Cru Beaujolais   The top grade of Beaujolais wine that comes from one of the ten highest-quality villages in Beaujolais.

Cuvee   Literally, a vatful. Signifies a selection of wine that may or may not have been blended. Also describes a batch of wine with the same characteristics.

Dessert Wines   Some wines have sufficiently high sugar content to be drunk with or after a dessert. In general, as aperitifs they would blunt the appetite; with a main dish they would taste strange. Dessert wines range from Sauterne to Trockenbeerenauslese and fortified wines such as Port.

D.O.C.   An abbreviation for Denominazione di Origine Controllata, the government agency that controls wine production in Italy. The biggest difference between the A.O.C. of France and the D.O.C. of Italy is that the D.O.C. has aging requirements.

D.O.C.G.   An abbreviation for Denominazione di Origine Controllata Grantita. The Italian government allows this marking to appear only on the finest wines. The "G" stands for "guaranteed."

Dry   Used to describe a wine with the absence of sweetness from residual sugar. Also lacking in fruit.

Earthy   Taste of the earth where the grapes are grown.

Eiswein   German wine made from Beerenauslese or Trockenbeerenauslese grapes that have frozen on the vine due to cold weather and have been quickly harvested (the night of the frost) and pressed (early that morning or at dawn).

Elegant   A wine that displays great finesse and balance. Lacking intensity, but complex and interesting.

En Cave   French term for "in the cellar."

Enology   Science or study of wine and wine making.

Estate-Bottled   Wine that is made, produced, and bottled by the owner. One hundred percent of the wine is from grapes grown on the land owned or controlled by the winery in a given viticultural area. The entire operation, from crushing the grapes to bottling the wine, takes place there.

Fat   Wine that is heavy, but lacking in complexity and firmness.

Finesse   A term used to describe a wine that has great balance and harmony and delivery.

Finish   Aftertaste, a sensation that remains after swallowing the wine.

Flat   Acidity, insipid; in champagne, without effervescence.

Flinty   Used to describe Chablis: dry, clean, sharp.

Flowery   Having an intense aroma of lilacs, honeysuckle, or other flowers while tasting the wine.

Fortified Wine   A wine that has additional neutral grape brandy that raises the alcohol content, such as port, sherry, and Marsala.

Forward   A wine that is mature before its time, soft and pleasant at a young age.

Foxy Wine   Native American grape taste. This term is mostly associated with New York wines. The taste and flavor of the wine from this region is referred to as foxy. The term is generally felt to be from the translation of the *Vitis Labruscia*. Labruscia is the fox grape—meaning foxes liked to eat off the vine.

Fruity   Having the flavor of grapes and sometimes suggesting other kinds of fruit. A term erroneously used for sweet wines.

Grafting   Horticultural technique, used in uniting European (Vitis Vinifera) vines with American phylloxera resistant (Vitis Labrusca).

Grand Cru   A wine that comes from an excellent vineyard, which has the best soil and slope conditions in Burgundy. One step above a Premier Cru.

Grape   A vinous fruit that grows in clusters. Generally growers produce grapes for the table or the bottle, but these are basically for main types, for wine, table, raisins and unfermented grape juice. Any kind of grape can be made into wine, used at table, or made into grape juice. But in fact no good wine grape does well as a table grape, or vice versa. Table grapes and wine grapes are two distinct categories of Vitis Vinifera, the patriarch of 90 percent of the world's cultivated vines, known to the ancients and first cultivated by the Egyptians who brought wine cultivation and wine making to a high degree of perfection.

Green   Young, immature, and undeveloped wine.

Hard   A term used to describe a wine that is immature and tannic.

Herbaceous   Describes wines with aromas and flavors that hint at grass or hay.

Hermitage   A Rhône district south of the Côte Rotie and also noted for dark, rich, long-aging red wines from Syrah.

Hock   Originally an English name for German white wine. It began as hochamore, from Hochheim on the Main. It was much liked by Queen Victoria and thus became a very fashionable wine in England.

Hybrids   Cross between two grape species, Vitis Labrusca and Vitis Vinifera.

Intense   Having strong, well-defined flavor and texture. Robust.

Jug Wines   The phrase "jug wine" refers to simple, uncomplicated, everyday drinking wine. Inexpensive wines were once bottled in jugs rather than conventional wine bottles—hence the name jug wine.

Kabinett   German (cabinet) wines made from fully mature grapes which have a fruity quality. They are the driest of the wines with special attributes.

Legs   Long drops running down the inside of the glass show good body, particularly when the wine adheres to glass. This demonstrates the density of the wine.

Light   Low in alcohol, lacking in body, dull.

Long-vatted   A term used for a wine fermented with the grape skins for a long period of time to acquire a rich red color.

Malic   Describes the applelike aroma from the malic acid present in wines made from insufficiently ripened grapes.

Medoc   Bordeaux's biggest district famous for long-aging, Cabernet-based red wines of its great chateaux. Look for the names of the Medoc's four villages—Margaux, Saint-Julien, Pauillac, and Saint Estephe—on the most celebrated wines. Medoc is the appellation of origin of wines made from grapes grown anywhere in the district.

Methode Champenoise   The method of making sparkling wine that was developed in Champagne in France and has been copied the world over. A secondary fermentation in the bottle results in bubbles of carbon dioxide becoming trapped in the wine. The wine makers of Champagne have fought to maintain the exclusivity of their name, and, following an EC directive, the term may no longer appear on any wine from outside the region.

Mise en Bouteilles   French wine term for "bottled at."

Moldy   An unpleasant taste extracted by wine from fungus on grapes or from musty casks.

Montrachet   An extraordinary twenty-acre vineyard in the Cote de Beaune of the Cote d'Or that produces the most famous and expensive dry white Burgundy wines.

Mosel   The principal river of the Mosel-Saar-Ruwer wine region of Germany. Wines from the steep hillside vineyards of this coolest of viticultural areas range from the ordinary to the highest quality in white Rieslings in dry to very sweet styles. (Spelled Moselle in French and English.)

Mulled Wine   Any wine, although red is the more usually chosen, which is brought almost to the boiling point, then poured back into a jug in which some sugar lumps have been melted in a little hot water. A slice or two of lemon is added, and the wine is stirred and sprinkled with a little grated nutmeg.

Must   A term indicating the crushed grapes and juice before termination.

Natural Wines   This method involves the simple fermentation of grape juice, without the addition of alcohol or sugar (beyond the very small amount of sugar allowed by law to supplement the natural sugar of some wines in certain years). Natural wines are usually dry wines.

Nose   The term used to describe the aroma and pronounced bouquet of the wine.

Nutty   A term frequently used to describe the unique taste of sherry; a "fino" or Amontillado is said to have a green walnut taste.

Oaky   Aroma and flavor of oak barrels used for aging. Also woody.

Oenophile   A person who is involved in the science, study, appreciation, and tasting of wines (Enology).

Off   Turned bad often due to microbial infection of the wine from dirty equipment.

Oxidized   Deteriorated from exposure to air, often indicated by brownish color and the odor of rotting hay.

Pasteurization   To "stabilize" low-quality wines and get rid of any microorganisms, wine can sometimes be pasteurized, that is, heat-sterilized in the same way as milk is treated.

Petillant   A wine that is slightly sparkling.

Phylloxera   A beetlelike creature that brought devastation to the European vineyards. A native of the eastern United States. No one understood what was happening, only that all the European vines planted withered and died. There was, however, a vine native to the United States which gave bad wine but was immune from these attacks. The beetle found its way to Europe, probably on an experimental vine, and its progeny swept through the vineyards doing terrible damage. Someone realized that the roots of the despised American vine were immune, and after much argument, millions of American vines were grafted onto the surviving European stock. The new roots resisted the scourge. It is acknowledged that but for the American vines there would have been no wine, and, of course, but for the American beetle there would have been no phylloxera.

Pomerol   Smallest Bordeaux wine district noted for rich, flavorful wines from Merlot and Cabernet Franc.

Port   Port comes from the Douro region in Northern Portugal. True port is named Porto or Oporto from the name of the port through which it is shipped. There are basically two types of port—wood port, which includes ruby port, a dark and fruity variety blended from young nonvintage wines. Tawny port is lighter and more delicate, blended from many vintages, and aged in casks up to twenty years. Port is nearly always decanted to avoid sediment. Once a bottle of port is opened, it should be consumed within one week.

Pouilly-Fuisse   The highest quality white wine from Chardonnay grapes grown near Macon in southern Burgundy.

Qualitatswein   A German term meaning quality wine.

Refreshment Wines   "Fun" wines or "quaffing" wines are created to be drunk unceremoniously, often without food accompaniment, without even the anticipation of a meal. They are drunk instead of water, milk, punch, beer, fruit juice, or cola. Many new wines are sold under upbeat brand names and are meant to be chilled ice cold or drunk on ice as refreshment wines.

Riddling   One step of the champagne-making process in which the bottles are turned gradually each day until they are almost upside down, with the sediment almost in the neck of the bottle.

Saint Emillion   Small Bordeaux district noted for its high proportion of fine wines from the varieties Merlot and Cabernet Franc. Chateau Cheval Blanc is one of the best vineyards.

Sake   The traditional wine of Japan, it is made from white rice, malt and water. Sake is to the Japanese what champagne is to the French or whiskey is to the Irish. Sake is pale amber in color, sweet and rich in flavor, and is the one traditional beverage taken with meals. At one time no one would consider drinking sake alone, so the word came to mean drinking parties. It is served in tiny porcelain cups not much larger than an egg cup. Formerly it was drunk cold, but when sake of inferior quality began to be served, it was warmed to disguise its poor quality. Today it is always served warm or even hot.

Sancerre   A French township and popular Loire wine made from Sauvignon Blanc. Closely resembles its neighbor Pouilly-Fume.

Sauternes   A sweet wine from the Bordeaux region of France made from semillon and sauvignon blanc grapes infected with Botrytis Cinerea (noble rot).

Sec   A very sweet style of champagne.

Shiraz   The Australian name for Syrah.

Solera System   This is the system used to produce and age Spanish sherries. It is accomplished by utilizing a system of oak barrels set up in tiers, up to thirteen layers high (youngest on top tier, oldest on the bottom).The wine in the bottom barrel is then replaced by the tier above and so on, so that the older wines are refreshed, and the younger wines gain complexity.

Sommelier   The French term for cellar master or wine steward.

Sparkling Wines   Carbonation, caused by the presence of carbon dioxide in a wine, is created by a change in production method. In the case of champagne, it is the corking of the bottles for the second fermentation which prevents the carbon dioxide release during the fermentation escape. Or, if bulk method, the addition of carbon dioxide bubbles to the wine in an automated, mechanical way, forcing the wine to become "supercharged."

Spatlese   German (late harvest) wines are made from grapes picked after the completion of the normal harvest, when they are more mature. These wines have a richer, sweeter taste.

Spumante   The Italian word for sparkling, as in wine.

Sturdy   A wine that indicates it can stand aging.

Sulphur/"Sulfites"   Sulfur dioxide blocks the metabolic process of many bacteria, therefore preventing their development and spread. In addition, in wine production sulfur dioxide renders inactive the naturally occurring yeasts and other microorganisms that collect on the skin of the grape before harvest. The addition of sulfites is closely monitored by wine producers, and wine chemists are constantly searching for ways to avoid using any chemicals. Sulphur dioxide is now used either in gaseous form or diluted in water. Too much sulphur dioxide produces a smell of rotten eggs and induces headaches.

Swirling   Swirling of the wine in the glass aids the unleashing of the fragrance and flavor of the wine. Normally done when "scrutinizing" the wine's aroma. But for most people, the initial "sniffing" will suffice.

Table Wines   These wines are enjoyed with food. A table wine can be inexpensive or expensive, red or white (or somewhere in between), still or sparkling. This category is certainly the largest.

Tannin   A natural compound that comes from the skins, stems, and pips of the grapes and also from the wood that the wine is aged in.

Tartaric Acid   Natural acid found in grapes. When the wine is chilled or cool-fermented, it can crystallize out as cream of tartar.

Tawny Port   A port that is lighter, softer, and aged longer than ruby port.

Tonneaux   French word for barrels.

Trocken   The German word for dry.

Trockenbeerenauslese   German ("shriveled hand-picked selected harvest") wines are made from noble rot grapes, harvested individually, which have been allowed to dry on the vine, shriveling and appearing like raisins, concentrating the sweet grape juice and flavor. They are very expensive and very sweet.

Valpolicella   Produced in northern Italy, this dry red wine is light bodied and has a fragrant bouquet and fruity flavor. It's best served young and is sometimes viewed as Italy's version of a French Beaujolais.

Varietal Wine   A wine that is labeled with the predominant grape used to produce the wine, for example, wine from Chardonnay (predominantly labeled "Chardonnay").

V.D.Q.S.   An abbreviation for Vins Delimites de Qualite Superieure, a classification of French wine, one step below A.O.C.

Vermouth   A white wine which has been cooked with a number of different herbs and flavorings, sweetened or not, but with a mildly bitter aftertaste which is supposed to promote the flow of saliva and thus prepare the diner to enjoy and digest the meal that is to follow. For many years the two main types of vermouth were the French, the lighter and drier of the two, and the Italian, sweeter and darker. They were made almost exclusively in France and in Italy immediately north and south of the Alps. However, Vermouths are now produced in all wine-making lands. Once opened, vermouth does not keep indefinitely.

Vin de Garde   French for "good for keeping."

Vin de Pays   A French classification of wine one step below V.D.Q.S.

Vin de Primeur   French term for young, new wine.

Vineyard   A plantation of grape vines.

Viniculture   The art and science of wine production.

Vintage   A vintage indicates the year the grapes were harvested, so every year is a vintage year. A vintage chart reflects the weather conditions for various years. Better weather results in a better rating for the "vintage." Nonvintage wine is made from the juice of grapes harvested from several years. There is no year noted on the label of a nonvintage wine.

Vintner   A dealer in wines, also a grower.

Viticulture   A branch of agriculture that deals with the science and art of grape growing.

Vitis Labrusca   A native American grape species.

Vitis Vinefera   A European grape species used to make European and California wine.

Vouvray   Can be dry to sweet and still to sparkling. The white "chameleon" wine from the Loire Valley region of France. Any of various white wines made in and around the French village of Vouvray in the Loire Valley, usually from Chenin Blanc grapes. These wines can vary greatly, with a broad range including dry, semisweet, sweet, slightly sparkling, or fully sparkling. Vouvrays can range from average to excellent, depending on the vintner.

Wine Bottles   The standard wine bottle is 750 ml (milliliters), which is almost exactly equivalent of an American fifth (4/5 of a quart or 25.6 ounces). In response to stricter driving/alcohol limits in many states, the wine industry is introducing a new 500 ml bottle size. This new size is midway between a standard bottle. A half bottle (12.8 ounces) is equivalent to about 17 ounces, or two-thirds of a standard bottle.

Magnum:	(2 in 1) equivalent to 2 standard bottles in 1
Jeroboam:	(4 in 1) equivalent to 4 standard bottles in 1
Gallon:	(5 in 1) equivalent to 5 standard bottles in 1
Rehoboam:	(6 in 1) equivalent to 6 standard bottles in 1

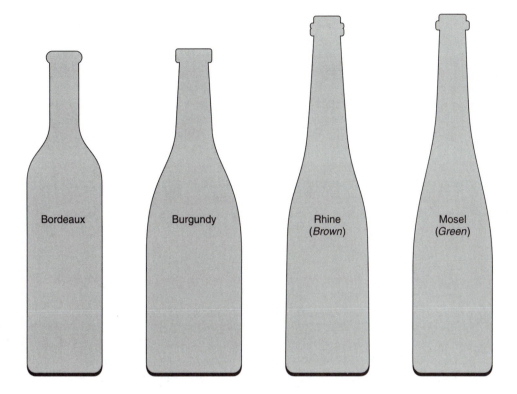

| Bordeaux | Burgundy | Rhine (*Brown*) | Mosel (*Green*) |

Methuselah: (8 in 1) equivalent to 8 standard bottles in 1
Salmanazar: (12 in 1) equivalent to 12 standard bottles in 1
Balthazar: (16 in 1) equivalent to 16 standard bottles in 1
Nebuchadnezzar: (20 in 1) equivalent to 20 standard bottles in 1

Wine Labels   In ancient times wine bottles were not labeled. It was usual to write the name of the wine on a piece of parchment and stick it on to the bottle with gum. With the appearance of glass decanters, something more elegant was required, and the silver bottle ticket made its appearance. This in turn went out of fashion with the coming of the stick-on wine labels on bottles.

Yeasty   Young wine, tasting of its yeasts.

Yield   The quantity of wine produced by a particular vineyard. The greater the quantity, generally, the lower the quality or the lighter the wine, due to a more rapid maturing process.

Glossary of Terms

Accompaniments   Items that accompany a course; food item mandated by the chef.

Active listening   Encouraging the speaker to continue talking by giving interested responses that show that you understand the speaker's meaning and feelings.

A la carte   Foods prepared to order. Each dish priced separately.

Alcohol   Naturally occurring and easily synthesized compound that induces intoxication when consumed.

Alcoholic   In wine terms, used to describe a wine that has too much alcohol for its body and weight, making it unbalanced.

Ale   A top-fermented barley malt product with a pale, bright color and a pronounced hop flavor.

American service   The food is prepared and dished onto individual plates in the kitchen, carried into the dining room, and served to guests. This method of service is quicker and guests receive the food hot and beautifully presented by the chef.

Antioxidants   Phenolic compounds present in grape color and tannin that provide protection to the human body, inhibiting LDL cholesterol and stimulating HDL cholesterol.

Appetizer   A small portion of food or drink served before a meal to stimulate the appetite.

Back-of-the-House   Refers to the support areas behind the scenes, in a hotel or restaurant, including, housekeeping, laundry, engineering, chefs, and kitchen support team. Also refers to individuals who operate behind the scene to make a guest's stay pleasant and safe.

Bacteria   Organisms that can cause fermentation or spoilage of foods; pathogenic types cause diseases in man.

Banquet   A dining function in which all guests are served at one time, and all factors are predetermined.

Bain-marie   A hot water bath for keeping foods hot.

Beer   An alcoholic beverage obtained by fermentation of malted cereals.

Beeswing   A light sediment, mostly the mucilage grapes, sometimes found in old ports; it does not settle upon the glass of the bottle, like crust, but it does not foul the wine when it passes from the bottle into the decanter. It is quite tasteless, although the crust is bitter.

Bin number   The number of the shelf or case in which wines are stored; a means of identifying and ordering wines.

Blanc   French word for white.

Blazer   An oval, rectangular, or round pan mostly used for tableside cooking.

Blend   To mix food thoroughly in a processor so that the resulting mixture is uniform in texture, color, and flavor.

Bock beer   A heavy, sweet beer, dark brown in color, rich in taste, usually served in the spring.

Body language   Expression of attitudes and feelings through body movements and positions.

Bonded   A term used by the U.S. Bureau of Alcohol, Tobacco and Firearms (ATF) in reference to wines on which the federal taxes have not yet been paid. A "bonded area" denotes the borders within which wine may be stored.

Buffet   A display of ready-to-eat foods presented on a table or sideboard where guests select their food items. Guests may serve themselves or be aided by a service person.

Call package   In bar operations, it is the group of spirits that the bar offers to guests who ask for specific name brands.

Captain   Team member who is responsible for an area of the dining room. This area is also known as a "station."

Carbonated water   Water charged with carbon dioxide gas, for sodas and for drinks.

Carbon dioxide   A gas obtained by fermentation of yeast or by the action of soda and an acid, and used to leaven baked products.

Casserole   A heavy oven-proof dish of metal or earthenware, and, by extension, a dish cooked in it.

Cellar   The place where wine is stored; may or may not be below ground.

Chafing dish   A two-part container and serving vessel for food, with a heat source beneath it; the upper compartment contains the food, the lower boiling water.

Charmat   Method of making sparkling wine, also known as cuve close. Sugar and yeast are placed in a large vat for secondary fermentation to take place. The wine is then chilled, filtered, transferred under pressure to a second tank, sweetened with liqueur d'expedition, and bottled.

Chill   To cool, but not freeze, in a refrigerator or over cracked ice.

China   Plates and cups of opaque material.

Cloche   A bell-shaped glass used to cover food for service.

Commis   An assistant in a classical restaurant team.

Communication   The process of passing along information and understanding from one person to another person or group.

Continental breakfast   Coffee, bread and butter, and sometimes jam; often complimentary.

Cover   A single place setting on a guest's table.

Cradle   A metal or wicker basket used for holding wine during decanting (see decanting) and sometimes for serving wine. Usually used for red wines.

Creamer   A container for cream, milk, or nondairy coffee whitener.

Crumbing   The act of removing food particles from a guest's table with the use of a plate and a folded napkin or crumber.

Crumbing a table   Removing debris from a table during a meal, often using a special device. Table crumbers or "silent butlers" or a clean napkin are often used.

Cuisine   Food cooked and served in styles from around the world.

Cultural empathy   Being sensitive to cultural differences and similarities by seeking to understand others' approach to life and their ways of thinking and living.

Decanter   A bottlelike vessel for liquids, with a stopper; meant to be used more than once. Usually used for old wines.

Decanting   The process of separating the wine from its sediment after several years of bottle aging. Done by pouring the wine into a separate container, leaving the sediment in the bottle.

Delegation   The process of distributing work to others and providing them with the appropriate resources and authority to do the task.

Disabled person   Any person who has or is considered to have a physical or mental impairment that substantially limits one or more of such person's major life activities.

Diversity   The physical and cultural dimensions that separate and distinguish individuals and groups: age, gender, physical abilities, and qualities, ethnicity, race and sexual preference.

Dram shop legislation   Includes laws and procedures that govern the legal operation of establishments that sell measured alcoholic beverages.

Draught beer   Beer dispensed from kegs through piping and a faucet, as opposed to beer in bottles and cans.

Dupe   Short for duplicate check.

Duplicate check   A copy of the guest's original check, used by servers to obtain food from the kitchen.

Empowerment   Giving team members permission to make decisions. In the foodservice industry, empowering team members to satisfy the guest.

Enology   Science or study of wine and wine making.

Entree   In the United States, the main course of a meal.

Enzyme   A substance in a living organism that causes changes in organic substances.

Estufa   Large heating chambers or ovens used to make Madeira.

Expediter   An individual who calls servers' orders to cooks in a kitchen and facilitates the gathering of orders for servers.

Family style service   Enough portions for a table of patrons served on one platter or in one bowl from which patrons may help themselves. Usually means sizable portions of food.

Fermentation   The chemical process in which yeast acts on sugar or sugar-containing substances, such as grain or fruit, to produce alcohol or carbon dioxide.

Finger bowl   A bowl of warm water, with either perfume, lemon slice, or rose petals, served after finger-dirtying foods in some restaurants, or routinely at the end of the meal.

Finger foods   Appetizers and bits of foods that can be eaten without the aid of utensils.

Flambe   Food served flaming in ignited liquor, usually prepared tableside in French service.

Flatware   All table utensils. Collectively, all forks, spoons, and serving utensils used in the dining room.

Foodservice organization   Any establishment preparing and serving food utilizing professionals.

Frappe   Means an iced drink. Various liqueurs, for example crème de menthe, are served over shaved ice in a cocktail glass. The resulting concoction is sipped through a straw as the ice melts.

Free Pour   Method of pouring drinks, favored by bartenders but disliked by management because of the potential abuse.

French service   This form of service is generally reserved for haute cuisine (elegant) restaurants and complements an elegant ambience. The food is attractively arranged on platters and presented to guests, after which the preparation of the food is completed on a gueridon beside the guest's seats.

Front-of-the-house   Those areas of a restaurant where the server meets the guest, such as dining room, lobbies, guest rooms, meeting rooms, and so forth.

Function   Any use of banquet facilities.

Garnish   Anything (usually another food) used to embellish, trim, or decorate another food or drink.

Gueridon   Wheeled cart from which food is served in the dining room.

Guest   Someone we entertain in our home, someone whom we desire to please.

Hors d'oeuvres   Small tasty bits of food served as an accompaniment to cocktails or small amounts of food eaten before a meal or as a first course.

Induction training   The absorbing of new team members into the culture and philosophy of the organization.

Keg   Aluminum or wooden container for beer, containing thirteen gallons. Most modern brewing companies ship in half and quarter kegs.

Lager   Literally, German word meaning to store.

Lager beer   Beer that has been aged or stored.

Leadership   The ability to influence others to do something voluntarily rather than because it is required or because there is fear of the consequences of not doing it or expectation of reward for doing it.

Linen   Term used for all cloth handled in the dining room, usually pertaining to that which will be placed on dining tables.

Liqueurs   Preparations of alcohol, sugar, and some flavoring, used in drink preparation and as after-dinner drinks.

Liquor   A distilled, alcoholic beverage made from a fermented mash of various ingredients, including grains or other plants. Whiskey, gin, vodka, and rum are among the most popular.

Maitre d'   Master of. A contraction of maitre d'service or maitre d'hotel. In the United States, indicates a dining room manager; in France, a food and beverage manager.

Malt   The name given to barley after it has been germinated and the germ has been eliminated from the grain. By this process the grain starch is converted into sugar which is known as maltose. The end product is pure malt which is principally used for brewing beer and distilling spirits, but also makes a highly nutritive beverage when mixed with hot water.

Malt liquor   Malt beverage of beer characteristics, with a higher alcoholic content.

Mise en place   Preparation, everything ready, in kitchens refers to preparation prior to foodservice. A collection of items necessary to prepare menu items.

Mixed drink   An alcoholic beverage prepared by combining a liquor with wine, fruit juice, fruit, sugar, syrup, or the like; a cocktail.

Morale   Group spirit with respect to getting the job done.

Nectar   In classical mythology the wine of the gods, a distillation of refined dew. Today the name is given to any particularly delicious beverage and to the honey of plants.

Nonverbal communication   Use of gestures, facial expressions, or body language.

Organization   A collection of individuals who are working together to reach common goals.

Orientation   The programmed introduction of new team members into the organization by which they learn what is important to the organization, to the supervisor, and to fellow team members.

Par stock   The number of items thought to be suitable inventory for normal business.

Personal space   The area within two to three feet of a person.

pH   An indicator of acidity, with a range from one to fourteen (acid to alkaline).

Pilsner   Originally from Czechoslovakia, it is light in color, with a pronounced hop flavor.

Pilsner glass   A conical glass on a foot, usually used for beer.

Piquant   With a sharp seasoning or flavor.

Place setting   All the flatware, linen, and glasses needed to serve in sequence one guest at a table.

Point of sale (POS)   Computerized system that allows bars to set drink prices according to the specific price.

Porter   A top-fermented beer, heavier and darker than ale, with sweeter, malty flavor.

Pour-cost percentage   Similar to food cost percentage, except in beverage control.

Procedures   The written statements that spell out the details of what is to be done and how.

Quality   The concept that the product or service meets the stated and implied specifications.

Rechaud   Heating unit designed to be used on a gueridon for tableside cookery.

Reservation   An arrangement established between a guest and a restaurant for dining at a specific date and time.

Rouge   French word for red.

Russian service   The food is cooked in the kitchen, cut, placed onto a serving dish, and beautifully garnished. The dish then is presented to the guests and served individually by lifting the food onto the guest's plate with a serving spoon and fork. Russian service can be used at a banquet or a dinner party, where the servers may wear white gloves.

Salver   A round silver tray about one foot in diameter used for glasses, wine, drinks, and sometimes coffee; by extension, any small round tray of any material.

Season   To enhance the taste of a food by adding salt, herbs, spices, or other ingredients.

Service plate   A plate used to replace a show plate and used as an underliner for all courses preceding the entree.

Service set   A large fork and spoon held in specific ways and used to transfer food items from one service container to another.

Service station   Side stand. A small work area or supply closet in the dining room. Usually containing items used frequently during service.

Serviette   A plate covered with a neatly folded napkin or just a napkin used to carry items such as flatware to a guest's table.

Sexual harassment   Unwelcome advances, requests for sexual favors, and other verbal or physical conduct of a sexual nature when compliance with any of these acts is a condition of employment, or when comments or physical contact create an intimidating, hostile, or offensive working environment.

Sidework   All duties assigned service personnel in addition to table service.

Silencer   A pad or cloth, rubber or felt, placed between the table and the tablecloth to reduce noise.

Silver service   Another term for Russian service.

Smorgasbord   Literally means "Sandwich Table." A buffet featuring "Scandinavian" items, generally including canned and pickled fish. Also, a buffet restaurant that urges guests to eat as much as they want.

Sommelier   Wine steward.

Spotter   A professional who, for a fee, will observe the bar operation with an eye toward reporting any unusual or inappropriate behavior by the bartender.

Steep   To let a food stand in liquid in order to extract its flavor and color; usually refers to tea.

Stillroom   A continental term for an area similar to the servers' pantry.

Stout   Top-fermented, very dark in color, strong hop characteristic and fairly sweet taste.

Straight   In referring to mixed drinks, means undiluted.

Straight up   In referring to mixed drinks, means served without ice, although usually made with ice and strained into the serving glass so as to chill the drink.

Supervisor   An employee who is in a management position and has authority to perform such management duties as assigning work, hiring, firing, and making promotions and transfers, or who can effectively recommend such actions.

Suzette pan   A circular pan, the most frequently used pan for tableside cooking. Named after an opera singer who was being entertained by the Prince of Wales in A.D. 1900, who served the first flaming dessert.

Syrup   A sweet, sticky, thick liquid made by boiling sugar and lemon juice with water or by reducing the juice of certain fruits.

Table d' hote   From table of the host. In modern context, a menu in which the price of a complete meal changes according to the entree selected.

Tart   The word also is used to describe a sharp, sour taste.

Tips   To ensure prompt service; a percentage of the bill left for service. Tips may be kept by the worker to whom they are given, may be pooled so all workers share an equal portion, or may be divided into shares given to other team members.

TQM   Total quality management is a business and management philosophy/process in which all efforts are expended through concerted effort directed at servicing guests by continuous improvements, utilizing and maximizing human resources.

Turnover   The "turning over" of a table, meaning to have one party leave and "turn over" the table to the next party. To serve two or more parties of guests during a meal period at a single table.

Underliner   Any plate placed under a service item containing food or beverage.

Values   Strongly held beliefs that either define right or wrong or indicate preferences.

Vin   French word for wine.

Yeast   A plant that causes fermentation and gives off carbon dioxide; it is used to leaven products.

Appendix 1

International Coffees and Tableside Preparations

In many countries, coffee is the most popular hot beverage consumed. It is prepared in various forms, from the simplest methods to the more complex. Mainly used as a symbol of hospitality, a variety of tastes and flavors are sometimes added to coffee according to national, regional, or local tastes.

One of the most popular specialty coffees (those flavored especially with alcohol) in the world is Irish Coffee (or Gaelic Coffee). According to Christopher Sands, a senior lecturer at the Dublin Institute of Technology, this method of serving coffee was popularized in the early 1940s in Ireland at Shannon Airport. It now enjoys worldwide popularity.

Irish Coffee, well made, consists of hot strong black coffee, sugar to taste, with a measure of Irish Whiskey, all topped with cold fresh heavy cream.

Irish Coffee

Ingredients

1 ounce of Irish whiskey (only Irish Whiskey, made in Ireland, should be used)

2 tsp. sugar (traditionally Demerara brown sugar has been served with Irish coffee)

4 tbsp. top grade heavy pouring cream

Coffee (25 percent stronger than normal)

Method of Preparation

1. Warm the glass lightly over the flame.
2. Add sugar and Irish Whiskey to the heated glass and flame.
3. Pour in the coffee, one inch from the rim.

4. Pour the liquid heavy cream over the back of a spoon and gently float on top of the hot coffee. This has the best effect if the cream is cool, straight from the refrigerator.

5. Serve with an underliner but no spoon. Irish Coffee should not be stirred once the cream has been floated on top of the coffee.

Mexican Coffee

Ingredients

1/2 ounce of Bacardi rum

1/2 ounce of kahlua

2 tbsp. whipped cream

Coffee

Method of Preparation

1. Warm glass slightly, by rotating over the flame.

2. Add rum and kahlua to glass and flame.

3. Fill the glass with coffee one inch from rim. Top with whipped cream.

4. Serve with an underliner.

Brazilian Coffee

Ingredients

1/2 ounce Grand Marnier

1/2 ounce Tia Maria

1/2 ounce cognac

Whipped cream

Coffee

Method of Preparation

1. Warm glass.

2. Add Grand Marnier to glass.

3. Add Tia Maria, and flame.

4. Add coffee one inch to the rim, top with whipped cream.

5. Warm a ladle.

6. Pour cognac into the ladle.

7. Light the cognac in the ladle and pour over the cream.

8. Serve on an underliner.

Spanish Coffee

Ingredients

1/2 ounce cognac

1/2 ounce Grand Marnier

2 half slices of orange

2 tsp. sugar

Coffee

Method of Preparation

1. Warm the glass lightly over the flame.
2. Add cognac and Grand Marnier and flame.
3. Add sugar and coffee and stir.
4. Garnish with orange slice.

Isabelle Coffee

Ingredients

1/2 ounce kahlua

1/2 ounce cognac

Vanilla ice cream

Whipped cream

1 tsp. sugar

Coffee

Method of Preparation

1. Blend ice cream with whipped cream.
2. Add kahlua and cognac.
3. Pour the glass half full of coffee.
4. Add the rest of the ingredients to the coffee.
5. Serve with an underliner.

Cafe Royale

Ingredients

2 ounces cognac

2 ounces Tia Maria

2 tsp. sugar

Whipped cream

Coffee

1 tsp. powdered chocolate

Method of Preparation

1. Warm high-ball glass.
2. Add cognac and Tia Maria and flame.
3. Add sugar and stir.
4. Add coffee to one inch from the rim.
5. Add whipped cream.
6. Sprinkle the powdered chocolate over the top.
7. Serve on an underliner.

Banana Flambe

(two portions)

Ingredients

1 banana

1 ounce of butter

2 ounces of honey

1 ounce crème de cacao

1 ounce Jamaican Rum

2 scoops of vanilla ice cream

Method of Preparation

1. Melt the butter in the pan.
2. Slice the banana 1/2 inch thick into the pan.
3. Add honey and simmer lightly.
4. Add crème de cacao and flame with Jamaican rum.
5. Place a scoop of ice cream in a suitable serving dish.
6. Pour the banana mixture over it.
7. Serve on dessert dish with a dessert spoon and fork.

Cherries Jubilee

(two portions)

Ingredients

bing cherries
3 tsp. sugar
1 ounce of Kirsch
Vanilla ice cream

Method of Preparation

1. Warm the cherries in a (tableside) pan.
2. Add sugar and caramelize lightly.
3. Add Kirsch and flame.
4. Serve over vanilla ice cream on a dessert plate.

Crepe Suzette

(two portions)

Ingredients

4 ounces sweet butter
2 Oranges
1 Lemon
Sugar
Grand Marnier
4 crepes
Brandy

Method of Preparation

1. Place two teaspoons of sugar in the suzette pan with the butter, and brown it to a light caramel.
2. Add zest of orange and lemon.
3. Cut the orange and lemon in half and squeeze the juices into the pan, allow the liquid to become clear and syrupy.
4. One at a time, place the crepes in the pan and turn once.
5. Sprinkle lightly with sugar and fold into a triangle.
6. Add Grand Marnier and allow to reduce slightly

(recipe continued on the next page)

7. Add the brandy and flame (remove the pan from the source of the flame before setting alight).

8. Serve on hot dessert plates.

Poire Flambe

(two portions)

Ingredients

2 pears (Bartletts)

Sugar

2 ounces of Kirsch

1 glass of white wine

1 tbsp. crushed almonds

Method of Preparation

1. Peel and core the pears, cut them into two halves.
2. Poach the pears in the white wine.
3. Add about 8 tablespoons of sugar.
4. Cook until nappe (coating consistency)
5. Add Kirsch and flame.
6. Serve on a hot dessert plate and sprinkle with crushed almonds.
7. Serve with a fork and dessert spoon.

Appendix 2

Cocktail Recipes

Bacardi Cocktail

Shake and strain the following into prechilled cocktail glass:

1-1/2 oz. Bacardi white rum

1 oz. fresh lime

1 teaspoon Grenadine

Banana Daiquiri

Blend and pour into wineglass:

3/4 oz. rum

3/4 oz. banana liqueur

Dash of Grenadine

1 whole banana

1/2 cup shaved ice

Garnish with a banana slice.

Between-the-Sheets

Shake and strain the following into prechilled cocktail glass:

Dash of fresh lemon juice

1 oz. brandy

1 oz. Cointreau

1 oz. Bacardi rum

Brandy Alexander

Shake and strain the following into prechilled cocktail glass:

1 oz. brandy

1 oz. dark cacao

1 oz. cream

Sprinkle with nutmeg.

Campari Cocktail

Stir and strain the following into prechilled cocktail glass:

2 oz. gin

1/2 oz. Campari

Garnish with a lemon twist.

Champagne Cocktail

Build in a prechilled cocktail glass:

1 sugar cube

2 dashes angostura bitters

2/3 oz. cognac

Champagne

Place sugar in glass, dash with bitters, fill with champagne

Garnish with a lemon twist.

Cuba Libre

Build in highball glass with ice cubes:

1-1/2 oz. Bacardi white rum

Juice of 1 fresh lime

Coca-Cola

Squeeze lime wedge over glass and drop in.

Dry Martini

Stir and strain the following into prechilled cocktail glass:

2-3/4 oz. gin

1/4 oz. dry vermouth

Garnish with an olive.

Dubonnet Cocktail

Stir and strain the following into prechilled cocktail glass:

1-1/2 oz. gin

1-1/2 oz. Dubonnet

Garnish with a lemon twist.

Gin Fizz

Shake and strain the following over ice cubes in a highball glass:

1-3/4 oz. gin

Juice of 1/2 lemon

Add soda to fill.

Golden Cadillac

Shake and strain the following into a prechilled cocktail glass:

1 oz. white cacao

1 oz. Galliano

1 oz. cream

Golden Dream

Shake and strain the following into a prechilled cocktail glass:

1/2 oz. orange juice

1/2 oz. Cointreau

2/3 oz. Galliano

1/3 oz. cream

Grasshopper

Shake and strain the following into a prechilled cocktail glass:

1 oz. green crème de menthe

1 oz. white cacao

1 oz. cream

Harvey Wallbanger

Build over ice cubes in highball glass:

1-3/4 oz. vodka

5-1/2 oz. orange juice

2/3 oz. Galliano (floated)

Kir Royale

Pour slowly into champagne flute:
1/3 oz. creme de cassis
5 oz. champagne
Lemon twist

Manhattan

Stir and strain into prechilled cocktail glass:
1-1/4oz. Canadian Club whiskey
2/3 oz. sweet vermouth
Dash angostura bitters
Garnish with a cherry

Margarita

Blend and strain the following into prechilled cocktail glass:
1 oz. tequila
1/2 oz. Triple Sec or Cointreau
Rim glass with salt
1 oz. fresh lime juice

Old-Fashioned

Build the following over ice cubes in a brandy glass:
1-3/4 oz. bourbon
1 dash of angostura bitters
Soda water
1 sugar cube
Stir and garnish with a cherry and orange twist.

Pina Colada

Blend and strain the following into a prechilled wine glass:
1-3/4 oz. white Bacardi rum
1-3/4 oz. coconut cream
3-1/2 oz. pineapple juice
Cherry and pineapple garnish

Pink Lady

Shake and strain the following into prechilled cocktail glass:

1-3/4 oz. gin

1/2 oz. grenadine

1 egg white

2/3 oz. lemon juice

Rob Roy

Stir and strain into prechilled highball glass:

1-1/2 oz. sweet vermouth

1-1/2 oz. Scotch whiskey

1–2 dashes angostura bitters

Cherry garnish

Rusty Nail

Build over ice cubes in an old-fashioned glass:

1 3/4 oz. Scotch

1 oz. Drambuie

Screw Driver

Build over cubes in a highball glass:

1-3/4 oz. vodka

5-1/2 oz. orange juice.

Singapore Sling

Blend and strain over ice cubes in a cocktail glass:

2/3 oz. gin

2/3 oz. cherry brandy

1/3 oz. Benedictine

1/3 oz. Cointreau

1/3 oz. fresh lime juice

1/2 oz. fresh orange juice

2-1/2 oz. pineapple juice

Cherry and orange garnish

Stinger

Build over ice into prechilled old-fashioned glass:
1-1/2 oz. brandy
3/4 oz. white crème de menthe

Tequila Sunrise

Build over ice cubes in a highball glass:
1-3/4 oz. tequila
5-1/2 oz. orange juice
1–2 dashes grenadine

Tom Collins

Build over ice cubes in a cocktail glass:
1-1/4 oz. gin
1 oz. sweet and sour
Top with soda water
Juice of one lemon
Cherry and orange garnish

Appendix 3

Napkin Folds

The Boar's Head

1. Fold the napkin into thirds.
2. Fold edges A to center line B.
3. Fold the triangles C to center line.
4. Napkin after stage 3.
5. Take the napkin in both hands, turn napkin over with the points toward you and the plain side uppermost. Roll to form a cone.
6. Tuck corner A into corner B.
7. Place on the table with the opening down and the points away from the diner.

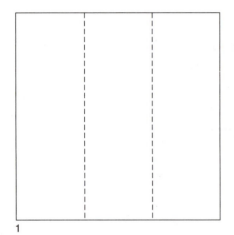

1

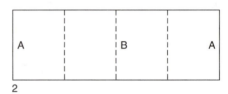

2

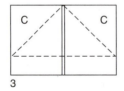

3

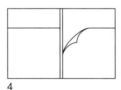

4

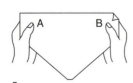

5

6

7

The Lazy Butler

1. Fold the napkin in thirds as shown.
2. Fold edges A to center line B.
3. Fold corners C to center line.
4. Napkin after stage 3.
5. Take the napkin in both hands, turn napkin over with the points toward you and the plain side uppermost. Roll to form a cone.
6. Tuck corner A into corner B.
7. Place on the table with the opening down and the points toward the diner.

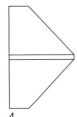

1

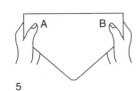

2

3

4

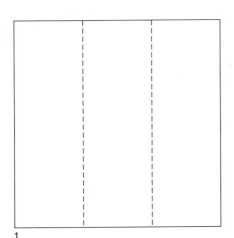

5

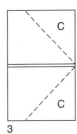

6

7

The French Pleat

1. Fold the napkin in thirds along the dotted lines to form a rectangle. Turn the napkin so the narrow side is toward you.
2. Fold ends A and B over one quarter of napkin along the dotted lines.
3. Fold B over once more to center.
4. Turn edge A over so that it meets the edge of the top of fold B.
5. Turn edge C under so that A is now the top. Position on plate.

Note: The name card or menu may be placed in between the steps of this fold.

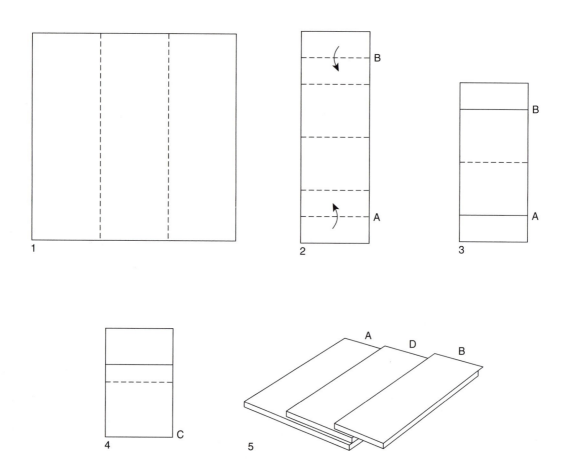

The Twirl

1. Fold the napkin into thirds along the dotted lines.
2. Lay both hands, palms up, on the napkin, taking corner A between the thumb and forefinger of the left hand and corner B with thumb and forefinger of the right hand.
3. Turn the hands palms down, retaining hold of the corners.
4. Turn hands in toward body in a circular motion.
5. Complete the motion. This will trap hands.
6. Release hands and place the napkin into a glass or arrange it flat on a show plate.

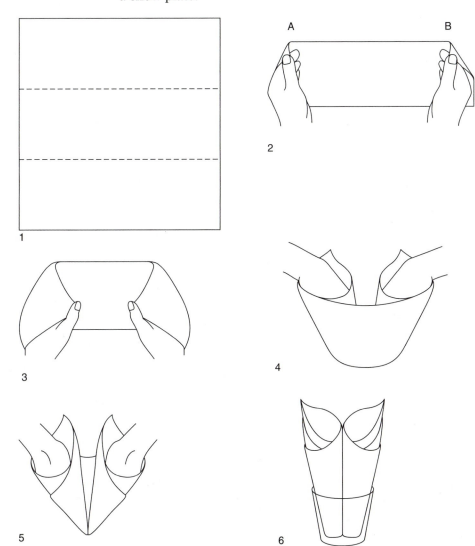

The Pocket Napkin Fold

1. Fold napkin into four sections, ensuring that the four loose edges are at A.
2. Fold down flap as indicated.
3. Fold along dotted line.
4. Fold down second flap.
5. Fold second flap along dotted line.
6. Tuck second fold under first fold.
7. Fold napkin along dotted line, putting fold underneath.
8. Fold napkin along dotted line.
9. Finished fold.

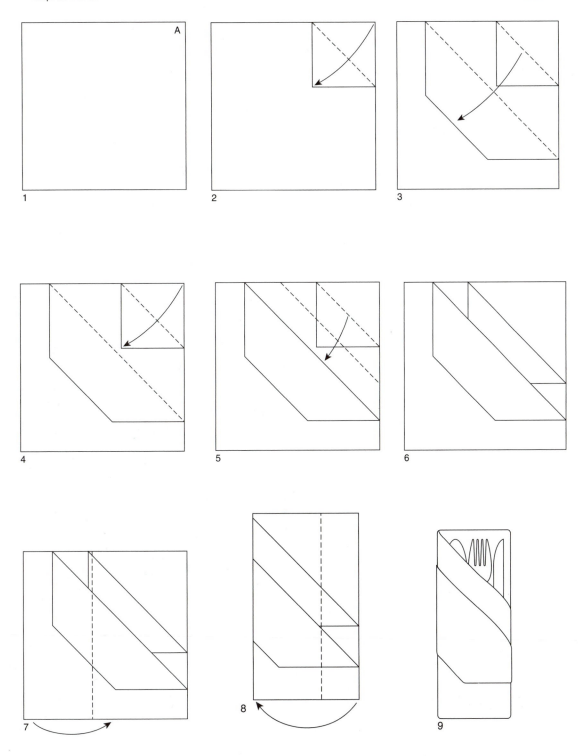

The Lotus

1. Lay napkin flat and fold along the dotted lines.
2. Turn through 45 degrees and fold along the dotted lines.
3. Turn again and fold along dotted lines.
4. Turn napkin over and fold along dotted lines.
5. Napkin after stage 4.
6. Place a tumbler over the points in the center.
7. Pull each of the twelve points gently away from underneath, taking opposite corners in turn.
8. Finished fold.

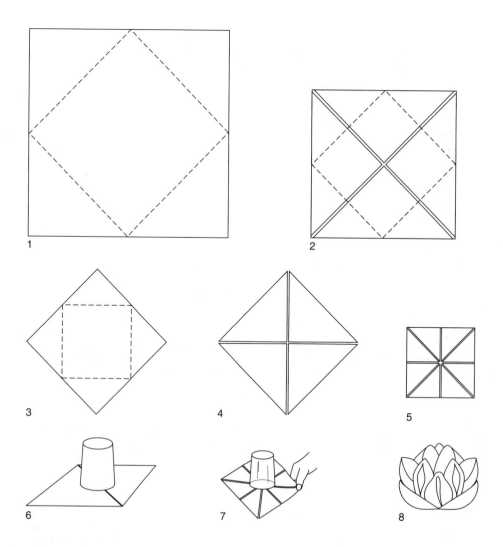

The Pixie's Slipper

1. Fold napkin into thirds.
2. Fold at lines A to bring sides B to the center.
3. Napkin after stage 2.
4. Turn the point to the right, folding along the center line.
5. Turn the napkin over, fold the portion BB up and away from you at the end of the dotted line shown in the previous diagram.
6. Fold CC in half toward you. This will make the heel.
7. Fold CC around the tuck into pleat D.
8. To finish this fold, insert the finger between the folds and curl this part around the slipper.

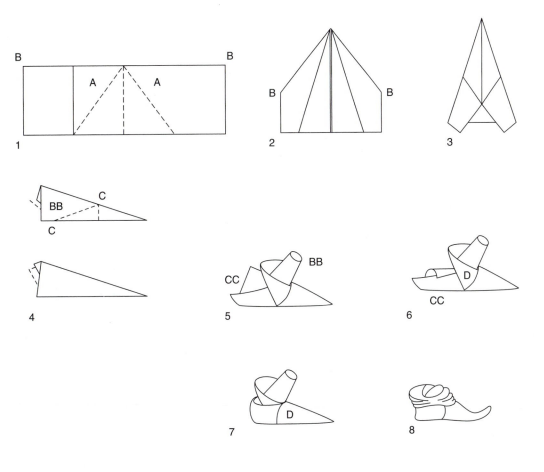

The Viking Hat

1. Fold the napkin in half diagonally, then fold corners A to B.
2. Fold two flaps marked A up to B.
3. Fold the two flaps marked A out to the dotted lines at B.
4. Fold A to B, ensuring that the fold falls along the bottom dotted line.
5. Fold bottom edge A along dotted line marked B, then tuck ends marked C around the back to make the napkin stand up.
6. Finished fold.

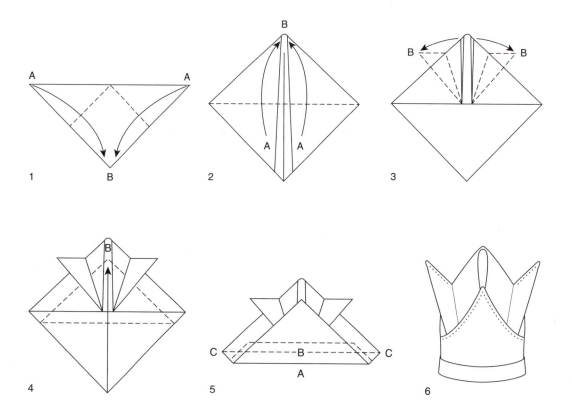

The Lily

1. Fold the napkin at the dotted line.
2. Fold corners A up at the dotted lines.
3. Fold B up at the dotted line.
4. Fold B down at the dotted line.
5. Napkin after stage 4.
6. Turn napkins so that side C to D is away from you. Fold corner C as shown. Fold D up at the dotted line and tuck into the pleat at C.
7. Stand the napkin on the table with point E up.
8. Pull down the pleats to produce the finished fold.

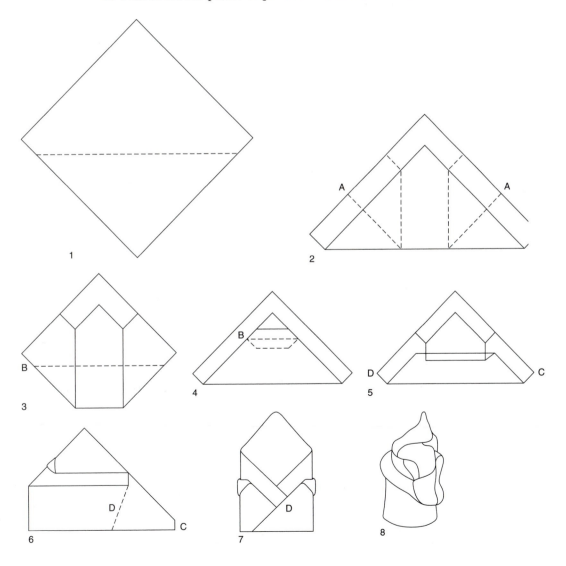

The Spear

1. Fold napkin into thirds as shown.
2. Fold corners A diagonally to center line.
3. Fold back corners A.
4. Keeping the two sides flat on the table, press them toward the middle. This will make the center line stand up. Fold sections B under at the dotted line.
5. Open out the center fold and arrange on the table with point away from the diner.

1

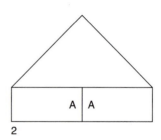

2

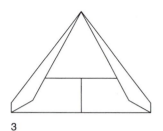

3

4

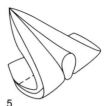

5

The Cone

1. Fold the napkin into thirds.
2. Fold corners A and B upward to center line.
3. Fold corners C to D and E to F.
4. Place fingers of left hand inside the fold and turn down point GH at the dotted line to form a cuff.
5. Mold the napkin into a cone and set it on the table with the points of the cuff facing the diner.

1

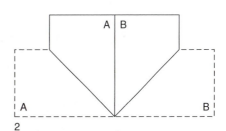

2

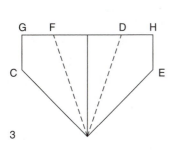

3

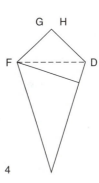

4

5

The Bishop's Hat

1. Fold the napkin in half.
2. Fold corners A to B and C to D.
3. Fold the top back at the dotted line.
4. Turning the points to the top, bring the left-hand corner around and tuck it behind the front flap.
5. Napkin after stage 4.
6. Turn the napkin around and repeat stage 4.
7. Finished fold.

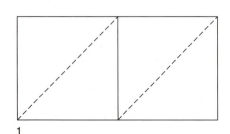

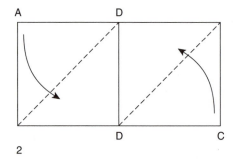

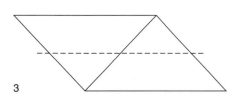

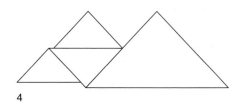

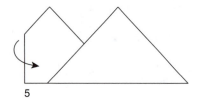

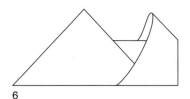

Bibliography

Adams, Leon. *The Wines of America*, 4th. ed. New York: McGraw-Hill, 1990.

Applied Foodservice Sanitation, 4th ed., Lansing, Michigan: The Educational Foundation of the National Restaurant Association, 1992.

Bakos, Joan B. and Guy E. Karrick. *Dining in Corporate America: Handbook of Noncommercial Foodservice Management*. Rockville, MD: Aspen Pub., 1989.

Baldy, Marian W. *The University Wine Course*. San Francisco, CA: The Wine Appreciation Guild, 1995.

Bank, John. *The Essence of Total Quality Management*. Prentice Hall International (UK) Ltd, 1992.

Barbee, Cliff and Valerie Bott. "Customer Treatment as a Mirror of Employee Treatment." *Advanced Management Journal* (spring 1991).

Barker, Joel Arthur. *Paradigms: The Business of Discovering the Future*. New York: Harper Collins, 1993.

Bennus, Warren and Burt Nanus. *Leaders: The Strategies for Taking Charge*. New York: Harper Collins, 1985.

Blanchard, Ken, John Carlos & Alan Randolph. *Empowerment Takes More Than a Minute*. Berrett-Koehler Publishers San Fransicso. 1996.

Blanchard, Ken., & Michael O'Connor. *Managing By Values*. Berret-Koehler Publishers, San Francisco, 1997.

Boulton, Roger B., Vernon L. Singleton, Linda F. Bisson, and Ralph E. Kunkee. *Principles and Practices of Winemaking*. New York: Chapman & Hall, 1996.

Broadbent, Michael. *The Great Vintage Wine Book*, 2nd ed. New York: Alfred A Knopf, 1992.

———. *The Pocket Guide to Wine Tasting*. New York: Simon & Schuster, 1989.

Calbrese, Salvatore. *Classic Cocktails*. New York: Sterling Publishing Co., Inc., 1997.

C.E.R.T. *Customer Relations*. Dublin, Ireland: CERT, 1990.

Chesser, Jerald. *The Art and Science of Culinary Preparation*. St. Augustine, FL: The American Culinary Federation Educational Institute, 1992.

Christensen, Julia. "The Diversity Dynamic: Implications for Organizations in 2005." *Hospitality Research Journal* (1993): 17 no. 1, p. 43.

Cichy, Ronald, Martin P. Sciarini, & Mark E. Patton, "Food-Service Leadership: Could Attila Run a Restaurant," *The Cornell Hotel and Restaurant Administration Quarterly*, pp. 44, 1992.

Clark, Corbert A. *American Wines of the Northwest*. New York: William Morrow, 1989.

Cohen, William A. *The Art of the Leader*. Upper Saddle River, New Jersey: Prentice Hall, 1990.

Crosby, Philip. *Quality Is Free*. New York: McGraw Hill, 1978.

Cullen, Noel C. "Cooking with Wine." *National Culinary Review* (May 1994).

———. "Culinary Leadership." *National Culinary Review* (March 1994, p. 16).

———. "Customer Service: Life Beyond the Line." *Chef Magazine* (July 1994, p. 24).

———. "Making the Kitchen a Great Place to Work." *Chef Magazine* (December 1993, p. 21).

———. "Protecting Your People Investment." *Chef Magazine* (August 1994, p. 23).

———. "Reengineering The Executive Chef." *Chef Magazine* (October 1993, p. 16).

———. "Total Quality Management for the Modern Chef." *National Culinary Review* (August 1996, p. 19).

———. *"The World of Culinary Supervision, Training, and Management*. Upper Saddle River, New Jersey: Prentice Hall, 1996.

Davidow, William H. and Bro Utall. *Total Customer Service: The Ultimate Weapon*. New York: Harper Perennial, 1990.

De Pree, Max. *Leadership Is an Art*. New York: Dell Pub., 1989.

Drummond, Karen Eich. *The Restaurant Training Program*. New York: John Wiley, 1992.

Dumont, Raymond and John M Lannon. *Business Communications*, 2nd ed. Boston: Brown & Co,. 1987.

Eade, Vincent H. *Human Resources Management in the Hospitality Industry*. Scotsdale, AZ: Garsuch Sciarisbrick Pub., 1993.

Fernandez, John P. *Managing a Diverse Work Force: Regaining the Competitive Edge*. Lexington, MA: Heath and Co., 1991.

Finch, Christopher. *A Connoisseur's Guide to the World's Best Beer.* New York: Abbeville Press, 1989.

Food: The Social Experience, Vol. II. Providence, RI: Johnson & Wales University, 1992.

Fuller, John. *Chef's Manual of Kitchen Management,* 3rd ed., London: Batsford, 1975.

Holleman, Gary. *Food and Wine Online.* New York: Van Nostrand Reinhold, 1995.

Iland, Patrick and Peter Gago. *Australian Wine: From the Vine to the Glass.* Adelaide, South Australia: Patrick Iland Wine Promotions, 1997.

Keiser, James R. *Principles and Practices of Management in the Hospitality Industry,* 2nd ed. New York: Van Nostrand Reinhold, 1989.

Kelly, Edward. *Interviews with Author.* Boston 1997.

King, Carol A. *Professional Diningroom Management,* 2nd ed. New York: Van Nostrand Reinhold, 1988.

Kinlaw, Denis C. *Coaching for Commitment.* San Diego, CA: Pfeiffer, 1993.

Koplan, Steven, Brian Smith, and Michael Weiss. *Exploring Wine.* New York: Van Nostrand Reinhold, 1996.

Kotschevar, Lendal H. *Management by Menu.* Lansing, Michigan: Wm. C. Brown, 1987.

Kouzes, James M. & Barry Z. Posner. *Credibility: How Leaders Gain and Lose It, Why People Demand It.* Jossey Bass, San Fransicso: 1993.

Larousse Encyclopedia of Wine. Paris: Larousse, 1994.

Larousse Gatronomique. London: Hamlyn, 1971.

Levinson, Charles. *Food and Beverage Operation Cost Control and Systems Management.* Upper Saddle River, New Jersey: Prentice Hall, 1989.

Lipinski, Bob and Kathie Lipinski. *Professional Beverage Management.* New York: Van Nostrand Reinhold, 1996.

Litrides, Carol A. and Bruce H. Axler. *Food and Beverage Service.* New York: John Wiley & Sons, 1990.

———. *Restaurant Service: Beyond the Basics.* New York: John Wiley & Sons, 1994.

Maddux, Robert B. *Team Building: An Exercise in Leadership.* Crisp, Menlo Park, CA: 1992.

Magee, Malachy. *1000 Years of Irish Whiskey.* Dublin, Ireland: The O'Brien Press, 1980.

Maslow, Abraham. *Motivation and Personality,* 2nd ed. New York: Harper & Row, 1970.

Maxwell, John C. *Developing the Leader within You.* Nashville, TN: Nelson Pub., 1993.

McGee, Harold. *On Food and Cooking: The Science and Lores of the Kitchen.* New York: Scribner's, 1984.

Metz, Ferdinand E. "Success Has a Future Perspective." *Lessons in Leadership.* New York: Van Nostrand Reinhold, 1991.

Meyer, Sylvia, Edy Schmidt, and Christel Spuhler. *Professional Table Service.* Translated by Heinz Holtman. New York: Van Nostrand Reinhold, 1991.

Miller, Jack E., Mary Porter, and Karen E. Drummond. *Supervision in the Hospitality Industry,* 2nd ed. New York: John Wiley & Sons, 1992.

Miller, Jack E. and David K. Hayes. *Basic Food and Beverage Cost Control.* New York: John Wiley & Sons, 1994.

Morgan, William J. Jr. *Food and Beverage Management and Service.* Lansing, MI: Educational Institute of the American Hotel and Motel Association. 1981.

———. *Supervision and Management of Quantity Food Production: Principles and Procedures,* 4th ed. Berkeley, CA: McCutchan Publishing Corporation, 1995.

O'Malley, Patrick L. "Make Excellence a Habit." *Lessons in Leadership,* p. 106. New York: Van Nostrand Reinhold, 1991.

Pauli Eugen. *Classical Cooking the Modern Way,* 2nd. ed. New York: Van Nostrand Reinhold, 1989.

Peters, Tom. *Thriving on Chaos: Handbook for a Management Revolution.* New York: Harper & Row Pub., 1988.

Peterson, Jim L. "Self-Esteem Is Essential to Building a Team." *Lessons in Leadership,"* p. 46, New York: Van Nostrand Reinhold, 1991.

Picogna, Joseph L. *Total Quality Leadership: A Training Approach.* Morrissville, PA: International Information Associates Inc., 1993.

Professional Restaurant Service: Ecole Technique Hoteliere Tsuji. New York: John Wiley & Sons, Inc., 1991.

Rande, Wallace. *Introduction to Professional Foodservice.* New York: John Wiley & Sons, Inc., 1996.

Reid, Robert D. *Foodservice and Restaurant Marketing.* New York: Van Nostrand Reinhold, 1983.

Rey, Anthony M. and Ferdinand Wieland. *Managing Service in Food and Beverage Operations.* East Lansing, MI: The Educational Institute of the American Hotel & Motel Association, 1985.

Rinke, Wolf J. *The Winning Foodservice Manager: Strategies for Doing More with Less,* 2nd. ed., Rockville, MD: Achievement Pub., 1992.

Ritz Carlton publicity pamphlet. *The Ritz Carlton Co.* Boston, MA: 1993.

Rubash, Joyce. *The Master Dictionary of Food & Wine.* New York: Van Nostrand Reinhold, 1996.

Ryan Kathleen and Daniel K. Oestreich. *Driving Fear Out of the Workplace.* San Francisco, CA: Jossey-Bass, 1991.

Schwartz, Andrew E. *Delegating Authority.* New York: Barrons, 1992.

Scott, Cynthia D. and Dennis T. Jaffe. *Empowerment.* London, England: Crisp Publications Inc., 1991.

Seely, James. *The Wines of South Africa.* London: Faber and Faber, 1997.

Sherman, Arthur, George Bohlander, and Herbert Crudden. *Managing Human Resources,* 8th ed. Cincinnati, Ohio: South-Western Pub. Co., 1988.

Shriver, Stephen J. *Managing Quality Services,* East Lansing, MI: The Educational Institute of the American Hotel & Motel Association, 1988.

Sullivan, Jim and Phil Roberts. *Service That Sells: The Art of Profitable Hospitality.* Denver, CO: Pencom Inc., 1991.

Sutcliffe, Serena. *Champagne.* New York: Simon & Shuster, 1988.

Strianese, Anthony J. *Dining Room Management,* 2nd ed. New York: Delmar Publishers, 1997.

Tanke, Mary L. *Human Resources Management for the Hospitality Industry.* Albany, NY: Delmar Pub., Inc., 1990.

Taylor, Jennifer. *The Essential Wine Buff.* London: Robert Hale, 1996.

Taylor, Derek. "Cesar Ritz and Auguste Escoffier vs the Savoy Hotel Company." *International Hospitality Management Journal,* 15, no. 1, p. 91 (March 1996).

Trager, James. *The Food Chronology.* New York: Henry Holt Pub., 1995.

U.S. Department of Labor. Bureau of Statistics, 1991.

Van Hoof, Hubert B., Marilyn E. McDonald, Lawrence Yu, and Gary K. Vallen. *A Host of Opportunities: An Introduction to Hospitality.* Boston: Irwin, 1996.

Van Kleek, Peter E. *Beverage Management & Bartending.* Boston, MA: CBI Pub., 1981.

Vine, Richard P. *Wine Appreciation,* 2nd ed. New York: John Wiley & Sons, Inc., 1997.

Voss, Roger. *The Pocket Guide to Fortified and Dessert Wines.* New York: Simon & Schuster, 1989.

Walker, John R. *Introduction to Hospitality.* Upper Saddle River, NJ: Prentice Hall, 1996.

Walton, Sally J. *Cultural Diversity in the Workplace.* New York: Irwin, 1994.

Webb, Susan L. *Step Forward: Sexual Harassment in the Workplace.* New York: Master Media, 1991.

Weinstein, Jeff. "Personnel Success." *Restaurants & Institutions* (December 1992).

Wood, Tom. "Total Quality Management." *Hosteur,* 3, no. 1 (spring 1993).

Woods Robert H. and Judy Z. King. *Quality Leadership and Management in the Hospitality Industry*. East Lansing, MI: The Educational Institute of the American Hotel & Motel Association, 1996.

Worthington, E. R. and Anita E. Worthington. *People Investment*. Central Point, Oregon: The Oasis Press, 1993.

Zraly, Kevin. *Windows on the World Complete Wine Course,* 2nd ed. New York: Sterling, 1992.

Index